CHILTON'S Repair and Tune-Up Guide

Opel
1971-75

ILLUSTRATED

Prepared by the

Automotive Editorial Department

Chilton Book Company

Chilton Way
Radnor, Pa. 19089
215—687-8200

president and chief executive officer **WILLIAM A. BARBOUR;** executive vice president **RICHARD H. GROVES;** vice president and general manager **JOHN P. KUSHNERICK;** managing editor **JOHN H. WEISE, S.A.E.;** assistant managing editor **KERRY A. FREEMAN, S.A.E.;** editors **DAVID P. GALLUCCIO** and **JOHN G. MOHAN;** technical editor **Ronald L. Sessions**

CHILTON BOOK COMPANY   RADNOR, PENNSYLVANIA

Copyright © 1976 by Chilton Book Company
All Rights Reserved
Published in Radnor, Pa. by Chilton Book Company
and simultaneously in Ontario, Canada
by Thomas Nelson & Sons, Ltd.

Manufactured in the United States of America

34567890   54321098

Chilton's Repair & Tune-Up Guide: Opel 1971–75
ISBN 0-8019-6574-8
ISBN 0-8019-6575-6 (pbk.)

Library of Congress Catalog Card No. 76-28578

ACKNOWLEDGMENT

The Chilton Book Company wishes to thank the Buick Division
of General Motors Corporation for its technical advice and
cooperation in the production of this guide.

Although information in this guide is based on industry
sources and is as complete as possible at the time of publica-
tion, the possibility exists that the manufacturer made later
changes which could not be included here. While striving for
total accuracy, Chilton Book Company can not assume respon-
sibility for any errors, changes, or omissions that may occur in
the compilation of this data.

Contents

Chapter One
General Information and Maintenance

Introduction

After a small beginning as a sewing machine manufacturer in 1862, Adam Opel rapidly expanded the family company into the production of bicycles and, when he recognized the potential of the automobile, Opel was quick to begin production. The Opel family rapidly matched twentieth century ideas by introducing, in 1924, the continent's first mass production conveyor system for manufacturing automobiles.

The 1920's was an affluent era when most auto manufacturers were building large high powered luxury cars for the post war wealthy. Opel's farsightedness led him to introduce the Opel 4PS, a small car designed for the working classes.

By 1929, General Motors Corporation was interested enough to buy the company from the Opel family. Within ten years the Opel A.G. (incorporated) company became Europe's largest producer of automobiles.

Second World War bombing destroyed most of the Opel plants and after the war their truck plant was disassembled by the Russians while they occupied Brandenburg.

Opels were once again on the streets of Europe within a decade and by 1958 Opels were being exported to the United States and other parts of the world. In Bochum, West Germany ground was broken in 1960 for a new factory and, by 1962, Opel

Opel GT
(Model 77)

Opel 1900 Rallye
(Model 57R)

Opel 1900 Sport Coupe
(Model 57)

Opel 1900 Sedan
(Model 51)

Opel 1900 Wagon
(Model 54)

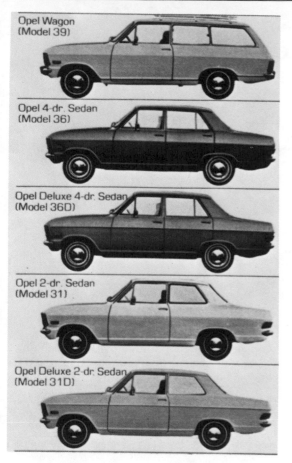

Opel Wagon (Model 39)

Opel 4-dr. Sedan (Model 36)

Opel Deluxe 4-dr. Sedan (Model 36D)

Opel 2-dr. Sedan (Model 31)

Opel Deluxe 2-dr. Sedan (Model 31D)

Kadetts were rolling off the assembly line. 1964 saw production of half a million units and Opel had re-established itself in the world automotive market.

In the United States little is heard of Opel models which are not imported. However Adam Opel A.G. has a complete line of large cars topped by the impressive Diplomat V8. The Opel Kapitan and Admiral are models designed for the basic car and middle line markets.

Until recently the Opel Kadett was the company's most successful car in the U.S.; but 1971 saw the introduction of the 1900 series which was readily accepted by American consumers. The sporty GT is in demand by enthusiasts and has proven that a car manufacturer can produce a wide variety of automobiles to suit different tastes without sacrificing dependability or quality. The GT was discontinued after 1973.

Serial Number Identification

VEHICLE

The Opel identification plate does not specify the year in which the vehicle was manufactured. There are, however, several identification markings on the car which will enable you to determine the year and model of your vehicle.

ADAM OPEL A.G.	RUSSELSHEIM WERK BOCHUM
1900-A	579762754
645	750
1380	303 PP 791

Model identification plate

The Opel identification plate will provide you with the proper model and a serial number. This plate is located on the front of the cowl between the battery and the heater on Opels; on 1900 and Manta models it is found inside the right front inner fender panel; on GT models it is on the top right side of the cowl. The first two digits represent the model of the car.

   31—Kadett 2dr sedan
   31D—Deluxe 2dr sedan
   39—Station Wagon
   51—1900 2dr sedan
   53—1900 4dr sedan
   54—1900 Station Wagon
   57—2dr Manta Sport Coupe
   57R—2dr Manta Ralleye Sport Coupe
   57L—Manta Luxus
   77—GT

In accordance with Federal Law, an additional tag is affixed vertically to the left front door inner panel. This tag specifies the month and year in which the car was built. Additionally, there is a narrow identification tag at the top left of the instrument panel visible from outside the vehicle. This is a GM tag and is deciphered in the following manner.

The first four digits are the General Motors model designations.

   0L11—Opel 1900 2dr Sedan
   0L60—Opel 1900 4dr Sedan
   0L15—Opel 1900 3dr Wagon
   0L77—Manta 2dr Sport Coupe
           Manta 2dr Ralleye Sport Coupe
           Manta Luxus
   0Y07—GT

Federal certification label location

The next three digits represent the engine code, model, year, and assembly plant respectively. The last six digits make up the actual serial number of the vehicle.

ENGINE

The engine number is stamped on a boss provided on the left side of the engine. There are only two designations and they are: 1.1 US for the 1100 cc engine and 1.9 US for the 1900 cc engine. The "US" code means the engine is equipped with the Opel Emission Control System.

Routine Maintenance

AIR CLEANER

The paper air filter element should be changed religiously every 24,000 miles. If your vehicle is operated in dusty areas, the air filter should be changed more often.
NOTE: *Do not run the engine with the air cleaner removed unless you are making carburetor adjustments (1.1 engine only).*

PCV SYSTEM

The PCV valve should be washed in solvent and blown clean with compressed air at least once a year or every 12,000 miles. If you do a lot of city driving and your engine spends a lot of time idling, you should perform this operation every 6000 miles. If

the valve becomes too loaded with deposits and cannot be effectively cleaned, it must be replaced.

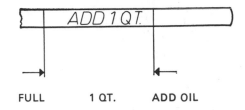

OIL GAUGE ROD
FOR SAFE OPERATION
OIL LEVEL MUST SHOW
ON THIS SECTION

FULL   1 QT.   ADD OIL

FLUID LEVEL CHECKS

Engine Oil

Each time you refill the gas tank you should check the motor oil level and you should never let it drop below the 1 qt low mark on the dipstick. Always check the oil with the engine off and, if the car has been running, let it stand for a few minutes so that the oil can drip back into the crankcase. Always add oil of the same grade as is in the crankcase.

If you get an erroneous reading while checking the oil level, try inserting the dipstick so that the curved handle is toward the firewall. This will give you a true reading.

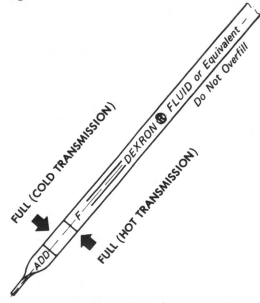

Automatic transmission dipstick

Transmission

STANDARD

On the side of the transmission you will find a plug; by removing it you can check the fluid level. The fluid should be level with the bottom of the hole from which the plug was removed.

AUTOMATIC

Check the automatic transmission fluid level with the transmission in Park or Neutral and the engine hot and idling. Remove the transmission dipstick and be sure the fluid is at or near the full mark. Add fluid if necessary through the filler tube where the dipstick is inserted.

Brake Master Cylinder

The master cylinder is located on the engine side of the firewall and on top of it is a plastic fluid reservoir. The reservoir is marked for minimum and maximum levels. Add fluid as necessary to keep the level between marks.

Brake master cylinder

Coolant

CAUTION: *Never remove the radiator cap from the radiator when the engine is hot.*
The coolant level should be kept at 2 in. below the top of the filler neck. Do not overfill as coolant will be lost due to expansion.

Rear Axle

The rear axle also has a plug which is located near the center of the differential. When the plug is removed, the fluid should reach the bottom of the plug hole.

Battery

The battery should have its' level maintained by adding clear water to the level prescribed on the battery filler caps. Take care when adding water as any acid spilled on the case will damage it.

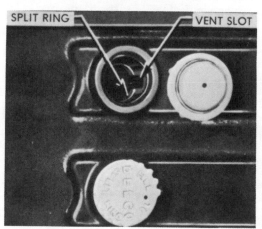

Battery filler well

TIRES AND WHEELS

Inspect the tires regularly for cracks or abrasions and look for bits of glass or other material that may damage the tire if not

Capacities

| Year | Model | Engine Displacement Cu in. (cc) | Engine Crankcase (qts) | | Transmission (pts) | | Drive Axle (pts) | Gasoline Tank (gals) | Cooling System (qts) |
			With Filter	Without Filter	Manual	Automatic			
1971	Kadette	1100 cc	3	2¾	1¼	4½	1½	10½	5
1971	Gt, 1900	1900 cc	3¼	3	2½	4½	2½	10½	6
1972–75	All	1900 cc	3¼	3	2½	5	2½	11½	6

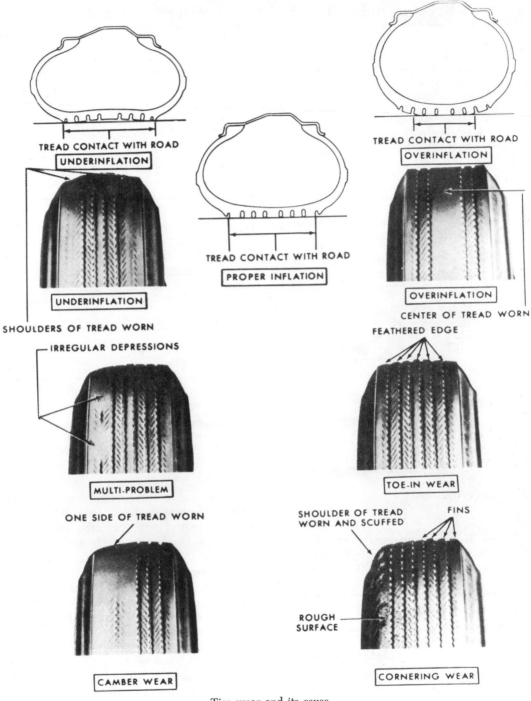

TREAD CONTACT WITH ROAD
UNDERINFLATION

UNDERINFLATION

SHOULDERS OF TREAD WORN

IRREGULAR DEPRESSIONS

MULTI-PROBLEM

ONE SIDE OF TREAD WORN

CAMBER WEAR

TREAD CONTACT WITH ROAD
PROPER INFLATION

TREAD CONTACT WITH ROAD
OVERINFLATION

OVERINFLATION
CENTER OF TREAD WORN

FEATHERED EDGE

TOE-IN WEAR

SHOULDER OF TREAD
WORN AND SCUFFED   FINS

ROUGH
SURFACE

CORNERING WEAR

Tire wear and its cause

removed. Check the tire pressures when the tires are cold and be sure to maintain proper inflation. The tires will indicate damage or wear in front end and suspension parts so by observing their wear you may head off serious trouble. Any time the tires seem to be wearing unevenly or if they seem to be wearing out too quickly, make efforts to investigate the cause.

Periodically check the lug nuts for tightness and look at the wheels to see if they are dented or bent.

Recommended Tire Inflation Pressures (psi-cold)

| Model and year | Standard inflation for all loads up to full rating | | Optional inflation for reduced loads | |
	Front	Rear	Front	Rear
All Opel with 1.1 Engine	22	32	22	25
1971 with 1900 Engine	25	32	25	25
1972 All except GT	25	32	25	25
1973–74 1900 and Manta	24	30	22	26
1973–74 Manta Rallye, Luxus, and Wagon	26	32	23	27
1975 Coupes	24	30	22	26
1975 Wagon	27	35	23	26
All GT	19	23	—	—

Note: Tire inflation can increase up to 6 psi when hot.
For high speed driving increase tire pressure 4 psi but do not exceed 32 psi.
Check air with tires cold.

4-Tire Rotation

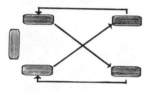

5-Tire Rotation

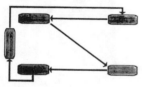

Tire rotation all models

FUEL FILTER

There is no maintainence for the fuel filter other than replacing it at least every 12,000 miles.

Lubrication

OIL AND FUEL RECOMMENDATIONS

The type of engine oil used will have an effect on engine wear, oil economy, combustion chamber deposits, and the overall reliability and performance of the engine. Only oil with the SE specification of the American Petroleum Institute should be used. This SE is stamped directly on the top of the oil can. You should choose the viscosity of oil which will give you the best protection for the time it is used. Attention paid to predetermining the sort of

Recommended SAE Viscosity Number

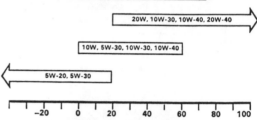

Temperature Range Anticipated Before Next Oil Change, °F

NOTE: SAE 5 W-20 oils are not recommended for sustained high-speed driving.
SAE 30 oils may be used at temperatures above 40° F.

Oil viscosity selection

driving and driving conditions you will expose the engine to will result in longer engine life and better performance.

All US Opel engines through 1974, are designed to run on regular grade gas (91 Octane or higher). All 1975 US Opel engines are designed to be run on unleaded fuel only. Contrary to the belief that using higher grade gas will benefit the engine, it is important to keep in mind that the engine is designed to run on regular grade gas and the use of high test may indeed do some damage. Using high test gas may greatly increase the carbon deposits in the combustion chamber and on the pistons. It is best to use low-lead, regular grade gasoline.

OIL CHANGES

Engine

Under normal use it is recommended that you change the oil in your Opel every

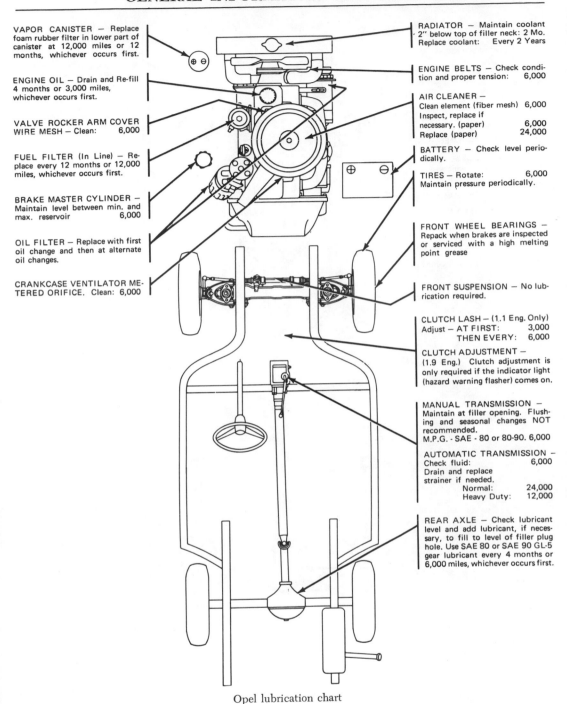

VAPOR CANISTER — Replace foam rubber filter in lower part of canister at 12,000 miles or 12 months, whichever occurs first.

ENGINE OIL — Drain and Re-fill 4 months or 3,000 miles, whichever occurs first.

VALVE ROCKER ARM COVER WIRE MESH — Clean: 6,000

FUEL FILTER (In Line) — Replace every 12 months or 12,000 miles, whichever occurs first.

BRAKE MASTER CYLINDER — Maintain level between min. and max. reservoir   6,000

OIL FILTER — Replace with first oil change and then at alternate oil changes.

CRANKCASE VENTILATOR METERED ORIFICE. Clean: 6,000

RADIATOR — Maintain coolant 2" below top of filler neck: 2 Mo. Replace coolant: Every 2 Years

ENGINE BELTS — Check condition and proper tension: 6,000

AIR CLEANER —
Clean element (fiber mesh) 6,000
Inspect, replace if
necessary. (paper)   6,000
Replace (paper)   24,000

BATTERY — Check level periodically.

TIRES — Rotate: 6,000
Maintain pressure periodically.

FRONT WHEEL BEARINGS — Repack when brakes are inspected or serviced with a high melting point grease

FRONT SUSPENSION — No lubrication required.

CLUTCH LASH — (1.1 Eng. Only)
Adjust — AT FIRST: 3,000
         THEN EVERY: 6,000

CLUTCH ADJUSTMENT —
(1.9 Eng.) Clutch adjustment is only required if the indicator light (hazard warning flasher) comes on.

MANUAL TRANSMISSION — Maintain at filler opening. Flushing and seasonal changes NOT recommended.
M.P.G. - SAE - 80 or 80-90. 6,000

AUTOMATIC TRANSMISSION —
Check fluid: 6,000
Drain and replace
strainer if needed.
          Normal: 24,000
          Heavy Duty: 12,000

REAR AXLE — Check lubricant level and add lubricant, if necessary, to fill to level of filler plug hole. Use SAE 80 or SAE 90 GL-5 gear lubricant every 4 months or 6,000 miles, whichever occurs first.

Opel lubrication chart

3000 miles and replace the oil filter every 6000.

Drain the oil when the engine is hot so that small particles in the lubrication system will be removed and the oil will flow more readily. Remove the drain plug in the oil pan on the underside of the engine and collect the oil in a suitable container. Opels use a spin-on type oil filter; to facilitate easier removal an oil filter strap wrench can be purchased very inexpensively. Simply use the wrench to turn the filter counterclockwise and it will come off. Clean the oil filter gasket surface with a rag and make sure the old gasket is completely removed. Put a small amount of clean oil on the gasket surface of the new filter and spin it on until it contacts the

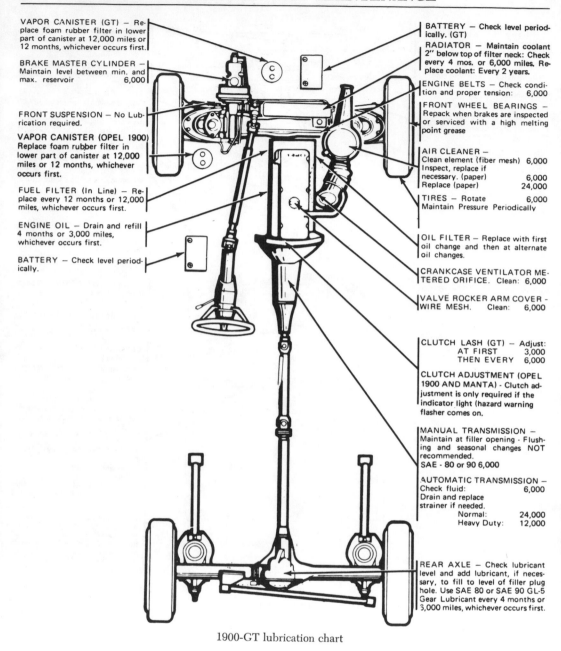

VAPOR CANISTER (GT) — Replace foam rubber filter in lower part of canister at 12,000 miles or 12 months, whichever occurs first.

BRAKE MASTER CYLINDER — Maintain level between min. and max. reservoir   6,000

FRONT SUSPENSION — No Lubrication required.

VAPOR CANISTER (OPEL 1900) Replace foam rubber filter in lower part of canister at 12,000 miles or 12 months, whichever occurs first.

FUEL FILTER (In Line) — Replace every 12 months or 12,000 miles, whichever occurs first.

ENGINE OIL — Drain and refill 4 months or 3,000 miles, whichever occurs first.

BATTERY — Check level periodically.

BATTERY — Check level periodically. (GT)

RADIATOR — Maintain coolant 2" below top of filter neck: Check every 4 mos. or 6,000 miles. Replace coolant: Every 2 years.

ENGINE BELTS — Check condition and proper tension: 6,000

FRONT WHEEL BEARINGS — Repack when brakes are inspected or serviced with a high melting point grease

AIR CLEANER —
Clean element (fiber mesh) 6,000 Inspect, replace if necessary. (paper)   6,000
Replace (paper)   24,000

TIRES — Rotate   6,000 Maintain Pressure Periodically

OIL FILTER — Replace with first oil change and then at alternate oil changes.

CRANKCASE VENTILATOR METERED ORIFICE. Clean: 6,000

VALVE ROCKER ARM COVER - WIRE MESH.   Clean: 6,000

CLUTCH LASH (GT) — Adjust:
AT FIRST   3,000
THEN EVERY   6,000

CLUTCH ADJUSTMENT (OPEL 1900 AND MANTA) - Clutch adjustment is only required if the indicator light (hazard warning flasher comes on.

MANUAL TRANSMISSION — Maintain at filler opening - Flushing and seasonal changes NOT recommended.
SAE - 80 or 90 6,000

AUTOMATIC TRANSMISSION — Check fluid: 6,000
Drain and replace strainer if needed.
Normal: 24,000
Heavy Duty: 12,000

REAR AXLE — Check lubricant level and add lubricant, if necessary, to fill to level of filler plug hole. Use SAE 80 or SAE 90 GL-5 Gear Lubricant every 4 months or 6,000 miles, whichever occurs first.

1900-GT lubrication chart

block. From the point of contact turn the filter one turn clockwise to seal it. Do not use an oil filter wrench to install the new filter as the gasket will be damaged.

Fill the engine with clean oil and start it but do not run the engine above idle speed until the oil pressure warning light goes out. After running the engine, check the oil filter area for leaks, recheck the oil level in the crankcase, replace the dipstick, and you are finished.

Transmission

MANUAL

The lubricant in the standard transmission should not be changed unless it somehow becomes contaminated. Such an instance might arise from not tightening the filler plug, or possibly from having the transmission out of the car and sitting somewhere.

Automatic

The fluid in the automatic transmission should be changed every 24,000 miles under normal use and every 12,000 miles if a lot of stop-and-start driving is done. The transmission fluid should be drained when the fluid is hot. Drive the car around for ten or fifteen minutes, stopping and starting so that the transmission runs through its whole range several times. Open the drain plug on the transmission oil pan and let the bulk of the fluid run out. The transmission fluid in the torque converter will not drain completely so it is a good idea to measure the amount of fluid drained so you have an idea of how much you will have to replace. Use only fluid which is marked Dexron ® or Type A to refill the transmission.

Rear Axle

Other than keeping the fluid level at its proper height, the rear axle lubricant needs no attention. The only exception is when the vehicle is used for towing a trailer. The high temperatures developed in the differential will make it necessary to change the gear oil every 12,000 miles. This is done simply by removing the plug on the bottom of the rear axle housing, draining the fluid, and refilling through the filler plug located above the drain plug near the center of the housing.

CHASSIS GREASING

There are no high pressure grease fittings on Opels but there are several points which should be lubricated at regular intervals. The chassis pivot points are sealed and self lubricating; however the various bushings and suspension bumpers should be lubricated with a good quality silicone lubricant approximately every 60 days.

WHEEL BEARINGS

The front wheel bearings require careful lubrication and adjustment every 12,000 miles. They should be checked and lubricated if necessary any time the brakes are inspected or replaced. See Chapter Nine for complete instructions.

INLINE FUEL FILTER

Removal and Installation

The fuel filter should be removed and replaced every 12 months or 12,000 miles. In 1971–74 models, it is located in the engine compartment in the line from the fuel pump to the carburetor and is removed by loosening the hose clamps and pulling the filter from the hoses. Be careful not to spill any fuel when removing it. On 1975 models, the filter is directly in front of the fuel tank and must be reached from underneath the car. You must remove its support bracket, then disconnect the hose clamps before you can remove it. Since the system will be under pressure, some gas will squirt out when you remove it so it is a good idea to have a catch basin ready and wear eye protection.

Pushing, Towing, Jump Starting

In some emergency situations it may become necessary to have your car pushed or jumped by a booster battery. There are some basic things to remember in these situations that will prevent personal injury or damage to your car.

If your car has a manual transmission, it may be push started in the following manner. Turn the ignition switch to the ON position and put the transmission in Third gear; hold the clutch in until the car is moving at ten to fifteen miles per hour—then release the clutch. Never attempt to tow the car behind another vehicle in an attempt to start it. The forward surge when the car starts could create a very bad situation.

NOTE: *Cars with automatic transmissions cannot be pushed started.*

In the event that starting the car with the aid of a booster battery is necessary, use only a battery of the same voltage as your own (12 V). Then:

Attach one end of the booster cable to the positive terminal of the booster battery. Attach the other end to the positive terminal of the car's battery. Attach the end of the other cable to the negative terminal of the booster battery and make the final connection on a solid chassis ground on your car. Do not let the cables touch

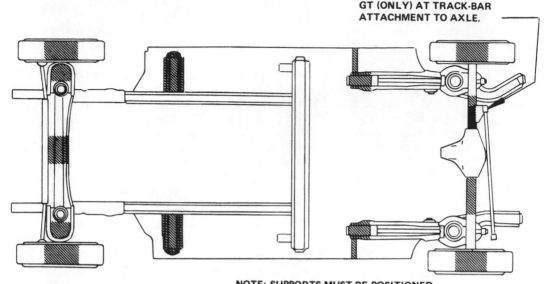

DO NOT LIFT OR SUPPORT
GT (ONLY) AT TRACK-BAR
ATTACHMENT TO AXLE.

NOTE: SUPPORTS MUST BE POSITIONED
SO AS TO DISTRIBUTE LOAD AND SUPPORT
VEHICLE IN A STABLE MANNER.

Vehicle lifting—all models

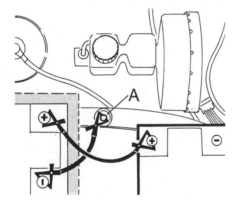

Booster battery hook up

each other. Reverse this procedure to remove the cables.

CAUTION: *Jump starting the battery in any other manner may result in damage to either the electrical system or to yourself. Never jump start a frozen battery as doing so may cause the battery to explode. Never expose the battery to open flame or electrical spark as it creates highly explosive hydrogen gas.*

Towing

Cars with manual transmissions may be towed with the transmission in Neutral. Cars with automatic transmissions should not be towed on the rear wheels at any speed over 30 mph. Towing must be short.

Jacking and Hoisting

In the course of performing routine maintenance on your Opel you undoubtedly will have to raise the car in the air to carry out certain procedures. Other than changing tires, the jack provided in your car should only be used to raise the vehicle, not support it for work. This is especially important when you are under the car. It is very embarrassing and painful to find yourself trapped under a car. The same sort of cynical warning is applied to using cinder blocks as they will crack if the weight of the car is not evenly distributed.

When working under the car a number of devices are available for home garage use that will safely support the vehicle while you are under it. Screw operated scissor jacks, small hydraulic jacks, and locking jackstands will all make for a safe job. If you are industrious and plan to do a lot of work on the car, you can fabricate or purchase steel or heavy wooden ramps.

Any of the methods that you use should first be considered from the safety standpoint. Do not adopt an "it can't happen to me attitude" because it can and will if you don't take the time to safely support the car.

Chapter Two

Tune-Up and Troubleshooting

Tune-Up Specifications

Year	Engine Cu in. Displace-ment	Spark Plugs Type	Gap (in.)	Point Dwell (deg)	Point Gap (in.)	Ignition Timing (deg) MT	AT	Fuel Pump Pres-sure (psi)	Com-pres-sion Pres-sure (psi)	Idle Speed (rpm) MT	AT	Valve Clearance (in.) In	Ex
1971	1.1 Liter	AC① 42FS	0.030	50 ± 2	0.018	TDC	TDC	3	③	950	950	0.006	0.010
1971	1.9 Liter	AC① 42FS	0.030	50 ± 2	0.018	TDC	TDC	3½	③	900	900	②	②
1972–74	1.9 Liter	AC① 42FS	0.030	50 ± 2	0.018	TDC	TDC	3½	③	900	850	②	②
1975	1.9 Liter	AC 42.6 FS	0.030	50 ± 3	0.016	TDC	TDC	31–44	③	950	950	②	②

① If carbon fouling exists, use AC 43FS
② Hydraulic lifters—zero lash plus one turn
③ Lowest reading—75% of highest (see chart in text)

Tune-Up Procedures

In order to keep your Opel in good running condition and to extract the full measure of performance and economy from the engine, it is essential that it be properly tuned at regular intervals. A regular tune-up will keep your engine running smoothly and will avoid the annoying breakdowns and poor performance that are common in an untuned motor. There is no reason for this maintenance to cost you a lot of money; with a little patience and a few tools you can keep your Opel running smoothly and cleanly.

A tune-up restores power and performance that can be lost as various parts wear or fall out of adjustment through normal use. You can save time and money and achieve lasting results by following an exact and methodical plan for analyzing and correcting malfunctions. This chapter on tune-up and troubleshooting will provide you with specific information on tuning your Opel as well as information which is more basic and will help you develop your own system of diagnosis and correction.

The areas considered in a tune-up are compression, ignition, and carburetion. These items should be considered in that order and carburetion should never be adjusted until one is certain that the compression and ignition are satisfactory.

We will then begin this section of the chapter with compression.

Testing Compression

A compression gauge measures the pounds per square inch (psi) of pressure that is exerted by the piston in the cylinder as the engine is cranked. A gauge may be purchased at reasonable cost from many suppliers or possibly rented from a garage or automotive parts outlet. If a gauge is unobtainable and your engine is running very poorly, it is worth your while to have the compression checked by someone who does have the equipment. Providing you can secure a gauge, proceed to paragraph 6.1 in the Troubleshooting section at the back of this chapter.

SPARK PLUGS

Spark plugs can be a most useful diagnostic tool when performing a tune-up. Once removed they can be compared with the samples shown in the Troubleshooting section at the end of this chapter. If the plugs in your car appear to be in good condition and show only normal wear and deposits, they can be cleaned and reinstalled. Spark plugs rarely last more than 10,000 miles and because of the low cost of replacement, it is a good idea to replace them at every major tune up.

When replacing spark plugs, keep in mind that their function is to provide a spark inside the cylinder which ignites the compressed air fuel mixture. It is essential to engine performance that the spark plugs be in good condition and that they are gapped precisely.

The best tool you can have for changing spark plugs is a ⅜ in. drive spark plug socket equipped with a rubber insert which prevents breakage of the ceramic insulators. The socket can be turned with a ratchet handle and will provide ample mobility inside the engine compartment.

There are a variety of methods for changing the spark plugs but perhaps the easiest is to change one spark plug at a time. Remove the rubber boot and spark plug connector from one plug and, using the spark plug socket, remove the plug from the cylinder head. Turn the plug slowly so as not to damage the threads in the cylinder head. Examine the plug for deposits and check the condition of the electrode. Take a new spark plug and gap it with a wire gauge according to the specifications listed in the "Tune-Up Specifications Chart".

The wire of the gauge should pass between the center electrode and the side electrode with just a slight drag. Use the tool on the end of the spark plug gauge to adjust the side electrode. Be sure that the area around the spark plug hole is clean before you insert the new plug. Thread the new plug in the cylinder head and tighten with the ratchet.

CAUTION: *Do not overtighten the spark plug. Replace the connector and boot and move on to the next spark plug. When you have replaced all the plugs, recheck all the connectors to be sure they are secure.*

BREAKER POINTS AND CONDENSER

The ignition distributor breaks the primary current, distributes the high voltage surges induced in the coil secondary winding to the spark plugs according to the engine firing order, and sets ignition timing in relation to engine rpm and load. The engine output is, to a large extent, influenced by the ignition timing. Maximum engine performance is obtained when the combustion process is well under way as the piston starts down on the power stroke. If the spark is too far advanced, the engine knocks which causes a drop in engine power output as well as overheating. If the spark is retarded, part of the energy developed during combustion is wasted and this results in reduced power output, excessive fuel consumption, and overheating.

The Opel distributor is equipped with a plastic cover under the rotor which helps keep the inside of the distributor cap free of condensation thus lowering voltage loss for easier starting. There is also a hood which fits over the upper part of the distributor with an outlet for the ignition cables which also cuts down on the amount of moisture which can reach the distributor. When servicing the distributor, be sure to put these back on as they aid greatly in the engine's ability to stay in tune.

Before beginning the actual tune-up, there are two very important rules which should be observed. When replacing the breaker point assembly, remember to replace the condenser and when you adjust the points remember that you are changing the ignition timing. Therefore if you adjust the points, you must adjust the timing.

Breaker Point Removal and Installation

Snap the retaining clips off of the distributor cap and lift the cap up and away from the distributor. It is not necessary to remove the ignition wires from the cap in order to do this but if for any reason you should find it necessary to remove the wires, it is best to use masking tape to number the wires and the corresponding towers on the cap. This will ensure that the wires will be replaced in their proper position. After lifting the cap, inspect it for cracks, excessive wear on the rotor contacts, and carbon tracks. If any of these conditions exist, it will be advisable to replace the cap with a new one.

Next, remove and inspect the rotor and look at the contacts. If they look very worn and burned or if the rotor seems to be loose on the distributor shaft, it too should be replaced. If there are only light burn marks on the rotor, use a piece of emery paper to remove the marks and reuse it. Lift off the plastic cover from the distributor housing and the points will be visible. Check the breaker points for burning, pitting, or wear and check the contact heel which rests on the distributor cam for

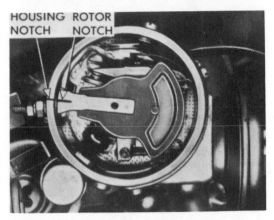

1.1 distributor showing firing position for No. 1 cylinder

wear. If defects are noted, remove the original points and condenser and wipe the distributor housing out with a clean dry rag. When removing the hold-down screws from the points and condenser, use a magnetic screwdriver so as not to lose the small screws.

1975 Opel distributors are slightly changed from previous models. The combination vacuum advance-retard unit has been replaced with a single-purpose unit. This change resulted in a repositioning of the breaker points, however they are serviced the same as the old ones. To replace the condenser, you should use either an offset screwdriver or a screwdriver with a very short handle. If you could find one of these types which is also magnetic it would be good, since the condenser screw is tiny and easily lost.

Installation of the new contact points and condenser is a simple operation.

1. Your new contact point set should come with a small quantity of distributor cam lubricant; spread this lubricant on the heel of the contact points and on the distributor cam prior to installing the points.

2. Position the point set on the breaker plate making sure that the small dowel on the point set rests in the hole in the breaker plate. Again using the magnetic screwdriver, replace the hold-down screw.

3. Replace the condenser in a similar fashion making the proper electrical connections secure.

4. Turn the crankshaft pulley so that the heel of the contact points is resting on the high point of one of the distributor cam lobes and, with a feeler gauge, set the breaker point gap at 0.016. This will be a

1.9 distributor showing firing position for No. 1 cylinder and relationship between cutout on distributor shaft and notch on distributor housing

fairly accurate setting and the final setting to be achieved with a dwell meter.

5. Return the rotor and distributor cap to the distributor making sure that the ignition cables are secure in the cap.

The following sections will describe the dwell angle setting and timing which should be checked after replacing the contact points.

DWELL ANGLE

The dwell angle is the number of degrees of distributor cam rotation through which the breaker points remain fully closed (conducting electricity). Increasing the point gap decreases dwell while decreasing the point gap increases dwell.

Using a dwell meter of known accuracy, connect the red lead (+) wire of the meter to the distributor primary wire on the positive (+) side of the coil and connect the black ground wire of the meter to a good ground on the engine.

The dwell angle may be checked either with the distributor cap and rotor installed and the engine running or with the cap and rotor removed and the engine cranking at starter speed. The meter gives a constant reading with the engine running. With the engine cranking, the reading will fluctuate between zero degrees dwell and the maximum figure for that angle. While cranking, the maximum figure is the correct one for that setting. Never attempt to adjust the points when the ignition is on; doing so will result in a shock.

To change the dwell angle, loosen the point retaining screw slightly and make the appropriate correction. Tighten the screw and test the dwell with the engine cranking. If the dwell appears to be correct, replace the rotor and distributor cap and check the dwell again with the engine running.

Run the engine up to high rpm and let it slow again; the dwell should not drift out of specification. If it does, it indicates that there are worn distributor parts.

After adjusting the dwell angle, the timing should be checked as a 1° increase in dwell results in an ignition timing retard of 2° and vice versa.

IGNITION TIMING

Providing the distributor has not been removed from the engine and that the engine will run, even if poorly, you can ad-

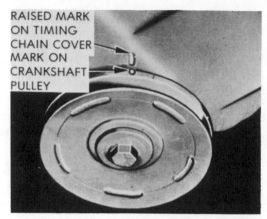
Timing marks—1.1 engine

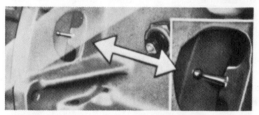
Timing marks—1.9 engine (1971–74)

1975 Opel timing marks

just the ignition timing in the following manner. If the distributor has been removed, please turn to Chapter Three and read the section on distributor removal and replacement before attempting to adjust the ignition timing.

The ignition timing should be checked each time the points are adjusted or replaced and as a part of every regular tune-up at 6000 mile intervals. The timing marks on the 1900 engine consist of a steel ball embedded in the flywheel and a pointer located on the right side of the flywheel facing the engine or, on 1975 models, a pointer on a bracket attached to the engine and a timing mark located on the crankshaft pulley. The 1100 engine has timing marks on the rear edge of the crankshaft pulley and on the timing case cover.

Connect a timing light to the No. 1 spark plug and to the battery according to the manufacturer's instructions. Disconnect and plug the vacuum advance unit and retard unit hoses. On the 1975 distributors, disconnect and plug the single hose going to the distributor. After connecting a tachometer from the distributor side of the coil to a ground, set the idle to the specification listed in the "Tune-Up Specifications Chart". With the engine running, aim the timing light at the timing marks. If the timing marks do not coincide, stop the engine and loosen the distributor hold-down bolt at the base of the distributor; then start the engine again. With the timing light pointed at the timing marks, grasp the distributor by the vacuum advance mechanism and slowly rotate it until the marks are aligned. Stop the engine and firmly tighten the hold-down bolt. As a final test, start the engine again and observe the timing marks to be sure that the setting has not changed.

Reconnect the hoses and remove the timing light from the engine.

VALVE LASH ADJUSTMENT

Adjusting the valves at every major tune-up or every 6000 miles is a good practice and it will prevent more serious trouble if minor discrepancies are corrected before they become severe. To determine at any time whether or not your valve train requires adjustment, just sit in the driver's seat leaving the valve cover in place and the hood of the car closed. Start the engine and allow it to reach operating temperature, thus allowing the mechanical components to expand fully and the oil and coolant to circulate. After about twenty minutes warm up time, begin running the engine at various speeds and listen for regular tapping occurring in direct proportion to the engine rpm. If you detect such noise, raise the hood and, using a length of heater hose as a stethoscope, see if you can locate the faulty valves. If a valve is merely out of adjustment, it will tap regularly; if it is sticking or warped or if the stem is bent, the noise will be intermittent and the engine will suffer most at low rpm under heavy load. The "Engine Rebuilding" section of this book contains information on the correction of these ailments by replacing the valves.

Valve adjustment is one major factor which determines how far the valves will open into the cylinder. If the clearance between the rocker arm and the valve is too great, part of the lift of the camshaft will be used up in removing the excess clearance; thus the valves will not be open far enough. This will result in a loud valve tap as well as poor performance when the valve train components take up the slack. Since the intake valves open less, the quantity of air/fuel mixture introduced into the cylinder will be less and the less the exhaust valve opens, the greater the back pressure. This will also prevent the air/fuel mixture from entering the cylinder in the correct proportions.

If the valve clearance is too small, the intake and exhaust valves will not fully seat on the cylinder head when they close. When a valve seats on the cylinder head it does two things: it seals the combustion chamber so none of the gases in the cylinder can escape and it cools itself by transferring some of the heat it absorbed from the combustion process through the cylinder head and into the cooling system. Therefore, if the valve clearance is too small, the engine will run poorly (due to gases escaping from the combustion chamber) and the valves will overheat and warp since they cannot transfer the heat properly.

Valve adjustments must be made as accurately as possible but it is better to have the valve train slightly loose than slightly tight as burned valves may result from overly tight adjustments.

1.1 LITER OHV ENGINE

Adjust the valves with the engine at operating temperature and running at slow idle. Remove the valve cover and gasket and, starting with No. 1 cylinder, adjust the intake valves to 0.006 in. clearance and the exhaust valves to 0.010 in. clearance between the valve and the rocker arm.

CAUTION: *As with any operation which requires that the engine be running, use extreme care to avoid the fan assembly.*

The adjusting operation requires an open-end wrench of the proper size for the rocker arm locknut and a screwdriver. Use the wrench to loosen the locknut and

Adjusting valves—1.1 engine

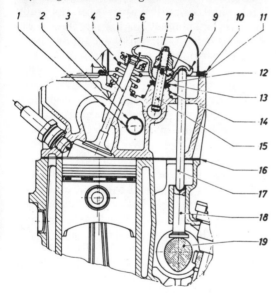

Sectional view of 1.9 engine showing parts related to valve adjustment

1. Calibrated bore in
   water line
2. Water line
3. Valve
4. Valve spring
5. Valve cap
6. Valve key
7. Adjusting nut (make
   valve adjustment here)
8. Ball seat
9. Rocker arm
10. Rocker arm cover
11. Rocker arm cover
    gasket
12. Lubrication hole
13. Spacer
14. Detent spring
15. Rocker arm stud
16. Cylinder head gasket
17. Push-rod
18. Valve lifter
19. Camshaft

Rotor positioning for valve adjustment—1.9 engine

No. 1
No. 2
No. 3
No. 4

a feeler gauge to check the clearance. The screw, when turned, will make the adjustment. When the setting has been made, hold the adjusting screw with the screwdriver and simultaneously tighten the locknut with the wrench. Check your adjustment.

1.9 LITER CIH ENGINE

The 1900 cc Opel engine utilizes hydraulic lifters which do not require as much service as the solid type. However, if adjustment becomes necessary, it can be done with the engine not running. It makes no difference whether the engine is hot or cold so proceed in this manner:

1. Remove the distributor cap so that the rotor can be observed. Trace the position of the rotor through the ignition cables to determine which cylinder is firing with the rotor in this position; that cylinder is at TDC (top dead center).

2. Back off the adjusting nut of those two valves until clearance exists between the valve stem, rocker arm, and lifter.

3. Begin tightening the adjusting nut slowly until there is no clearance in the valve train parts; then tighten the nut one full turn past that point. This will put the adjustment in the center of the lifters' travel and no further adjustment will be necessary.

CARBURETOR

Idle Speed and Mixture Adjustments

As a part of a regular tune-up it may be necessary to adjust the carburetion to attain peak performance. The carburetor should never be adjusted until all other phases of engine tune-up have been completed. If you attempt to adjust the carburetors before adjusting the timing and dwell or if you try to compensate for poor compression, you will have trouble for sure. The result will be frustrating because you won't be able to make the engine run properly and you will put the carburetion so far out of adjustment that it will require professional assistance to get you back on the street.

Therefore, check all other systems and adjust as required before touching the carburetor.

It will be easier for you to adjust the carburetor if you understand how it works and what effect the adjustments you make have on the engine and on the car's overall performance.

The carburetor is a device whose only function is to mix the liquid fuel with air in the correct proportions to provide a combustible mixture for the engine to compress and ignite. A partial vacuum is created by the downward movement of the pistons on their intake stroke. This partial vacuum draws a stream of air through the carburetor into which a jet of fuel is introduced; this air/fuel mixture is drawn into the engine by the action of that same vacuum. The amount of air/fuel mixture which enters the engine is controlled by throttle plates in the bottom of the carburetor. When the engine is not running, these throttle plates are completely closed. The plates are connected by various kinds of linkage to the accelerator pedal inside your car. When you start the engine, put the car in gear, and step on the gas to get under way you are opening the throttle plates of the carburetor to admit more air/fuel mixture into the engine. The farther you open the throttle plates, the greater the engine speed.

As we said before, when the engine is not running, the throttle plates are closed; but some sort of mechanism is required to keep the engine running when your foot is not on the gas pedal (idling). This mechanism is the idle speed screw which contacts the throttle lever on the outside of the carburetor and keeps the throttle plates open a specified amount when your foot is not on the accelerator. Its correct name is the curb idle adjusting screw and there are instructions in this section on how to adjust it.

Since it is difficult for the engine to draw the air/fuel mixture from the carburetor with the throttle valves only slightly open at idle, an idle mixture passage is provided in the carburetor. This passage delivers air/fuel mixture to the engine from a hole which is located in the bottom of the carburetor below the throttle plates. This idle mixture passage has an adjusting screw which regulates the amount of air/fuel mixture that enters the engine at idle. This section will also describe this adjustment.

NOTE: *Carburetor adjustment must be effected only when the engine is at normal operating temperature; it is useless to attempt adjustment if the engine is cold or if it is overheated.*

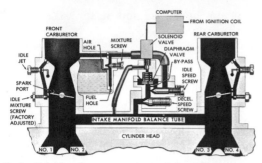

Twin Solex carburetor system—1.1 engine

1.1 LITER TWO CARBURETOR ENGINE

The twin carburetor system is balanced at the factory so you should not touch the individual throttle stop screws or the idle mixture needles. If for some reason the adjustments are disturbed, the carburetors will have to be synchronized before performing the following adjustments. (See appropriate paragraph in this section.)

1. Connect a tachometer between the distributor side of the coil and a ground.

2. Start the engine and run at fast idle until the upper radiator inlet is hot.

3. Adjust the idle speed to 875 rpm using the idle speed screw in the center unit between the carburetors.

4. On the left side of the front carburetor you will see an idle mixture screw. Adjust it to obtain the highest rpm reading on the tachometer. If the idle speed exceeds 1000 rpm, reduce the idle speed using the idle speed screw on the center unit. Again adjust the front carburetor.

5. Once adjusted in this manner, reduce the idle speed by 50 rpm. This is accomplished by turning the mixture screw in slightly from the high rpm setting.

NOTE: *On this installation, neither of the two throttle stop screws should be adjusted in any way.*

Center unit mixture adjusting screw

Center unit air speed screw

1.9 LITER ENGINE

CAUTION: *Federal and state emission control regulations require that exhaust emissions fall within certain limitations. If your carburetor is equipped with limiter caps on the mixture adjustment screws and you do not have access to an exhaust analyzer, it is recommended that you do not attempt to adjust the carburetor. Have the carburetor adjusted by authorized personnel.*

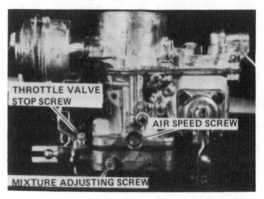

Solex two barrel carb as used on 1.9 engine and adjusting screws

The throttle valve has been set at the factory and it should not require adjustment but should it become necessary to adjust it, use the following procedure.

Fully close the idle air adjusting screw until it is seated. Adjust the idle mixture needle and throttle stop screw to 400–600 rpm to obtain the best possible mixture.

NOTE: *Now that the throttle stop screw has been set, do not move it. All further adjustments will be made with the idle air and mixture screws.*

1. Connect a tachometer between the distributor side of the coil and a ground.

2. Run the engine until the upper radiator hose is full of hot coolant. Be sure that the choke valve is fully open.

3. Be sure that the parking brake is secure and make all adjustments in Neutral or Park.

4. Adjust the idle air speed adjusting screw to obtain 850 rpm for automatic transmission cars and 900 rpm for manual. The idle air speed screw is located in the main body of the carburetor on the right-hand side.

5. Adjust the idle mixture needle as required to get the highest tachometer reading.

6. If the idle speed increases to over 1000 rpm, reduce it using the idle air speed screw and then readjust the idle mixture needle to obtain the highest rpm reading.

7. Lean out the mixture slightly by turning the idle mixture just enough to reduce engine speed by about 30 rpm.

ELECTRONIC FUEL INJECTION

All 1975 Opels are equipped with an electronic fuel injection system. All adjustments should be left to a qualified dealer who has the service tools needed to work on the system. For additional information, see Chapter 4.

Synchronization Of Twin Carburetors

Prior to adjusting the carburetors, the engine must be at operating temperature. Loosen the screw on the coupling between the carburetors, leaving clearance between the screw and the shaft pick-up.

NOTE: *On cars equipped with the Opel Emission Control System, shut off the center unit by pulling the hose from the front carburetor to the center unit and plugging the carburetor nipple and the intake manifold vacuum port.*

Back out the throttle idle adjust screw and close the idle mixture screw on the front carburetor so that the engine is running only on the rear carburetor. Start the engine and adjust the rear carburetor so that the engine runs as smoothly as possible at 700 rpm. Reverse the procedure and adjust the front carburetor in the same manner.

NOTE: *Record the number of turns as the idle mixture screw is closed on the rear carburetor.*

Back out the idle mixture screw on the rear carburetor the number of turns recorded and adjust the idle, using the rear throttle screw, to 1000 rpm. Replace the coupling screw so that no clearance remains.

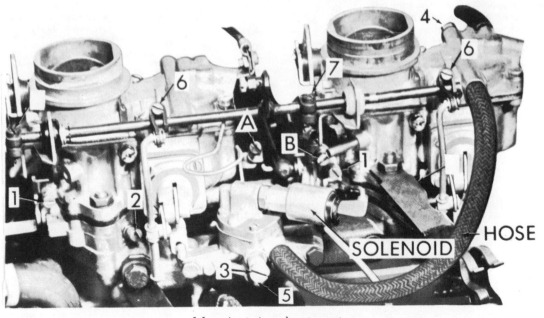

1.1 engine twin carburetor system

A. Carburetor linkage coupling screw	2. Idle mixture screw	6. Accelerator pump eccentric adjusting screw
B. Choke stop screw	3. Center unit air speed screw	7. Choke butterfly adjusting screw
1. Throttle stop screw	4. Center unit mixture screw	
	5. Deceleration mixture screw	

Engine Tune-Up

Engine tune-up is a procedure performed to restore engine performance, deteriorated due to normal wear and loss of adjustment. The three major areas considered in a routine tune-up are compression, ignition, and carburetion, although valve adjustment may be included.

A tune-up is performed in three steps: *analysis*, in which it is determined whether normal wear is responsible for performance loss, and which parts require replacement or service; *parts replacement or service*; and *adjustment*, in which engine adjustments are returned to original specifications. Since the advent of emission control equipment, precision adjustment has become increasingly critical, in order to maintain pollutant emission levels.

Analysis

The procedures below are used to indicate where adjustments, parts service or replacement are necessary within the realm of a normal tune-up. If, following these tests, all systems appear to be functioning properly, proceed to the Troubleshooting Section for further diagnosis.

—Remove all spark plugs, noting the cylinder in which they were installed. Remove the air cleaner, and position the throttle and choke in the full open position. Disconnect the coil high tension lead from the coil and the distributor cap. Insert a compression gauge into the spark plug port of each cylinder, in succession, and crank the engine with

Maxi. Press. Lbs. Sq. In.	Min. Press. Lbs. Sq. In.	Max. Press. Lbs. Sq. In.	Min. Press. Lbs. Sq. In.
134	101	188	141
136	102	190	142
138	104	192	144
140	105	194	145
142	107	196	147
146	110	198	148
148	111	200	150
150	113	202	151
152	114	204	153
154	115	206	154
156	117	208	156
158	118	210	157
160	120	212	158
162	121	214	160
164	123	216	162
166	124	218	163
168	126	220	165
170	127	222	166
172	129	224	168
174	131	226	169
176	132	228	171
178	133	230	172
180	135	232	174
182	136	234	175
184	138	236	177
186	140	238	178

Compression pressure limits
© Buick Div. G.M. Corp.)

the starter to obtain the highest possible reading. Record the readings, and compare the highest to the lowest on the compression pressure limit chart. If the difference exceeds the limits on the chart, or if all readings are excessively low, proceed to a wet compression check (see Troubleshooting Section).

—Evaluate the spark plugs according to the spark plug chart

in the Troubleshooting Section, and proceed as indicated in the chart.

—Remove the distributor cap, and inspect it inside and out for cracks and/or carbon tracks, and inside for excessive wear or burning of the rotor contacts. If any of these faults are evident, the cap must be replaced.

—Check the breaker points for burning, pitting or wear, and the contact heel resting on the distributor cam for excessive wear. If defects are noted, replace the entire breaker point set.

—Remove and inspect the rotor. If the contacts are burned or worn, or if the rotor is excessively loose on the distributor shaft (where applicable), the rotor must be replaced.

—Inspect the spark plug leads and the coil high tension lead for cracks or brittleness. If any of the wires appear defective, the entire set should be replaced.

—Check the air filter to ensure that it is functioning properly.

Parts Replacement and Service

The determination of whether to replace or service parts is at the mechanic's discretion; however, it is suggested that any parts in questionable condition be replaced rather than reused.

—Clean and regap, or replace, the spark plugs as needed. Lightly coat the threads with engine oil and install the plugs. CAUTION: *Do not over-torque taper-seat spark plugs, or plugs being installed in aluminum cylinder heads.*

—If the distributor cap is to be reused, clean the inside with a dry rag, and remove corrosion from the rotor contact points with fine emery cloth. Remove the spark plug wires one by one, and clean the wire ends and the inside of the towers. If the boots are loose, they should be replaced.

If the cap is to be replaced, transfer the wires one by one, cleaning the wire ends and replacing the boots if necessary.

—If the original points are to remain in service, clean them lightly with emery cloth, lubricate the contact heel with grease specifically designed for this purpose. Rotate the crankshaft until the heel rests on a high point of the distributor cam, and adjust the point gap to specifications.

When replacing the points, remove the original points and condenser, and wipe out the inside of the distributor housing with a clean, dry rag. Lightly lubricate the contact heel and pivot point, and install the points and condenser. Rotate the crankshaft until the heel rests on a high point of the distributor cam, and adjust the point gap to specifications. NOTE: *Always replace the condenser when changing the points.*

—If the rotor is to be reused, clean the contacts with solvent. Do not alter the spring tension of the rotor center contact. Install the rotor and the distributor cap.

—Replace the coil high tension lead and/or the spark plug leads as necessary.

—Clean the carburetor using a spray solvent (e.g., Gumout Spray). Remove the varnish from the throttle bores, and clean the linkage. Disconnect and plug the fuel line, and run the engine until it runs out of fuel. Partially fill the float chamber with solvent, and reconnect the fuel line. In extreme cases, the jets can be pressure flushed by inserting a rubber plug into the float vent, running the spray nozzle through it, and spraying the solvent until it squirts out of the venturi fuel dump.

—Clean and tighten all wiring connections in the primary electrical circuit.

Additional Services

The following services *should* be performed in conjunction with a routine tune-up to ensure efficient performance.

—Inspect the battery and fill to the proper level with distilled water. Remove the cable clamps, clean clamps and posts thoroughly, coat the posts lightly with petroleum jelly, reinstall and tighten.

—Inspect all belts, replace and/or adjust as necessary.

—Test the PCV valve (if so equipped), and clean or replace as indicated. Clean all crankcase ventilation hoses, or replace if cracked or hardened.

—Adjust the valves (if necessary) to manufacturer's specifications.

Adjustments

—Connect a dwell-tachometer between the distributor primary lead and ground. Remove the distributor cap and rotor (unless equipped with Delco externally adjustable distributor). With the ignition off, crank the engine with a remote starter switch and measure the point dwell angle. Adjust the dwell angle to specifications. NOTE: *Increasing the gap decreases the dwell angle and* *vice-versa.* Install the rotor and distributor cap.

—Connect a timing light according to the manufacturer's specifications. Identify the proper timing marks with chalk or paint. NOTE: *Luminescent (day-glo) paint is excellent for this purpose.* Start the engine, and run it until it reaches operating temperature. Disconnect and plug any distributor vacuum lines, and adjust idle to the speed required to adjust timing, according to specifications. Loosen the distributor clamp and adjust timing to specifications by rotating the distributor in the engine. NOTE: *To advance timing, rotate distributor opposite normal direction of rotor rotation, and vice-versa.*

—Synchronize the throttles and mixture of multiple carburetors (if so equipped) according to procedures given in the individual car sections.

—Adjust the idle speed, mixture, and idle quality, as specified in the car sections. Final idle adjustments should be made with the air cleaner installed. CAUTION: *Due to strict emission control requirements on 1969 and later models, special test equipment (CO meter, SUN Tester) may be necessary to properly adjust idle mixture to specifications.*

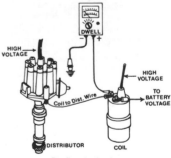

Dwell meter hook-up

Trouble-shooting

The following section is designed to aid in the rapid diagnosis of engine problems. The systematic format is used to diagnose problems ranging from engine starting difficulties to the need for engine overhaul. It is assumed that the user is equipped with basic hand tools and test equipment (tach-dwell meter, timing light, voltmeter, and ohmmeter).

Troubleshooting is divided into two sections. The first, *General Diagnosis*, is used to locate the problem area. In the second, *Specific Diagnosis*, the problem is systematically evaluated.

General Diagnosis

PROBLEM: Symptom	Begin diagnosis at Section Two, Number ———
Engine won't start:	
Starter doesn't turn	1.1, 2.1
Starter turns, engine doesn't	2.1
Starter turns engine very slowly	1.1, 2.4
Starter turns engine normally	3.1, 4.1
Starter turns engine very quickly	6.1
Engine fires intermittently	4.1
Engine fires consistently	5.1, 6.1
Engine runs poorly:	
Hard starting	3.1, 4.1, 5.1, 8.1
Rough idle	4.1, 5.1, 8.1
Stalling	3.1, 4.1, 5.1, 8.1
Engine dies at high speeds	4.1, 5.1
Hesitation (on acceleration from standing stop)	5.1, 8.1
Poor pickup	4.1, 5.1, 8.1
Lack of power	3.1, 4.1, 5.1, 8.1
Backfire through the carburetor	4.1, 8.1, 9.1
Backfire through the exhaust	4.1, 8.1, 9.1
Blue exhaust gases	6.1, 7.1
Black exhaust gases	5.1
Running on (after the ignition is shut off)	3.1, 8.1
Susceptible to moisture	4.1
Engine misfires under load	4.1, 7.1, 8.4, 9.1
Engine misfires at speed	4.1, 8.4
Engine misfires at idle	3.1, 4.1, 5.1, 7.1, 8.4

PROBLEM: Symptom	Probable Cause
Engine noises: ①	
Metallic grind while starting	Starter drive not engaging completely
Constant grind or rumble	*Starter drive not releasing, worn main bearings
Constant knock	Worn connecting rod bearings
Knock under load	Fuel octane too low, worn connecting rod bearings
Double knock	Loose piston pin
Metallic tap	*Collapsed or sticky valve lifter, excessive valve clearance, excessive end play in a rotating shaft
Scrape	*Fan belt contacting a stationary surface
Tick while starting	S.U. electric fuel pump (normal), starter brushes
Constant tick	*Generator brushes, shreaded fan belt
Squeal	*Improperly tensioned fan belt
Hiss or roar	*Steam escaping through a leak in the cooling system or the radiator overflow vent
Whistle	*Vacuum leak
Wheeze	Loose or cracked spark plug

①—It is extremely difficult to evaluate vehicle noises. While the above are general definitions of engine noises, those starred (*) should be considered as possibly originating elsewhere in the car. To aid diagnosis, the following list considers other potential sources of these sounds.

Metallic grind:
  Throwout bearing; transmission gears, bearings, or synchronizers; differential bearings, gears; something metallic in contact with brake drum or disc.

Metallic tap:
  U-joints; fan-to-radiator (or shroud) contact.

Scrape:
  Brake shoe or pad dragging; tire to body contact; suspension contacting undercarriage or exhaust; something non-metallic contacting brake shoe or drum.

Tick:
  Transmission gears; differential gears; lack of radio suppression; resonant vibration of body panels; windshield wiper motor or transmission; heater motor and blower.

Squeal:
  Brake shoe or pad not fully releasing; tires (excessive wear, uneven wear, improper inflation); front or rear wheel alignment (most commonly due to improper toe-in).

Hiss or whistle:
  Wind leaks (body or window); heater motor and blower fan.

Roar:
  Wheel bearings; wind leaks (body and window).

Specific Diagnosis

This section is arranged so that following each test, instructions are given to proceed to another, until a problem is diagnosed.

INDEX

Group		Topic
1	*	Battery
2	*	Cranking system
3	*	Primary electrical system
4	*	Secondary electrical system
5	*	Fuel system
6	*	Engine compression
7	**	Engine vacuum
8	**	Secondary electrical system
9	**	Valve train
10	**	Exhaust system
11	**	Cooling system
12	**	Engine lubrication

*—The engine need not be running.
**—The engine must be running.

SAMPLE SECTION

Test and Procedure	Results and Indications	Proceed to
4.1—Check for spark: Hold each spark plug wire approximately ¼″ from ground with gloves or a heavy, dry rag. Crank the engine and observe the spark.	→ If no spark is evident: —————	→ 4.2
	→ If spark is good in some cases: —————	→ 4.3
	→ If spark is good in all cases: —————	→ 4.6

DIAGNOSIS

Test and Procedure	Results and Indications	Proceed to
1.1—Inspect the battery visually for case condition (corrosion, cracks) and water level.	If case is cracked, replace battery:	1.4
	If the case is intact, remove corrosion with a solution of baking soda and water (CAUTION: *do not get the solution into the battery*), and fill with water:	1.2
1.2—Check the battery cable connections: Insert a screwdriver between the battery post and the cable clamp. Turn the headlights on high beam, and observe them as the screwdriver is gently twisted to ensure good metal to metal contact. **Testing battery cable connections using a screwdriver**	If the lights brighten, remove and clean the clamp and post; coat the post with petroleum jelly, install and tighten the clamp:	1.4
	If no improvement is noted:	1.3

1.3—Test the state of charge of the battery using an individual cell tester or hydrometer.

Spec. Grav. Reading	Charged Condition
1.260-1.280	Fully Charged
1.230-1.250	Three Quarter Charged
1.200-1.220	One Half Charged
1.170-1.190	One Quarter Charged
1.140-1.160	Just About Flat
1.110-1.130	All The Way Down

State of battery charge

Electrolyte temperature (°F)	Specific gravity correction
+120	+.016
+100	+.012
	+.008 ADD to reading
	+.004
+80	no correction
	−.004
+60	−.008
	−.012
+40	−.016
	−.020
+20	−.024
	−.028
0	−.032
	−.036
−20	−.040 SUBTRACT from reading

The effect of temperature on the specific gravity of battery electrolyte

If indicated, charge the battery. NOTE: *If no obvious reason exists for the low state of charge (i.e., battery age, prolonged storage), the charging system should be tested:*   1.4

Test and Procedure	Results and Indications	Proceed to
1.4—Visually inspect battery cables for cracking, bad connection to ground, or bad connection to starter.	If necessary, tighten connections or replace the cables:	2.1

Tests in Group 2 are performed with coil high tension lead disconnected to prevent accidental starting.

Test and Procedure	Results and Indications	Proceed to
2.1—Test the starter motor and solenoid: Connect a jumper from the battery post of the solenoid (or relay) to the starter post of the solenoid (or relay).	If starter turns the engine normally:	2.2
	If the starter buzzes, or turns the engine very slowly:	2.4
	If no response, replace the solenoid (or relay).	3.1
	If the starter turns, but the engine doesn't, ensure that the flywheel ring gear is intact. If the gear is undamaged, replace the starter drive.	3.1
2.2—Determine whether ignition override switches are functioning properly (clutch start switch, neutral safety switch), by connecting a jumper across the switch(es), and turning the ignition switch to "start".	If starter operates, adjust or replace switch:	3.1
	If the starter doesn't operate:	2.3
2.3—Check the ignition switch "start" position: Connect a 12V test lamp between the starter post of the solenoid (or relay) and ground. Turn the ignition switch to the "start" position, and jiggle the key.	If the lamp doesn't light when the switch is turned, check the ignition switch for loose connections, cracked insulation, or broken wires. Repair or replace as necessary:	3.1
	If the lamp flickers when the key is jiggled, replace the ignition switch.	3.3

Checking the ignition switch "start" position

Test and Procedure	Results and Indications	Proceed to
2.4—Remove and bench test the starter, according to specifications in the car section.	If the starter does not meet specifications, repair or replace as needed:	3.1
	If the starter is operating properly:	2.5
2.5—Determine whether the engine can turn freely: Remove the spark plugs, and check for water in the cylinders. Check for water on the dipstick, or oil in the radiator. Attempt to turn the engine using an 18″ flex drive and socket on the crankshaft pulley nut or bolt.	If the engine will turn freely only with the spark plugs out, and hydrostatic lock (water in the cylinders) is ruled out, check valve timing:	9.2
	If engine will not turn freely, and it is known that the clutch and transmission are free, the engine must be disassembled for further evaluation:	Next Chapter

Tests and Procedures	*Results and Indications*	*Proceed to*
3.1—Check the ignition switch "on" position: Connect a jumper wire between the distributor side of the coil and ground, and a 12V test lamp between the switch side of the coil and ground. Remove the high tension lead from the coil. Turn the ignition switch on and jiggle the key.	If the lamp lights:	3.2
	If the lamp flickers when the key is jiggled, replace the ignition switch:	3.3
	If the lamp doesn't light, check for loose or open connections. If none are found, remove the ignition switch and check for continuity. If the switch is faulty, replace it:	3.3

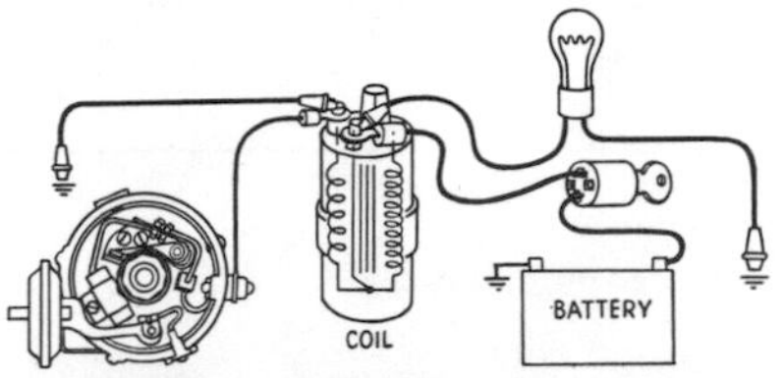

Checking the ignition switch "on" position

| 3.2—Check the ballast resistor or resistance wire for an open circuit, using an ohmmeter. | Replace the resistor or the resistance wire if the resistance is zero. | 3.3 |

| 3.3—Visually inspect the breaker points for burning, pitting, or excessive wear. Gray coloring of the point contact surfaces is normal. Rotate the crankshaft until the contact heel rests on a high point of the distributor cam, and adjust the point gap to specifications. | If the breaker points are intact, clean the contact surfaces with fine emery cloth, and adjust the point gap to specifications. If pitted or worn, replace the points and condenser, and adjust the gap to specifications:
 NOTE: *Always lubricate the distributor cam according to manufacturer's recommendations when servicing the breaker points.* | 3.4 |

| 3.4—Connect a dwell meter between the distributor primary lead and ground. Crank the engine and observe the point dwell angle. | If necessary, adjust the point dwell angle: NOTE: *Increasing the point gap decreases the dwell angle, and vice-versa.* | 3.6 |
| | If dwell meter shows little or no reading: | 3.5 |

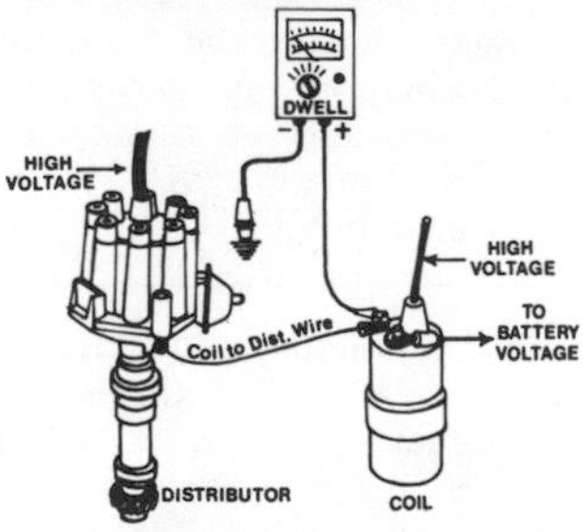

Dwell meter hook-up

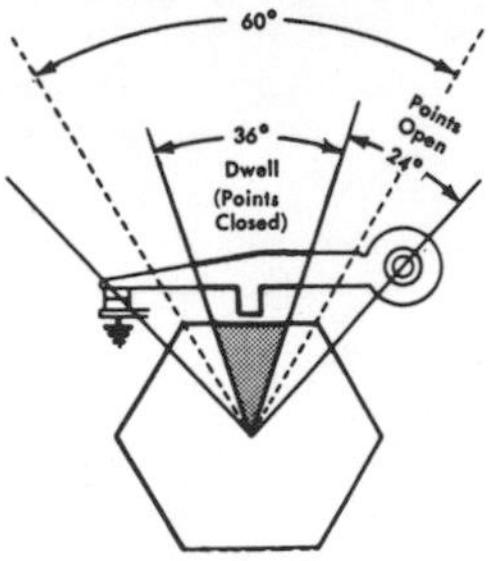

Dwell angle

| 3.5—Check the condenser for short: Connect an ohmmeter across the condenser body and the pigtail lead. | If any reading other than infinite resistance is noted, replace the condenser: | 3.6 |

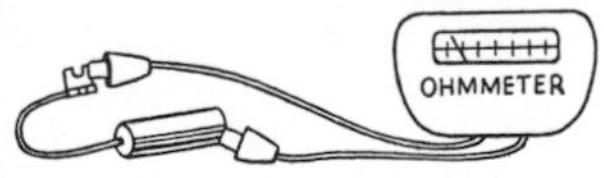

Checking the condenser for short

Test and Procedure	Results and Indications	Proceed to
3.6—Test the coil primary resistance: Connect an ohmmeter across the coil primary terminals, and read the resistance on the low scale. Note whether an external ballast resistor or resistance wire is utilized. **Testing the coil primary resistance**	Coils utilizing ballast resistors or resistance wires should have approximately 1.0Ω resistance; coils with internal resistance should have approximately 4.0Ω resistance. If values far from the above are noted, replace the coil:	4.1
4.1—Check for spark: Hold each spark plug wire approximately $\frac{1}{4}''$ from ground with gloves or a heavy, dry rag. Crank the engine, and observe the spark.	If no spark is evident: If spark is good in some cylinders: If spark is good in all cylinders:	4.2 4.3 4.6
4.2—Check for spark at the coil high tension lead: Remove the coil high tension lead from the distributor and position it approximately $\frac{1}{4}''$ from ground. Crank the engine and observe spark. CAUTION: *This test should not be performed on cars equipped with transistorized ignition.*	If the spark is good and consistent: If the spark is good but intermittent, test the primary electrical system starting at 3.3: If the spark is weak or non-existent, replace the coil high tension lead, clean and tighten all connections and retest. If no improvement is noted:	4.3 3.3 4.4
4.3—Visually inspect the distributor cap and rotor for burned or corroded contacts, cracks, carbon tracks, or moisture. Also check the fit of the rotor on the distributor shaft (where applicable).	If moisture is present, dry thoroughly, and retest per 4.1: If burned or excessively corroded contacts, cracks, or carbon tracks are noted, replace the defective part(s) and retest per 4.1: If the rotor and cap appear intact, or are only slightly corroded, clean the contacts thoroughly (including the cap towers and spark plug wire ends) and retest per 4.1: If the spark is good in all cases: If the spark is poor in all cases:	4.1 4.1 4.6 4.5
4.4—Check the coil secondary resistance: Connect an ohmmeter across the distributor side of the coil and the coil tower. Read the resistance on the high scale of the ohmmeter. **Testing the coil secondary resistance**	The resistance of a satisfactory coil should be between $4K\Omega$ and $10K\Omega$. If the resistance is considerably higher (i.e., $40K\Omega$) replace the coil, and retest per 4.1: NOTE: *This does not apply to high performance coils.*	4.1

Test and Procedure	Results and Indications	Proceed to
4.5—Visually inspect the spark plug wires for cracking or brittleness. Ensure that no two wires are positioned so as to cause induction firing (adjacent and parallel). Remove each wire, one by one, and check resistance with an ohmmeter.	Replace any cracked or brittle wires. If any of the wires are defective, replace the entire set. Replace any wires with excessive resistance (over 8000Ω per foot for suppression wire), and separate any wires that might cause induction firing.	4.6
4.6—Remove the spark plugs, noting the cylinders from which they were removed, and evaluate according to the chart below.	See below.	See below.

	Condition	Cause	Remedy	Proceed to
	Electrodes eroded, light brown deposits.	Normal wear. Normal wear is indicated by approximately .001″ wear per 1000 miles.	Clean and regap the spark plug if wear is not excessive: Replace the spark plug if excessively worn:	4.7
	Carbon fouling (black, dry, fluffy deposits).	If present on one or two plugs:		
		Faulty high tension lead(s).	Test the high tension leads:	4.5
		Burnt or sticking valve(s).	Check the valve train: (Clean and regap the plugs in either case.)	9.1
		If present on most or all plugs: Overly rich fuel mixture, due to restricted air filter, improper carburetor adjustment, improper choke or heat riser adjustment or operation.	Check the fuel system:	5.1
	Oil fouling (wet black deposits)	Worn engine components. NOTE: *Oil fouling may occur in new or recently rebuilt engines until broken in.*	Check engine vacuum and compression: Replace with new spark plug	6.1
	Lead fouling (gray, black, tan, or yellow deposits, which appear glazed or cinderlike).	Combustion by-products.	Clean and regap the plugs: (Use plugs of a different heat range if the problem recurs.)	4.7

	Condition	Cause	Remedy	Proceed to
	Gap bridging (deposits lodged between the electrodes).	Incomplete combustion, or transfer of deposits from the combustion chamber.	Replace the spark plugs:	4.7
	Overheating (burnt electrodes, and extremely white insulator with small black spots).	Ignition timing advanced too far.	Adjust timing to specifications:	8.2
		Overly lean fuel mixture.	Check the fuel system:	5.1
		Spark plugs not seated properly.	Clean spark plug seat and install a new gasket washer: (Replace the spark plugs in all cases.)	4.7
	Fused spot deposits on the insulator.	Combustion chamber blow-by.	Clean and regap the spark plugs:	4.7
	Pre-ignition (melted or severely burned electrodes, blistered or cracked insulators, or metallic deposits on the insulator).	Incorrect spark plug heat range.	Replace with plugs of the proper heat range:	4.7
		Ignition timing advanced too far.	Adjust timing to specifications:	8.2
		Spark plugs not being cooled efficiently.	Clean the spark plug seat, and check the cooling system:	11.1
		Fuel mixture too lean.	Check the fuel system:	5.1
		Poor compression.	Check compression:	6.1
		Fuel grade too low.	Use higher octane fuel:	4.7

Test and Procedure	Results and Indications	Proceed to
4.7—Determine the static ignition timing: Using the flywheel or crankshaft pulley timing marks as a guide, locate top dead center on the *compression* stroke of the No. 1 cylinder. Remove the distributor cap.	Adjust the distributor so that the rotor points toward the No. 1 tower in the distributor cap, and the points are just opening:	4.8
4.8—Check coil polarity: Connect a voltmeter negative lead to the coil high tension lead, and the positive lead to ground (NOTE: *reverse the hook-up for positive ground cars*). Crank the engine momentarily. **Checking coil polarity**	If the voltmeter reads up-scale, the polarity is correct:	5.1
	If the voltmeter reads down-scale, reverse the coil polarity (switch the primary leads):	5.1

Test and Procedure	Results and Indications	Proceed to
5.1—Determine that the air filter is functioning efficiently: Hold paper elements up to a strong light, and attempt to see light through the filter.	Clean permanent air filters in gasoline (or manufacturer's recommendation), and allow to dry. Replace paper elements through which light cannot be seen:	5.2
5.2—Determine whether a flooding condition exists: Flooding is identified by a strong gasoline odor, and excessive gasoline present in the throttle bore(s) of the carburetor.	If flooding is not evident: If flooding is evident, permit the gasoline to dry for a few moments and restart. If flooding doesn't recur: If flooding is persistant:	5.3 5.6 5.5
5.3—Check that fuel is reaching the carburetor: Detach the fuel line at the carburetor inlet. Hold the end of the line in a cup (not styrofoam), and crank the engine.	If fuel flows smoothly: If fuel doesn't flow (NOTE: *Make sure that there is fuel in the tank*), or flows erratically:	5.6 5.4
5.4—Test the fuel pump: Disconnect all fuel lines from the fuel pump. Hold a finger over the input fitting, crank the engine (with electric pump, turn the ignition or pump on); and feel for suction.	If suction is evident, blow out the fuel line to the tank with low pressure compressed air until bubbling is heard from the fuel filler neck. Also blow out the carburetor fuel line (both ends disconnected): If no suction is evident, replace or repair the fuel pump: NOTE: *Repeated oil fouling of the spark plugs, or a no-start condition, could be the result of a ruptured vacuum booster pump diaphragm, through which oil or gasoline is being drawn into the intake manifold (where applicable).*	5.6 5.6
5.5—Check the needle and seat: Tap the carburetor in the area of the needle and seat.	If flooding stops, a gasoline additive (e.g., Gumout) will often cure the problem: If flooding continues, check the fuel pump for excessive pressure at the carburetor (according to specifications). If the pressure is normal, the needle and seat must be removed and checked, and/or the float level adjusted:	5.6 5.6
5.6—Test the accelerator pump by looking into the throttle bores while operating the throttle.	If the accelerator pump appears to be operating normally: If the accelerator pump is not operating, the pump must be reconditioned. Where possible, service the pump with the carburetor(s) installed on the engine. If necessary, remove the carburetor. Prior to removal:	5.7 5.7
5.7—Determine whether the carburetor main fuel system is functioning: Spray a commercial starting fluid into the carburetor while attempting to start the engine.	If the engine starts, runs for a few seconds, and dies: If the engine doesn't start:	5.8 6.1

Test and Procedures	*Results and Indications*	*Proceed to*
5.8—Uncommon fuel system malfunctions: See below:	If the problem is solved:	6.1
	If the problem remains, remove and recondition the carburetor.	

Condition	*Indication*	*Test*	*Usual Weather Conditions*	*Remedy*
Vapor lock	Car will not re-start shortly after running.	Cool the components of the fuel system until the engine starts.	Hot to very hot	Ensure that the exhaust manifold heat control valve is operating. Check with the vehicle manufacturer for the recommended solution to vapor lock on the model in question.
Carburetor icing	Car will not idle, stalls at low speeds.	Visually inspect the throttle plate area of the throttle bores for frost.	High humidity, 32-40° F.	Ensure that the exhaust manifold heat control valve is operating, and that the intake manifold heat riser is not blocked.
Water in the fuel	Engine sputters and stalls; may not start.	Pump a small amount of fuel into a glass jar. Allow to stand, and inspect for droplets or a layer of water.	High humidity, extreme temperature changes.	For droplets, use one or two cans of commercial gas dryer (Dry Gas) For a layer of water, the tank must be drained, and the fuel lines blown out with compressed air.

Test and Procedure	*Results and Indications*	*Proceed to*
6.1—Test engine compression: Remove all spark plugs. Insert a compression gauge into a spark plug port, crank the engine to obtain the maximum reading, and record.	If compression is within limits on all cylinders:	7.1
	If gauge reading is extremely low on all cylinders:	6.2
	If gauge reading is low on one or two cylinders:	6.2
	(If gauge readings are identical and low on two or more adjacent cylinders, the head gasket must be replaced.)	

Testing compression
(© Chevrolet Div. G.M. Corp.)

Maxi. Press. Lbs. Sq. In.	Min. Press. Lbs. Sq. In.	Maxi. Press. Lbs. Sq. In.	Min. Press. Lbs. Sq. In.	Max. Press. Lbs. Sq. In.	Min. Press. Lbs. Sq. In.	Max. Press. Lbs. Sq. In.	Min. Press. Lbs. Sq. In.
134	101	162	121	188	141	214	160
136	102	164	123	190	142	216	162
138	104	166	124	192	144	218	163
140	105	168	126	194	145	220	165
142	107	170	127	196	147	222	166
146	110	172	129	198	148	224	168
148	111	174	131	200	150	226	169
150	113	176	132	202	151	228	171
152	114	178	133	204	153	230	172
154	115	180	135	206	154	232	174
156	117	182	136	208	156	234	175
158	118	184	138	210	157	236	177
160	120	186	140	212	158	238	178

Compression pressure limits
(© Buick Div. G.M. Corp.)

Test and Procedure	Results and Indications	Proceed to
6.2—Test engine compression (wet): Squirt approximately 30 cc. of engine oil into each cylinder, and retest per 6.1.	If the readings improve, worn or cracked rings or broken pistons are indicated:	Next Chapter
	If the readings do not improve, burned or excessively carboned valves or a jumped timing chain are indicated:	7.1
	NOTE: *A jumped timing chain is often indicated by difficult cranking.*	
7.1—Perform a vacuum check of the engine: Attach a vacuum gauge to the intake manifold beyond the throttle plate. Start the engine, and observe the action of the needle over the range of engine speeds.	See below.	See below

	Reading	Indications	Proceed to
	Steady, from 17-22 in. Hg.	Normal.	8.1
	Low and steady.	Late ignition or valve timing, or low compression:	6.1
	Very low	Vacuum leak:	7.2
	Needle fluctuates as engine speed increases.	Ignition miss, blown cylinder head gasket, leaking valve or weak valve spring:	6.1, 8.3
	Gradual drop in reading at idle.	Excessive back pressure in the exhaust system:	10.1
	Intermittent fluctuation at idle.	Ignition miss, sticking valve:	8.3, 9.1
	Drifting needle.	Improper idle mixture adjustment, carburetors not synchronized (where applicable), or minor intake leak. Synchronize the carburetors, adjust the idle, and retest. If the condition persists:	7.2
	High and steady.	Early ignition timing:	8.2

Test and Procedure	Results and Indications	Proceed to
7.2—Attach a vacuum gauge per 7.1, and test for an intake manifold leak. Squirt a small amount of oil around the intake manifold gaskets, carburetor gaskets, plugs and fittings. Observe the action of the vacuum gauge.	If the reading improves, replace the indicated gasket, or seal the indicated fitting or plug: If the reading remains low:	8.1 7.3
7.3—Test all vacuum hoses and accessories for leaks as described in 7.2. Also check the carburetor body (dashpots, automatic choke mechanism, throttle shafts) for leaks in the same manner.	If the reading improves, service or replace the offending part(s): If the reading remains low:	8.1 6.1
8.1—Check the point dwell angle: Connect a dwell meter between the distributor primary wire and ground. Start the engine, and observe the dwell angle from idle to 3000 rpm.	If necessary, adjust the dwell angle. NOTE: *Increasing the point gap reduces the dwell angle and vice-versa.* If the dwell angle moves outside specifications as engine speed increases, the distributor should be removed and checked for cam accuracy, shaft endplay and concentricity, bushing wear, and adequate point arm tension (NOTE: *Most of these items may be checked with the distributor installed in the engine, using an oscilloscope*):	8.2
8.2—Connect a timing light (per manufacturer's recommendation) and check the dynamic ignition timing. Disconnect and plug the vacuum hose(s) to the distributor if specified, start the engine, and observe the timing marks at the specified engine speed.	If the timing is not correct, adjust to specifications by rotating the distributor in the engine: (Advance timing by rotating distributor opposite normal direction of rotor rotation, retard timing by rotating distributor in same direction as rotor rotation.)	8.3
8.3—Check the operation of the distributor advance mechanism(s): To test the mechanical advance, disconnect all but the mechanical advance, and observe the timing marks with a timing light as the engine speed is increased from idle. If the mark moves smoothly, without hesitation, it may be assumed that the mechanical advance is functioning properly. To test vacuum advance and/or retard systems, alternately crimp and release the vacuum line, and observe the timing mark for movement. If movement is noted, the system is operating.	If the systems are functioning: If the systems are not functioning, remove the distributor, and test on a distributor tester:	8.4 8.4
8.4—Locate an ignition miss: With the engine running, remove each spark plug wire, one by one, until one is found that doesn't cause the engine to roughen and slow down.	When the missing cylinder is identified:	4.1

TUNE-UP AND TROUBLESHOOTING   33

Test and Procedure	Results and Indications	Proceed to
9.1—Evaluate the valve train: Remove the valve cover, and ensure that the valves are adjusted to specifications. A mechanic's stethoscope may be used to aid in the diagnosis of the valve train. By pushing the probe on or near push rods or rockers, valve noise often can be isolated. A timing light also may be used to diagnose valve problems. Connect the light according to manufacturer's recommendations, and start the engine. Vary the firing moment of the light by increasing the engine speed (and therefore the ignition advance), and moving the trigger from cylinder to cylinder. Observe the movement of each valve.	See below	See below

Observation	Probable Cause	Remedy	Proceed to
Metallic tap heard through the stethoscope.	Sticking hydraulic lifter or excessive valve clearance.	Adjust valve. If tap persists, remove and replace the lifter:	10.1
Metallic tap through the stethoscope, able to push the rocker arm (lifter side) down by hand.	Collapsed valve lifter.	Remove and replace the lifter:	10.1
Erratic, irregular motion of the valve stem.*	Sticking valve, burned valve.	Recondition the valve and/or valve guide:	Next Chapter
Eccentric motion of the pushrod at the rocker arm.*	Bent pushrod.	Replace the pushrod:	10.1
Valve retainer bounces as the valve closes.*	Weak valve spring or damper.	Remove and test the spring and damper. Replace if necessary:	10.1

*—When observed with a timing light.

Test and Procedure	Results and Indications	Proceed to
9.2—Check the valve timing: Locate top dead center of the No. 1 piston, and install a degree wheel or tape on the crankshaft pulley or damper with zero corresponding to an index mark on the engine. Rotate the crankshaft in its direction of rotation, and observe the opening of the No. 1 cylinder intake valve. The opening should correspond with the correct mark on the degree wheel according to specifications.	If the timing is not correct, the timing cover must be removed for further investigation:	

Test and Procedure	Results and Indications	Proceed to
10.1—Determine whether the exhaust manifold heat control valve is operating: Operate the valve by hand to determine whether it is free to move. If the valve is free, run the engine to operating temperature and observe the action of the valve, to ensure that it is opening.	If the valve sticks, spray it with a suitable solvent, open and close the valve to free it, and retest. If the valve functions properly: If the valve does not free, or does not operate, replace the valve:	10.2 10.2
10.2—Ensure that there are no exhaust restrictions: Visually inspect the exhaust system for kinks, dents, or crushing. Also note that gasses are flowing freely from the tailpipe at all engine speeds, indicating no restriction in the muffler or resonator.	Replace any damaged portion of the system:	11.1
11.1—Visually inspect the fan belt for glazing, cracks, and fraying, and replace if necessary. Tighten the belt so that the longest span has approximately ½″ play at its midpoint under thumb pressure. Checking the fan belt tension (© Nissan Motor Co. Ltd.)	Replace or tighten the fan belt as necessary:	11.2
11.2—Check the fluid level of the cooling system.	If full or slightly low, fill as necessary: If extremely low:	11.5 11.3
11.3—Visually inspect the external portions of the cooling system (radiator, radiator hoses, thermostat elbow, water pump seals, heater hoses, etc.) for leaks. If none are found, pressurize the cooling system to 14-15 psi.	If cooling system holds the pressure: If cooling system loses pressure rapidly, reinspect external parts of the system for leaks under pressure. If none are found, check dipstick for coolant in crankcase. If no coolant is present, but pressure loss continues: If coolant is evident in crankcase, remove cylinder head(s), and check gasket(s). If gaskets are intact, block and cylinder head(s) should be checked for cracks or holes. If the gasket(s) is blown, replace, and purge the crankcase of coolant: NOTE: *Occasionally, due to atmospheric and driving conditions, condensation of water can occur in the crankcase. This causes the oil to appear milky white. To remedy, run the engine until hot, and change the oil and oil filter.*	11.5 11.4 12.6

Test and Procedure	Results and Indication	Proceed to
11.4—Check for combustion leaks into the cooling system: Pressurize the cooling system as above. Start the engine, and observe the pressure gauge. If the needle fluctuates, remove each spark plug wire, one by one, noting which cylinder(s) reduce or eliminate the fluctuation. **Radiator pressure tester** (© American Motors Corp.)	Cylinders which reduce or eliminate the fluctuation, when the spark plug wire is removed, are leaking into the cooling system. Replace the head gasket on the affected cylinder bank(s).	
11.5—Check the radiator pressure cap: Attach a radiator pressure tester to the radiator cap (wet the seal prior to installation). Quickly pump up the pressure, noting the point at which the cap releases. **Testing the radiator pressure cap** (© American Motors Corp.)	If the cap releases within ± 1 psi of the specified rating, it is operating properly: If the cap releases at more than ± 1 psi of the specified rating, it should be replaced:	11.6 11.6
11.6—Test the thermostat: Start the engine cold, remove the radiator cap, and insert a thermometer into the radiator. Allow the engine to idle. After a short while, there will be a sudden, rapid increase in coolant temperature. The temperature at which this sharp rise stops is the thermostat opening temperature.	If the thermostat opens at or about the specified temperature: If the temperature doesn't increase: (If the temperature increases slowly and gradually, replace the thermostat.)	11.7 11.7
11.7—Check the water pump: Remove the thermostat elbow and the thermostat, disconnect the coil high tension lead (to prevent starting), and crank the engine momentarily.	If coolant flows, replace the thermostat and retest per 11.6: If coolant doesn't flow, reverse flush the cooling system to alleviate any blockage that might exist. If system is not blocked, and coolant will not flow, recondition the water pump.	11.6 —
12.1—Check the oil pressure gauge or warning light: If the gauge shows low pressure, or the light is on, for no obvious reason, remove the oil pressure sender. Install an accurate oil pressure gauge and run the engine momentarily.	If oil pressure builds normally, run engine for a few moments to determine that it is functioning normally, and replace the sender. If the pressure remains low: If the pressure surges: If the oil pressure is zero:	— 12.2 12.3 12.3

Test and Procedure	Results and Indications	Proceed to
12.2—Visually inspect the oil: If the oil is watery or very thin, milky, or foamy, replace the oil and oil filter.	If the oil is normal:	12.3
	If after replacing oil the pressure remains low:	12.3
	If after replacing oil the pressure becomes normal:	—
12.3—Inspect the oil pressure relief valve and spring, to ensure that it is not sticking or stuck. Remove and thoroughly clean the valve, spring, and the valve body.	If the oil pressure improves:	—
	If no improvement is noted:	12.4
12.4—Check to ensure that the oil pump is not cavitating (sucking air instead of oil): See that the crankcase is neither over nor underfull, and that the pickup in the sump is in the proper position and free from sludge.	Fill or drain the crankcase to the proper capacity, and clean the pickup screen in solvent if necessary. If no improvement is noted:	12.5
12.5—Inspect the oil pump drive and the oil pump:	If the pump drive or the oil pump appear to be defective, service as necessary and retest per 12.1:	12.1
	If the pump drive and pump appear to be operating normally, the engine should be disassembled to determine where blockage exists:	Next Chapter
12.6—Purge the engine of ethylene glycol coolant: Completely drain the crankcase and the oil filter. Obtain a commercial butyl cellosolve base solvent, designated for this purpose, and follow the instructions precisely. Following this, install a new oil filter and refill the crankcase with the proper weight oil. The next oil and filter change should follow shortly thereafter (1000 miles).		

Oil pressure relief valve
(© British Leyland Motors)

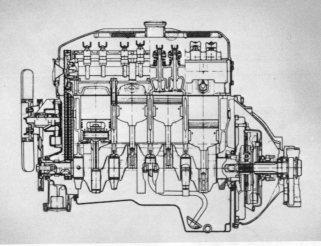

Engine and Engine Rebuilding

Engine Electrical

DISTRIBUTOR

Removal and Installation

1.1 ENGINE

1. Remove the distributor cap.

2. Align the notch in the tip of the rotor with the notch on the distributor housing and align the timing marks on the crankshaft pulley and the timing case cover. This ensures that the engine is in the No. 1 cylinder firing position.

CAUTION: *Once in this position do not disturb the engine.*

3. Disconnect the hose from the vacuum advance unit.

4. Disconnect the primary ignition wires.

5. Remove the distributor hold-down bolt and clamp.

6. Pull the distributor out of the engine. Providing the engine has not been disturbed and is still in the No. 1 firing position, the installation consists of inserting the distributor in the following manner.

1. Inspect the paper gasket on the distributor housing and replace it if necessary.

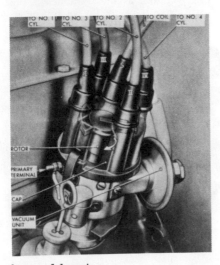

Distributor—1.1 engine

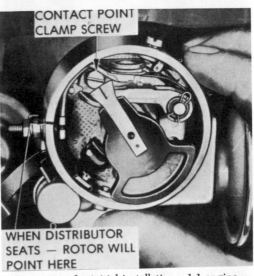

Rotor position for initial installation—1.1 engine

2. Turn the rotor so that the notch on the tip aligns with the contact point hold-down screw.

3. The vacuum advance unit should be pointing toward the rear of the engine and parallel with it.

NOTE: *As the distributor slides into the engine, the rotor will turn and when the housing bottoms on the engine block, the tip of the rotor should align with the notch on the housing.*

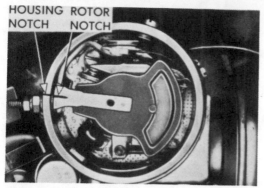

Rotor position for firing No. 1 cylinder—1.1 engine

4. Install the clamp and bolt but do not tighten. Align the marks on the rotor and housing and check the timing marks. Align to be exact.

If the engine has been disturbed while the distributor was not in place, you must get the No. 1 cylinder at top dead center before installing the distributor. Do this by turning the engine over by hand until the valves on the No. 1 cylinder are both loose and the timing marks are aligned.

1.9 ENGINE

In order to remove the distributor from the engine, the fuel pump must be removed as it will block the distributor drive gear. The fuel pump does not have to be removed on 1975 models, as it is an electric unit located in the gas tank.

Proceed in the same manner as described for the 1.1 engine. Remember that the 1.9 engine has different timing marks than the 1.1 engine.

ALTERNATOR

The alternator converts the mechanical energy which is supplied by the drive belt into electric energy by a process of electro-magnetic induction. When the ignition switch is turned on, current flows from the

Removing distributor—1.9 engine

Shaft position for initial installation—1.9 engine; the shaft will turn as the distributor is inserted which will cause the rotor tip notch to align with the notch in the housing

1.9 engine oil pump slot—positioning for installation

Cutaway showing the 1.9 distributor installed

battery, through the charging system light or ammeter, to the voltage regulator, and finally to the alternator. When the engine is started, the drive belt turns the rotating field (rotor) in the stationary windings (stator), inducing alternating current. This alternating current is converted into usable direct current by the diode rectifier. Most of this current is used to charge the battery and to power the electrical accessories of the vehicle. A small part is returned to the field windings of the alternator enabling it to increase its output. When the current in the field windings reaches a predetermined level, the voltage regulator grounds the circuit preventing any further increase. The cycle is continued so that the voltage remains constant.

Opel used three alternators: a 28, 35, and 45 amp model in its line from 1971–75. The Bosch 28 amp model was standard equipment in 1971; if the optional heated rear window was ordered, a Delco 35 amp alternator was supplied. From 1972–74, the Delco 35 amp alternator was the only one available. In 1975, this unit was replaced with a 45 amp Delco unit.

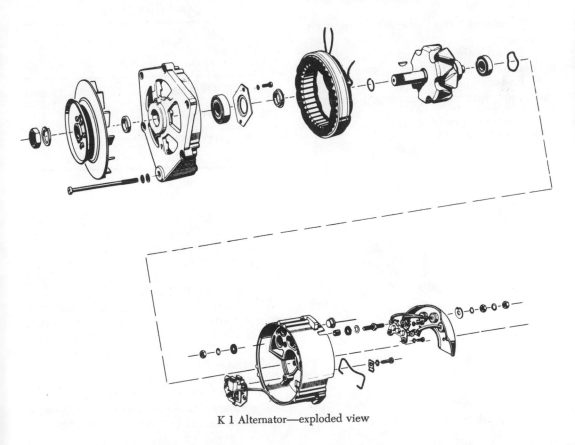

K 1 Alternator—exploded view

Alternator Precautions

1. If the battery is removed for any reason, make sure that it is reinstalled with the proper polarity observed. Reversing the battery connections may result in damage to the one-way rectifiers.

2. Make sure that the battery, alternator, and regulator leads are not disconnected when the engine is running.

3. Never attempt to polarize an alternator.

4. When boost charging a battery that is installed in the car, be sure the negative terminal is disconnected.

5. When using another battery to jump start the vehicle, be sure the batteries are connected in parallel. See Chapter One.

6. When arc welding is performed on any part of the car, be sure to disconnect the negative battery cable, the alternator leads, and the voltage regulator.

Removal and Installation

NOTE: *Always disconnect the battery before making any electrical repairs.*

1. Disconnect the battery ground strap.

2. Unplug the wiring connector from the alternator.

3. Disconnect the battery lead from the alternator.

4. Remove the adjusting brace bolt and related hardware.

5. Loosen the pivot bolt which is the lowermost bolt on the assembly and push

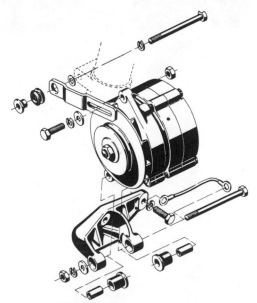

Alternator installation

the alternator toward the engine. Remove the belt from the pulley.

6. Swing the alternator back away from the engine and remove the pivot bolt and hardware. The alternator is off.

To install:

1. Hold the alternator in place on its mounting brackets and slide the pivot bolt through the brace and alternator. Tighten the bolt just finger tight.

2. Install the drive belt on the pulley.

3. Put the adjusting brace bolt in place but do not tighten.

4. You want the alternator drive belt to deflect approximately ½ in. at a point midway between the alternator and the water pump. Use a bar, a long screwdriver or, better yet, a wooden hammer handle to pull back on the alternator as close to the mounting bracket as possible.

5. When the proper tension is achieved, tighten the adjusting brace bolt.

6. Finally, tighten the pivot bolt and reconnect all electrical leads.

Alternator and Regulator Specifications

	Alternator		Regulator	
Year	Part No.	Contin-uous Output	Part No.	Setting @ 2500 RPM
1971–75	G114V28A22	28 Amp	ADI/14V	14 ± 0.5 Volts
	K114V35A20	35 Amp		
	K114V45A20	45 Amp		

VOLTAGE REGULATOR

The regulator consists internally of only one unit as it is a double contact voltage regulator. The alternator field is grounded inside the alternator and so the regulator contacts are in series with the field. Field current is supplied from the D terminal of the alternator; it passes through a red wire to the contacts in the regulator and comes out of the regulator through a brown wire into the DF terminal of the alternator and through the field winding.

The diodes of the alternator act as one-way check valves making a cutout relay unnecessary. Battery current can only flow as far as the diodes but cannot discharge

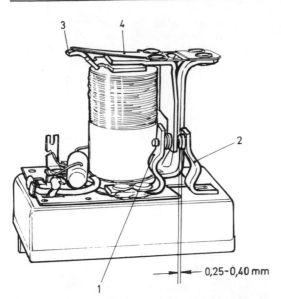

Bosch voltage regulator—internal parts (© Volvo of America Inc.)

1. Regulator contact for lower control range
2. Regulator contact for upper control range
3. Spring tensioner
4. Spring upper section:
   Steel spring
   Spring lower section
   Bimetal spring

through the alternator. However, when the alternator voltage is higher than the battery voltage, the current can flow freely in the other direction to charge the battery.

A current regulator is not necessary either because an alternator cannot supply more current than it was designed to. It cannot overheat and burn out due to excessive output.

Although the voltage regulator can be adjusted, the delicacy of the operation and the equipment required makes the job one which is better left to skilled personnel.

Removal and Installation

Simply remove the connector plug and unscrew the hold-down hardware to remove the regulator. Be sure that the negative battery cable is removed!

STARTER

The starter motor used on Opels between 1971 and 1974 is a Delco-Remy brush type equipped with an overrunning clutch and operated by a solenoid.

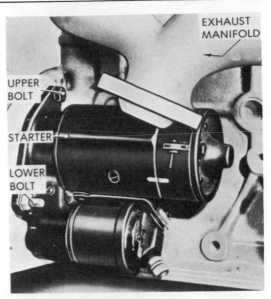

Starter—1.1 engine

Removal and Installation

1.1 ENGINE

As with all electrical repairs, disconnect the negative battery cable before removing the starter. On the 1.1 engine it is also necessary to remove the air cleaner and the choke control cable.

1. From under the car disconnect the wires attached to the starter, noting their location. Be sure to observe proper precautions when getting under the vehicle. Lower the car after removing the wires.

2. Remove the bolts which secure the exhaust manifold to the cylinder head and block the manifold so that it does not interfere with the starter.

3. Unbolt the right front motor mount so the engine can be raised 2 or 3 in. with a jack placed under the transmission or the clutch housing.

4. The starter can now be removed by removing its upper and lower bolts.

To install the starter: naturally, install the starter and the two bolts which secure it to the bellhousing—being certain to support the back end of the starter so that it goes in straight. Drop the engine back down on the motor mount and replace the nut, tightening it securely. Return the exhaust manifold to the cylinder head and finally attach the wires to the starter; put the air cleaner, choke control cable, and the battery cable all back in place.

Removing starter stud—1.9 engine

1.9 ENGINE

1. Disconnect the starter wiring.
2. Remove the starter support bracket.
3. Completely remove the lower starter bolt. Loosen the nut on the upper bolt, which is really a stud, but do not remove it. With the nut on the end of the threads use a soft (brass or plastic) hammer to drive the stud out of the bellhousing. When the stud has been driven out in this manner, the threads will not be damaged.
4. Take the nut off the end of the stud and the starter can be removed.

1.9 starter installation

To install, hold the starter in position and drive in the stud (upper). Install the nut on the upper stud and also install the lower bolt.

5. Install the support bracket. To ensure a stress free installation, install the bolt and two nuts only finger tight. Then tighten the bolt at the engine first and the two nuts on the starter end-frame last.

Starter Drive Replacement

SOLENOID REPLACEMENT

The starters on the 1.1 engine and the 1.9 engine are nearly the same insofar as the replacement of the drive unit and the solenoid are concerned. The following procedures will relate to both starters but whenever special instructions are required, they will appear in the text for the model to which they apply.

DISASSEMBLY

1. Remove the field frame cover band (1.1 only).
2. Support the starter in a vise so that the drive end is down.
3. Mark the end-frame to ensure proper reassembly of parts.
4. Remove the field coil lead from the bottom terminal of the solenoid.
5. Remove the through bolts. (On some

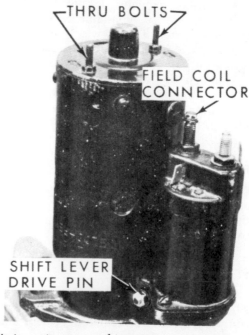

Starter motor supported in a vise

1971 and 1972 1.9 starters it is also necessary to remove the end-frame cover which has two small screws attaching it to the end frame.)

6. Remove the end frame.

7. If you have a 29mm socket you can place it over the commutator to prevent the brushes from falling out when you lift off the field frame.

Driving back the retaining ring

Using a 29mm socket to hold the brushes while removing the field frame

2. Slide the pinion stop retainer down over the shaft with the recessed side outward.

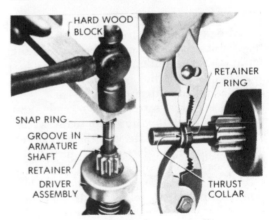

Pinion stop retainer and snap-ring installation

8. Remove the two screws which attach the solenoid to the drive housing.

9. Remove the solenoid and spring.

10. Remove the shift lever fulcrum bolt.

11. Remove the shift lever assembly and the armature out of the drive housing.

12. To remove the drive unit from the armature, place a cylinder of the proper diameter (a piece of ½ in. pipe coupling will do) over the end of the shaft to bear against the pinion stop retainer. Tap the retainer toward the armature to uncover the snap-ring. Remove the snap-ring from the groove in the shaft then slide the retainer and drive unit from the shaft.

ASSEMBLY

1. Lubricate the armature shaft. Install the drive assembly with the pinion outward.

3. Place a new snap-ring on the drive end of the shaft and hold it in place with a hard wood block. Strike the block with a hammer to force the snap-ring over the end of the shaft, then slide the ring down into the groove in the shaft.

4. Place the thrust collar on the shaft with the shoulder next to the snap-ring and move the retainer into contact with the ring. Using pliers on opposite sides of the shaft, squeeze the retainer and thrust collar together until the snap-ring is forced into the retainer.

5. Lubricate the drive housing bushing

Battery and Starter Specifications

| Year | Battery | | | | Starter | | | | | | Brush Spring Tension (oz) |
| | Ampere Hour Engine Capacity | Volts | Terminal Grounded | Lock Test | | | No-Load Test | | | |
				Amps	Volts	Torque (ft lbs)	Amps	Volts	RPM	
1971	1.1	44	12	Negative	270–310	7.5–8.5	——	25–45	11.5	8000–9500	28–32
1971–73	1.9	44	12	Negative	280–320	6	——	35–45	12	6400–7900	40–46
1974–75	1.9	44	12	Negative	280–320	7.5	——	30–50	10.6	7300–8500	40–46

and install the armature and drive assembly in the housing.

6. Install the solenoid thrust spring and the solenoid.

7. Again utilizing the 29mm socket to hold the brushes in place, slide the field frame down onto the drive housing.

8. Install the end-frame and through bolts.

9. Install the lead to the solenoid.

10. Install the field frame cover band (1.1 only).

BATTERY

1. Remove the positive and negative battery cables. If they seem to be stuck to the terminals, use a puller to remove them.

2. Remove all the hold-down hardware and lift the old battery out of the car.

3. Clean the battery cable ends and wash out the battery tray with soapy water.

4. Put the new battery in the car, fasten all hold-down hardware, and install the battery cables in proper polarity.

5. Coat the cable and terminal connection with petroleum jelly to resist moisture.

CAUTION: *Remember, when you're working around the battery, that the electrolyte is SULFURIC ACID!*

Engine Mechanical

DESIGN

Opels have been equipped with two engines of very different design. The 1.1 engine which is standard equipment on 1971 Opel sedans and station wagons is a conventional overhead valve, in-line, four cylinder engine. The 1.9 engine which is standard for all 1900, GT, and Manta series cars and optional on all 1971 Opels is a unique cam-in-head design incorporating hydraulic lifters. Both engines have a compression ratio of 7.6:1 and are designed to run on regular gas except for the 1975s, which must use unleaded fuel. The 1.1 engine was dropped after 1971.

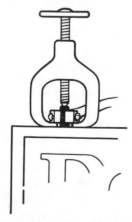

Battery cable puller properly installed on terminal

Sectional view of the 1.9 engine

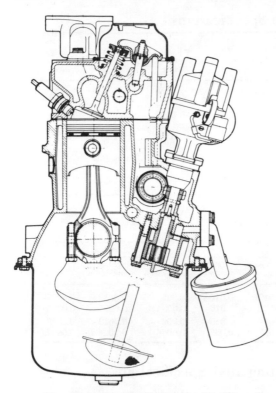

Front cross section—1.1 engine

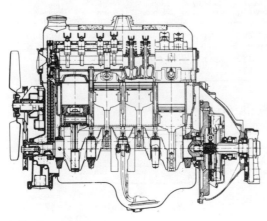

Side view—1.9 engine

Although the 1.1 engine is designed along very traditional lines, it has a number of highly efficient features which make it a very good example of small overhead valve engine design.

The cylinder head is made of chromium alloyed cast iron with intake and exhaust ports on the right side of the cylinder. The combustion chambers are machined to ensure smooth travel of the air/fuel mixture.

The crankshaft rides on three main bearings and the center bearing serves as the thrust bearing. The crank is forged out of

heat treated steel and the bearings are inductively hardened.

An example of the engineering mentioned appears in the pistons which are made of light alloy with a steel expansion strip integrally cast into them. This limits the thermal expansion of the piston to the extent that the piston clearance in the cylinder bore remains practically the same whether the engine is cold or at operating temperature.

The camshaft is driven off of the crankshaft which is a standard procedure; however, Opels feature an oil pressure operated chain tensioning mechanism which automatically adjusts the tension on the timing chain. This system eliminates the slack that develops from use and also provides excellent lubrication for the timing mechanism.

Opel's unique cam-in-head design for the 1.9 engine makes it one of the greatest innovations in valve train design. The cylinder head supports the camshaft with four main bearings. These bearings are sized in such a way as to correspond to the progressively sized journals of the camshaft. The camshaft may be installed only one way by this method and much confusion is eliminated.

The valves are located in the center of the combustion chamber as is the spark plug which provides for short flame travel and excellent combustion.

The forged, five main bearing crank has large diameter main and connecting rod bearing journals which make for little vibration and long life.

The full skirt autothermic type pistons have two horizontal slots which partially separate the head and skirt and provide for good expansion at all temperature ranges.

The cam is driven off of the crank by an endless duplex roller chain which is tensioned by both a spring and by oil pressure. This system is similar to that of the 1.1 engine and again provides good lubrication as well as removing the slack from the timing chain.

1.9 engines use a short hydraulic lifter which is fashioned in such a way as to allow the ball end of the rocker arm to ride in a cup on its upper surface. The position of the cam, the easily adjusted hydraulic lifters, and the integral valve guide arrangement make the 1.9 valve train one of the most rigid and easily adjusted in the business.

General Engine Specifications

Year	Model	Engine Cu In. Displacement	Carburetor Type	Horsepower @ rpm	Torque @ rpm (ft lbs)	Bore x Stroke (in.)	Compression Ratio
1971	1.1	65.8	2-Solex 1 Bbl w/manual choke	56 @ 5800	55 @ 4400	2.95 x 2.40	7.6 : 1
	1.9	115.8	1 Solex 2 Bbl w/automatic choke	90 @ 5200	111 @ 3400	3.66 x 2.75	7.6 : 1
1972–73	1.9	115.8	1-Solex 2 Bbl w/automatic choke	90 @ 5200	111 @ 3400	3.66 x 2.75	7.6 : 1
1974	1.9	115.8	1-Solex 2 Bbl w/automatic choke	75 @ 4800	92 @ 3100	3.66 x 2.75	7.6 : 1
1975	1.9	115.8	Electronic Fuel Injection	81 @ 5000	96 @ 2200	3.66 x 2.75	7.6 : 1

Piston and Ring Specifications
(All measurements in inches)

Year	Engine Cu in. Displacement	Piston Clearance	Ring Gap			Ring Side Clearance		
			Top Compression	Bottom Compression	Oil Control	Top Compression	Bottom Compression	Oil Control
1971	1.1	0.004–0.0012	0.012	0.012	0.010–0.016	0.0024–0.0034	0.0013–0.0025	0.0013–0.0025
1971–75	1.9	0.0014	0.014–0.022	0.014–0.022	0.015–0.055	0.0024–0.0034	0.0013–0.0024	0.0013–0.0024

Crankshaft and Connecting Rod Specifications
(All measurements are given in inches)

Year	Engine Cu In. Displacement	Crankshaft				Connecting Rod		
		Main Brg Journal Dia	Main Brg Oil Clearance	Shaft End-Play	Thrust on No.	Journal Diameter	Oil Clearance	Side Clearance
1971	1.1	2.1260	0.004–0.0022	0.004–0.008	Center (2)	1.77	0.0006–0.0025	0.004–0.010
1971–75	1.9	2.2832	0.009–0.0025	0.0017–0.0061	5	2.0464	0.0006–0.0025	0.0043–0.0095

Torque Specifications
(All readings in ft lbs)

Year	Engine Displacement	Cylinder Head Bolts	Rod Bearing Bolts	Main Bearing Bolts	Crankshaft Pulley Bolt	Flywheel-to-Crankshaft Bolts	Manifold		Cylinder Head-to-Timing Cover
							Intake	Exhaust	
1971	1.1 Liter	35①	20	45	30	25	15	15	——
1971–74	1.9 Liter	72①	36	72	72	43	33②		17
1975	1.9 Liter	72①	33	73	72	43	29②		17

① Cold; 1.9 engine 58 ft lbs warm   ② Combination manifold

Valve Specifications

Year	Engine Displacement (liters)	Seat Angle (deg)	Face Angle (deg)	SPRING TEST PRESSURE (lb @ in.)				STEM TO GUIDE CLEARANCE (in.)		STEM DIAMETER (in.)	
				Closed		Open					
				Intake	Exhaust	Intake	Exhaust	Intake	Exhaust	Intake	Exhaust
1971	1.1	45	44	33 @ 1.28	——	99 @ 0.91	——	0.0006–0.0018	0.0014–0.0026	0.2756–0.2760	0.2748–0.2752
	1.9	45	44	1.57 @ 81.6	1.36 @ 71.7	1.18 @ 153.2	0.96 @ 157	0.0014–0.0025	0.002–0.0039	0.3538–0.3543	0.3524–0.3528
1972	1.9	45	44	1.57 @ 81.6	1.36 @ 71.7	1.18 @ 153.2	0.96 @ 157	0.0014–0.0025	0.002–0.0039	0.3538–0.3543	0.3524–0.3528
1973–75	1.9	45	44	1.57 @ 93	1.36 @ 97	1.18 @ 182	0.96 @ 180	0.0010–0.0029	0.002–0.0039	0.3538–0.3543	0.3524–0.3528

ENGINE REMOVAL AND INSTALLATION

Removing the engine is not one of the easiest jobs to accomplish and it would be extremely advisable to have at least one assistant and more if they're available. Before beginning, get your equipment together; if you don't have at least two jackstands, a small hydraulic jack, and a good scissor jack . . . forget it. The front and rear of the car have to be supported at the same time and there is work to be done underneath.

CAUTION: *Do not attempt to remove the engine unless you can safely support the entire car about 20 in. off the ground.*

You will also need a chain hoist or similar device to lift the engine from the car.

1.1 Engine

1. Mark the hood hinge location and remove the hood.

2. Disconnect the battery cables.

3. Drain the radiator. Disconnect and remove the radiator, radiator hoses, and heater hoses.

4. Remove the shift lever by placing the shifter in Neutral, raising the boot cover, and unscrewing the locking cap. Push the locking cap down and turn it counterclockwise. Some models use a snap-ring to retain the shift lever. Remove the snap-ring and lift the shifter out.

5. Detach the throttle linkage from the carburetor and remove the rear support, fuel lines, vacuum lines, heater control cables, and electrical connections to the starter and generator.

6. Unbolt the exhaust pipe from the manifold.

7. Remove the oil filter housing and filter.

8. Jack up the front and rear of the car and support it in a safe manner.

9. Detach the clutch cable and remove it from the transmission.

10. Disconnect the back-up light switch and speedometer cable.

11. Remove the driveshaft.

12. Support the transmission and remove the transmission mounting bolts.

13. Attach suitable lifting equipment to the engine.

14. Disconnect both motor mounts.

Removing the 1.1 engine

NOTE: *The engine rubber motor mounts are the same, but the support bracket on the starter side is larger.*

15. Lift the engine out of the compartment.

16. To install the engine, lower the engine into the compartment.

17. With the engine still supported, install the motor mounts, but do not tighten.

18. Install the transmission mounting bolts. After all mounting bolts are in position, tighten all bolts.

19. Install the oil filter housing using a new gasket to prevent leakage.

20. Reversing the removal procedures, install all electrical connections, heater hose, linkage to carburetor, etc.

1.9 Engine, 1971–72 (except 1900)

Unfortunately things do not get any easier if your Opel happens to have the optional 1.9 engine. The only way to remove this engine from the car is to drop it and the front suspension out of the car from the bottom. It is not impossible to do this but I think it wise to mention that the equipment used at a service center to perform the job is quite elaborate. The job involves much time and care to perform but if you are patient and careful you can accomplish it.

1. Remove all connections to the engine and transmission. This includes battery cables, air cleaner, coil wire, electrical harness to the alternator, oil pressure switch, choke cable, and heater control valve. Disconnect all fuel lines, vacuum lines, and heater and coolant hoses.

2. Drain all remaining lubricant coolant from the engine.

3. Remove the gearshift lever.

4. Disconnect the speedometer cable.

5. Disconnect the clutch cable.

Remove the shift lever by removing the lock cap

Match mark driveshaft joint flanges before removing bolts; parking brake can be disassembled at the equalizer

6. Disconnect the driveshaft at the torque tube and remove it.

7. Remove the exhaust pipe at the manifold.

8. Remove all tailpipe and muffler hangers.

9. Remove the ground strap from the engine to the frame rails.

10. On two very good jackstands, support the front end of the car at the frame.

11. Disconnect the front brake hoses.

12. Remove the steering clamp pinch bolt. Mark the location of the shaft to the flange.

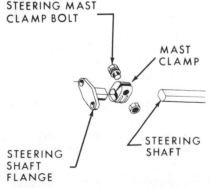

Steering mast flange

Mast guide stop bolt—Kadett shown

13. Remove the steering mast guide sleeve stop bolt from the mast jacket bracket. Pull the steering column out until it clears the mast flange.

NOTE: *At this point there is some maneuvering to be done. The suspension must be supported from above with a chain hoist or similar device and a floor jack must be placed under the crossmember. Use the floor jack to gently support the crossmember without raising the car off of the stands. The chain hoist will prevent the suspension from tilting when the engine and suspension are lowered.*

14. Disconnect the shock absorbers from their upper mounting.

15. Remove the transmission support bracket bolts.

16. Remove the front suspension crossmember attaching nuts and lower the assembly from the car.

At this point you can remove the engine from the suspension on the ground.

INSTALLING THE ASSEMBLY

First you will have to install the engine and transmission on the suspension member in preparation for putting the unit back in the car.

1. With the car still supported at the front, position the front crossmember under the frame. Possibly the best way to approach this is to have the entire assembly, engine and all, on a floor jack so you have some mobility.

2. Raise the assembly with the jack and again from above attach the chain hoist.

3. Using the hoist and the jack, position the assembly properly.

4. Attach the front member to the frame rails and torque the nuts to 36 ft lbs.

5. Reassemble the drive unit.

Opel 1900 Series and Manta

The removal of the engine and transmission on these models is a good deal easier than the older model Opels. They can be removed as a unit in a fairly conventional manner. Observe all safety precautions as outlined earlier in this chapter.

1. Remove the hood and scribe the location of the hinges so proper replacement can be effected.
2. Disconnect the negative battery cable.
3. Drain the coolant at the lower radiator hose.
4. Remove the upper and lower radiator hoses.
5. Remove the radiator and the fan shroud.
6. Disconnect the heater hoses.
7. Disconnect the brake booster vacuum hose.
8. Remove the air cleaner assembly and the evaporative emissions canister lines if applicable.
9. Disconnect all electrical connections to the engine.
10. Remove the console.
11. Remove the shift lever, boot, and plate.
12. Disconnect the fuel line at the fuel pump.
13. Remove the front splash pan.
14. Disconnect the back-up light switch, speedometer cable, and clutch cable.
15. Remove the driveshaft.
16. Disconnect the bellhousing support, the EGR line to the exhaust pipe, and the exhaust pipe.
17. Disconnect the transmission support.
18. Remove the engine mount bolts.
19. Using a chain hoist, lift the engine and transmission out of the car.
20. To reinstall the engine, simply lower the engine and transmission assembly back

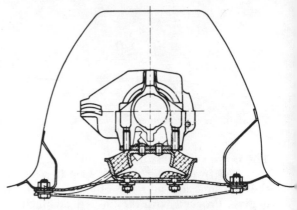

Transmission support bolts—1900 series

into the car and reinstall all components. There are no unusual procedures involved.

NOTE: *Before tightening the engine or transmission support bolts, put all support bolts in place finger tight. This will ensure a stress free installation.*

GT

The only way to remove the engine from the GT is from the underside of the car.

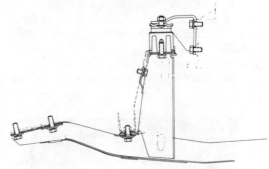

Left front engine suspension with crossmember—(GT)

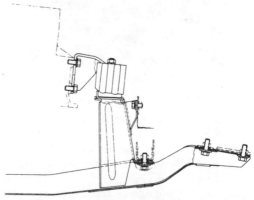

Right front engine suspension with crossmember —(GT)

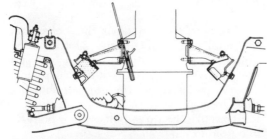

Engine mount bolts—1900 series

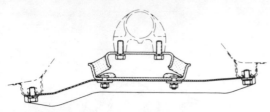

Transmission crossmember

There are two crossmembers which can be removed from under the car. One is under the transmission and the other under the engine. Proceed with the basic detachment of the engine and transmission from the rest of the car as outlined in the 1900 and Manta series engine removal paragraphs.

When you are ready to make the final removal, you will have to get the car up in the front with good solid support equipment such as heavy duty jackstands. A chain hoist and a good floor jack will also come in handy; you will be able to get by without the jack but not without the hoist. Take the weight off of the front motor mounts either by raising the jack slightly or by picking up some of the weight of the engine with the hoist. Unbolt the transmission crossmember from the transmission and the frame and do likewise with the engine crossmember. The engine and transmission can now be lowered out of the car.

Removing the 1.9 engine from an Opel GT

In order to get the engine back in the car it will have to be positioned from underneath. The easiest method would be with a floor jack. Raise the engine and transmission into the engine compartment and install the crossmembers and fastening bolts. Replace all components in their logical sequence.

INTAKE MANIFOLD
Removal and Installation
1.1 ENGINE

1. Disconnect the battery cables from the battery.
2. Remove the air cleaners and silencers and then remove the throttle rod from the carburetor and from the rear support.
3. From the carburetors, remove the fuel lines, bowden control wires, and vacuum hoses.
4. Disconnect the heater hose and the control wire from the heater temperature control valve.
5. Remove the joint carburetor linkage at the center. (See Chapter Four)
6. Remove the carburetors.
7. Remove the O-ring seals from between the carburetors and the manifold.

The center intake manifold bolt is located in the manifold below the carburetor

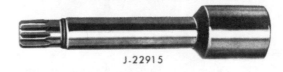

J-22915

J-23016

Serrated bits

8. In order to remove the bolts from the intake manifold, a special tool is required. You will notice that the bolts are the star type; the tool required to remove them is pictured and the number shown is the Opel special tool number. Using this tool, remove the three bolts which hold the manifold to the head.
9. Remove the manifold and the gasket.

10. Before installing the manifold, install a new intake manifold gasket and then place the manifold in position.

11. Tighten the serrated bolts using the proper tool. Begin with the center bolt and torque each bolt to 15 ft lbs.

12. Install new O-ring seals between the carburetors and the manifold.

13. Install the carburetors.

14. Install all carburetor connections.

15. Replace the air cleaners and silencers and connect the battery.

1.9 ENGINE

1971–74

The 1.9 engine utilizes a combination intake and exhaust manifold which must be removed from the engine as a unit. After removal, they can be separated.

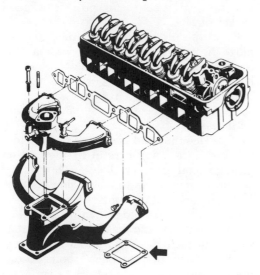

Combination manifold intermediate gasket

1. Disconnect the battery and remove the air cleaners.

2. Disconnect the throttle linkage at the carburetor.

3. Remove the vacuum advance hose at the carburetor connection.

4. Remove the PCV hose at the rocker arm.

5. Disconnect the E.G.R. hoses (if so equipped) from the carburetor and the intake manifold.

6. Unbolt the exhaust pipe from the manifold.

7. Remove the six bolts which hold the manifold to the head and remove the manifold and carburetor as a unit.

8. The manifolds may be separated by removing the carburetor and the four bolts which hold the manifolds together. In order to remove the star bolts, a special tool is necessary. Always replace the intermediate gasket between the manifolds when they are separated.

Always assemble the manifolds before installing and, to facilitate the installation, also mount the carburetor on the manifold.

1. Install a new gasket and hold the manifold in place against the head.

2. Install several bolts finger tight and begin tightening from the center out. (See the torque sequence illustration)

Manifold bolt tightening sequence—1.9 engine

3. Reinstall all parts removed in the disassembly procedure.

1975

1. Cover the fender with a heavy shop cloth to prevent damage.

2. Disconnect the wires at the cold start injector, the four fuel injectors, the throttle valve switch, temperature sensor, thermo time switch, auxiliary air valve, and the airflow meter.

3. Loosen the air outlet hose clamp and remove the hose at the airflow meter. Loosen the airflow meter retaining nut and the air cleaner top clips; remove the air cleaner top and flow meter.

4. Disconnect the throttle body housing inlet hose and move it aside.

5. Disconnect the Bowden wire from the accelerator linkage, and then disconnect the hoses from the auxiliary air valve, distributor vacuum hose at the "T" fitting, the air conditioning hose at the "T" fitting and the EGR vacuum hose at the carburetor.

6. Disconnect the fuel injection ground at the rear of the intake manifold, and the EGR pipe at the throttle body.

7. Disconnect the vacuum brake hose and remove the two accelerator linkage springs.

8. Disconnect the fuel return hose at both ends of the manifold.

9. Disconnect the fuel pressure regulator hose at the firewall, remove the intake manifold attaching bolts, and remove the intake manifold.

10. Installation is the reverse of removal, but remember to apply a sealing compound to the mounting bolt threads and to torque the bolts in the proper sequence.

EXHAUST MANIFOLD

Removal and Installation

1.1 ENGINE

The 'exhaust manifold may be removed easily by disconnecting the exhaust pipe at the manifold and removing the bolts which hold it to the cylinder head. It is also easily installed, but just remember to put a new gasket between the manifold and head and to torque the bolts from the center outward to 15 ft lbs.

1.9 ENGINE

1975

1. Remove the intake manifold.

2. Disconnect the exhaust pipe from the exhaust manifold.

3. Remove the exhaust manifold attaching bolts and remove the exhaust manifold.

4. Installation is the reverse of removal.

CYLINDER HEAD

Removal and Installation

1.1 ENGINE

1. Drain the radiator and the engine block. To do this satisfactorily, remove the drain plug at the right front of the block and also remove the lower radiator hose.
NOTE: *Never attempt to remove the cylinder head if the engine is warm, only do so when cold.*

2. Disconnect the wires from the spark plugs and remove the distributor cap with the wires still attached to it.

3. Remove the intake manifold.

4. Loosen the alternator adjusting bolt and remove the fan belt.

5. Remove the exhaust manifold.

6. Remove the temperature sending unit from the cylinder head.

7. Remove the heater hose from its connection on the head.

8. Remove the rocker arm cover, the rocker arms, and the pushrods.

9. Removing the cylinder head bolts requires a special tool since the bolts are star types. The tool is pictured here and identified by its Opel identification number.

10. Remove the cylinder head from the block.
NOTE: *When you put the cylinder head down on a bench, be careful not to damage the valves. Support the head on some wood blocks placed on the ends.*

Before installing the cylinder head, examine the condition of the cylinder walls to determine if further repairs are necessary. Clean the gasket surface of the block thoroughly and wipe it with a rag lightly dampened with solvent. This will remove any residual grease and provide a good gasket surface.

Raise the pistons one at a time and remove heavy carbon deposits with a thin scraper. You don't have to be too meticulous but a good cleaning will really help. Then replace the head as follows.

1. Coat the new cylinder head gasket with graphite grease.

2. Place the head gasket on the cylinder block surface being careful to align all oil passage and coolant holes. The gasket should be marked as to which side goes up. If it is an original equipment Opel part, the up side will be marked "Oben".

3. Install all the head bolts and start them into their threads without tightening.

4. Tighten the star head bolts to the proper torque following the sequence shown in the illustration.

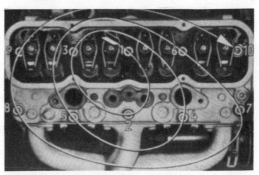

Cylinder head bolt tightening sequence—1.1 engine

5. Put the pushrods back into the engine making sure they are straight and falling directly on the lifters.

6. Install the rocker arms, ball seats, and adjusting nuts but do not tighten the adjusting nuts.

7. Adjust the valves while cold by following the directions in Chapter Two.

8. Install the intake manifold.

9. Install all components removed in the disassembly procedure.

10. Refill the engine with the proper coolant and check the engine oil level before starting.

1.9 ENGINE

1971–74

The removal of the 1.9 cylinder head is a little more involved than that of the 1.1 engine because of the timing chain. Use special care when removing or installing the timing chain or related parts. They are quite a bit more delicate than the rest of the parts involved.

1. Drain the coolant by removing the lower radiator hose and opening the plug on the right rear of the engine block.

2. Remove the hoses from the thermostat housing.

3. Remove the combination intake and exhaust manifold.

4. Remove the spark plug wires and the loom which holds them away from the cylinder head. Leave the wires attached to the distributor cap and remove the cap.

5. Remove the rocker arm cover.

6. The cylinder head bolts can be removed using a 12 mm serrated drive wrench (tool #J22915).

7. Remove the two cylinder head-to-timing cover bolts with a 6 mm hex head wrench (J23016).

8. Remove the plate attached to the front of the cylinder head with three bolts.

9. Remove the plastic screw in the end of the camshaft under the plate removed in Step 8.

10. Remove the three bolts which hold the camshaft sprocket to the camshaft and slide the sprocket off of the camshaft.

11. The cylinder head may now be removed.

Basically the installation involves only the reinstallation of the components removed. Pay special attention to the following:

1. Thoroughly clean all gasket surfaces.

2. Clean the piston tops.

3. On the front of the block there is a

rubber ring to the left of the timing chain; replace it with a new one.

Rubber gasket ring in timing case

1. Timing chain	5. Support timing mark
2. Camshaft sprocket	6. Support
3. Sprocket timing mark	7. Cylinder block
4. Timing case	8. Rubber gasket ring

4. Coat both sides of the new head gasket with a sealer (not gasket cement but rather a sealer designed for use on head gaskets.)

5. Place the new gasket on the cylinder block and install the cylinder head.

NOTE: *Rotate the camshaft so that the recesses are vertical to allow installation of the left row of bolts.*

6. Install the head bolts and tighten them sequentially in three stages, the final stage bringing the ft lb reading to 72.

RECESSES VERTICAL FOR REMOVAL OF
LEFT ROW OF CYLINDER HEAD BOLTS

NOTE: *The cylinder head-to-timing cover bolts must only be torqued to 17 ft lbs.*

7. Slide the camshaft sprocket, with the assembled chain, onto the camshaft and guide pin. Fasten the three attaching bolts. Install the nylon screw in the end of the camshaft. After the sprocket has been attached to the camshaft, check alignment to be sure that the chain has not slipped.

1.9 engine cylinder head bolt tightening sequence

8. Replace the front cover on the cylinder head. Check the camshaft end clearance and see that it is between 0.004 in. and 0.008 in.

1975

1. Remove the airflow meter and air cleaner assembly.
2. Remove the EGR valve hold-down bolt from the thermostat housing, and disconnect all the hoses and electrical connections from the thermostat housing and auxiliary valve.
3. Follow Steps 1–11 of the 1971–74 procedure.

ROCKER ARM STUDS

Removal and Installation

1.1 ENGINE

The rocker arm studs on the 1.1 engine are pressed into the cylinder head. To remove a damaged stud, place about 1 in. of washers over the stud and then fit a rocker arm adjusting nut on the top. Using a wrench, turn the nut against the washers to pull the stud out of the head. You may have to add more washers to gain enough height.

To install a new stud, simply oil the unthreaded end of the stud and use a rubber mallet to drive the stud into the head to a height 1⅛ in. above the edge of the cylinder head (not the rocker arm galley). If more driving force is necessary than can be obtained with the mallet, use a block of wood against the stud and drive it in with a heavier hammer being careful not to damage the stud or the threads.

NOTE: *Two types of studs are installed which differ in shaft thickness. The standard shaft diameter is 0.354 in. and the*

oversize *shaft is 0.360 in. Be sure you replace the stud(s) with the correct parts. One stud is constant in diameter from top to bottom, the other is slightly tapered.*

1.9 ENGINE

Rocker arm studs on the 1.9 engine are screwed into the cylinder head. One short portion of the stud is unthreaded so that it can be seated in the cylinder head. To remove a damaged stud, use a pair of vise grip pliers and turn the stud out of the head.

Seat the unthreaded portion of the stud with a rubber mallet. Screw the new stud into the cylinder head by locking two 10 x 1 metric nuts against each other on the top of the stud. Torque the stud to 29 ft lbs.

Valve Guides

The valve guides of both the 1.1 engine and the 1.9 engine are cast integrally with the cylinder head. If they are damaged or loose, the best way to repair them is to have the valve guides knurlized or to replace the valves with new ones that have oversized stems. This is discussed more fully in the section at the end of this chapter.

Cylinder Head Overhaul

It may be necessary to overhaul the cylinder head if the valves are in poor condition. You can either take the cylinder head to a qualified machinist and have the job done or you may want to do the job yourself. The "Engine Rebuilding" section at the back of this chapter provides the required instructions. Read them carefully before deciding how to approach the problem. If you begin the job and find you cannot do it correctly, you stand the chance of creating bigger problems. Time spent analyzing the work involved and matched against an honest evaluation of your skill will probably yield a better solution.

TIMING GEAR COVER

Removal and Installation

1.1 ENGINE

1. Loosen the alternator adjusting bolt and remove the fan belt from the alternator pulley, fan pulley, and crankshaft pulley.
2. Remove the bolt which secures the crankshaft pulley and remove the pulley.

It should come off by hand but if it doesn't, strike the back of it with a rubber hammer.

CAUTION: *Do not distort the pulley by using a metal hammer.*

3. Remove the timing chain cover and oil slinger by unfastening the attaching bolts.

Before installing the timing chain cover, thoroughly clean all gasket surfaces on the block and cover and apply a film of gasket sealer.

1. Slide the oil slinger onto the crankshaft so that the slot in the slinger aligns with the woodruff key in the crankshaft.

2. Place a new gasket on the timing cover and install the cover on the block with all bolts finger tight.

3. The bolts should be torqued down in stages using a criss-cross sequence to 5 ft lbs.

4. Install the crankshaft pulley and its retaining bolt and torque to 30 ft lbs.

ALL MODELS WITH 1.9 ENGINE EXCEPT GT

There does not seem to be any simple way of removing the timing gear cover on these models with the engine in the car. The prescribed methods will be outlined here. However, you have the option of removing the engine rather than performing these operations in the car. Refer to the "Engine Removal" section in this chapter and determine for yourself which method is most suitable.

1. The engine must be supported in the frame independent of its lower support which must be removed. This can be accomplished either with a hoist supporting the engine from above or with the holding tool shown.

2. Support the whole front end of the car by placing good jackstands under the jacking brackets. Support the front suspension under the crossmember with a good jack.

3. Unbolt the front motor mounts and allow the engine to be supported from above.

4. Remove the steering mast clamp bolt, marking the location of the shaft to the flange.

5. Remove the steering mast guide sleeve stop bolt from the mast jacket bracket, and pull the steering column out of the steering mast flange.

CAUTION: *Avoid any shocks to the steering mast as all the elements of the energy absorbing system are very sensitive to damage and must be handled with tremendous care.*

6. Disconnect the brake lines where they join the front brake hoses.

7. Disconnect the shock absorber mountings at the upper shock mounting bolts.

8. Remove the bolts which hold the front suspension to the frame and lower the unit from the car.

9. Remove the radiator and the fan shroud assembly.

10. Remove the cylinder head as outlined previously.

11. Remove the alternator belt and bracket.

12. Remove the crankshaft pulley nut and pulley.

13. Remove the oil pan.

14. Remove the water pump assembly.

15. Remove the timing chain cover bolts.

NOTE: *One of the bolts is covered by the water pump so do not forget to remove it.*

BOLT BEHIND WATER PUMP COVER – MUST BE REMOVED BEFORE TIMING CHAIN COVER CAN BE REMOVED

The 1.9 engine has a timing cover bolt behind the water pump

The installation procedure is straightforward; the following instructions provide the necessary information.

1. Install new timing case rubber gaskets against the cylinder block, using a little grease to hold them in place. The gasket will overlap slightly on the oil pan gasket.

2. Position the timing case cover on the guide pin at the upper left corner of the block. Insert the centering bolt through the timing chain cover into the lower right corner of the block.

3. Replace the timing chain cover bolts being careful not to overtighten.

4. Reverse the disassembly procedure replacing all components and paying strict

attention to the replacement of the front suspension. For further information on the front suspension, refer to Chapter Eight.

GT

The timing gear cover can be removed from GT models without removing the front suspension. The engine should be supported from above with a chain hoist or with engine holding fixture #J23375. Remove the engine support crossmember and then the oil pan. Proceed as outlined above for the Opel 1900 and Manta models.

Installation of Timing Cover Oil Seal

1.1 ENGINE

1. Remove the timing chain cover.
2. Support the timing cover on a bench so that the end containing the seal is not lying on a flat surface.
3. Drive out the outer seal retainer and the seal with a punch.

CAUTION: *Do not remove or disturb the inner seal retainer.*

Removing the timing chain cover oil seal on the 1.1 engine

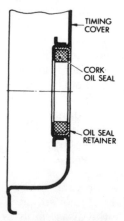

Installing timing cover oil seal—1.1 engine

4. Install the new seal through the front of the cover. Be sure it is driven in flush with the cover; use a block of wood, a seal driving tool, or some other soft drift so as not to damage the seal.
5. Replace the timing chain cover using a new gasket.

1.9 ENGINE

There are a number of special tools described in this installation and the decision as to whether or not you can successfully complete the job without them is, of course, up to you.

If you are replacing the seal with the engine installed in the car, proceed as follows.

1. Remove the fan belts.
2. Remove the crankshaft pulley bolt and the pulley.
3. Insert a screwdriver behind the seal and rest it on the crankshaft pin. Pry out the oil seal.
4. Lubricate the new oil seal and place it on the installer (#J22924).

Installing the timing cover oil seal on the 1.9 engine with the engine installed in the car

5. Place the installer on the crankshaft and use the crankshaft bolt and washer to force the seal into the timing chain cover.
6. Remove the installer, install the crankshaft pulley and bolt, and tighten the bolt to 72 ft lbs.
7. Replace all drive belts.

If you have removed the timing cover, you can drive the seal out with a drift. To replace the seal, put it in place and use either tool #J22924 or some other suitable device to drive the seal into the cover.

TIMING CHAIN AND TENSIONER
Removal and Installation

1.1 ENGINE

1. Remove the timing chain cover.
2. Remove the timing chain tensioner.

NOTE: *The tensioner is spring loaded so when you unbolt it from the block, be sure to hold it by the bumper and the body to avoid losing any of the internal parts.*

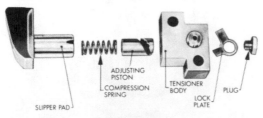

Timing chain tensioner parts

3. If you are going to replace the same chain you are removing, you must mark the chain so that when it is reinstalled it will rotate in the same direction. Put a paint mark on the forward side of the chain.
4. Remove the camshaft sprocket retaining bolt and washer.
5. Using a suitable puller, remove the chain and gears together.

NOTE: *There is a woodruff key on the crankshaft; upon removal of the crankshaft sprocket, inspect the key for cracks and wear. Replace if necessary.*

The crankshaft sprocket has 19 teeth and, because the camshaft rotates at half crankshaft speed, the camshaft sprocket has 38 teeth; after thus identifying the sprockets, assemble them in the chain and install as follows.

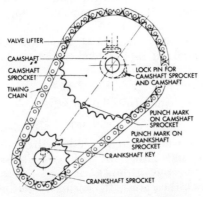

Timing chain and sprockets—1.1. engine

1. Install the crankshaft sprocket on the crankshaft so that the punch mark faces the front. Push it back over the woodruff key to its stop.
2. Install the camshaft sprocket on the camshaft and be certain that the punch mark is facing the front.
3. Turn the crankshaft and camshaft together with the timing chain and sprockets so that the punch marks are opposite each other.

NOTE: *Be sure that the timing chain is positioned so that the direction of rotation is the same as before it was removed. If any of the three components (either sprocket or the chain) are defective, they must be replaced as a unit. Do not replace any of the parts separately.*

4. After positioning the sprockets, tighten the camshaft sprocket bolt and lockplate to 30 ft lbs torque.

NOTE: *Before replacing the tensioner, inspect all of its parts; if any are defective, the entire assembly must be replaced.*

5. Assemble the timing chain tensioner as follows.

a. Insert the compression spring into the adjusting piston.

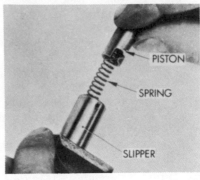

Installing the compression spring into the adjusting piston

b. Install the compression spring and adjusting piston into the plunger sleeve so that the helical slot of the adjusting piston and the guide of the plunger sleeve are aligned.

c. Using a $\frac{1}{8}$ in. allen wrench, turn the adjusting piston clockwise into the plunger sleeve until the guide pin emerges on top of the helical slot locking the unit for installation.

d. Slide the plunger sleeve into the tensioner body and install the body on the engine front plate.

e. After installing the tensioner body on the engine, remove the end plug, insert a ⅛ in. allen wrench, and turn the adjusting piston counterclockwise to release it. The timing chain tensioner is now properly adjusted. Install the end plug and lock plate.

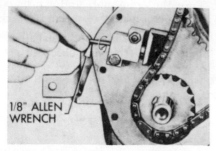

Release the adjusting piston after installing it on the engine

6. Slide the oil slinger back onto the crankshaft so that the slot on the slinger matches up with the woodruff key on the crankshaft.

7. Replace the timing cover with a new gasket.

8. Replace the fan belts.

1.9 ENGINE

1. Remove the timing case cover.

2. Remove the ignition distributor.

3. Remove the fuel pump.

4. Remove the timing chain tensioner assembly.

5. Pull off the crankshaft sprocket using an appropriate puller.

NOTE: *If you intend to use the old timing chain in the reassembly, put a paint mark on the front forward side so that the chain will rotate in the same direction when replaced. Clean and check all parts before reassembly. If either the sprockets or the chain need replacement, it is best to replace all three components.*

1. Turn the crankshaft so that the key for the sprocket is at the top and vertical.

2. Assemble the camshaft sprocket with the chain and put the chain on the crankshaft.

NOTE: *There is a mark on the camshaft pulley which should line up with the mark on the camshaft support bracket. Be sure the chain is parallel with the damper block.*

3. Install the chain tensioner.

4. Install the timing case cover following earlier instructions.

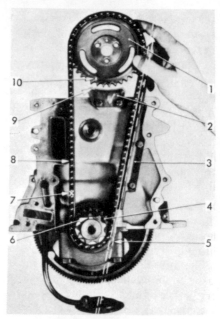

Timing chain and sprocket installation—1.9 engine

1. Camshaft sprocket
2. Camshaft sprocket support
3. Long damper block
4. Crankshaft sprocket
5. Chain and damper block in parallel
6. Crankshaft key
7. Paint mark on front of chain
8. Timing chain
9. Mark on camshaft sprocket support
10. Mark on camshaft sprocket

5. Install the cylinder head.

After the installation is complete and the camshaft sprocket has been attached to the camshaft, the engine will be set with No. 1 and No. 4 cylinders at TDC. The No. 4 cylinder will be in the firing position and No. 1 will be on the top of the exhaust stroke. To set the engine in the No. 1 firing position, rotate the crankshaft 360°. This will position the timing mark 180° from the original alignment of the camshaft sprocket and the mark on the camshaft support. It will also close the No. 1 cylinder intake and exhaust valves and align the pointer and steel ball on the flywheel.

CAMSHAFT

Removal and Installation

1.1 ENGINE

The camshaft is located in the cylinder block and cannot be removed unless the engine is out of the car. If it is necessary to replace the camshaft bearings, it is best to have it done at a machine shop. Once in-

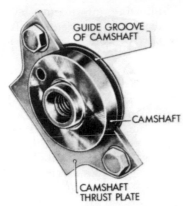

The camshaft thrust plate on the 1.1 engine mounts in a guide groove on the camshaft with the closed end facing the crankshaft

stalled, the bearings must be align-bored in the block. Be absolutely certain that the bearings are defective before assuming they must be replaced.

1. Take the engine out of the car and locate it in a work area that is relatively free from dirt which may damage the engine.

2. Remove the rocker arm cover, rocker arm adjusting nuts, rocker arm ball seats, and pushrods.

3. Remove the timing chain cover.

4. Remove the ignition distributor.

5. Invert the engine so the lifters will not interfere.

6. Remove the camshaft thrust plate.

7. Remove the engine front plate and then the camshaft.

To install the camshaft, liberally lubricate it and the bearings with engine oil and slide the camshaft into the engine. Put a new gasket on the engine front plate and reinstall it. The camshaft thrust plate should sit in the groove of the camshaft with the closed side facing the crankshaft. The camshaft thrust plate bolts should be tightened to 5 ft lbs when replaced. Install the timing chain cover and tensioner with new gaskets. Install the rocker arm parts and the distributor. After installing the engine in the car, adjust the valves and set the timing.

1.9 ENGINE

The 1.9 engine is a cam-in-head design which makes removal of the camshaft relatively easy.

Remove the cylinder head, place it on a bench, and support it in such a way that the valves are not in contact with the work surface. Loosen the self locking rocker arm nuts and swing the rocker arms off of the valve lifters.

NOTE: *The position of each valve lifter must be carefully noted as they must be replaced in the same bore when reinstalled.*

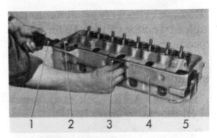

1. CAMSHAFT
2. FRONT ACCESS HOLE
3. LATERAL ACCESS HOLE
4. CYLINDER HEAD
5. REAR ACCESS HOLE

Removing the 1.9 camshaft from the cylinder head

After removing the valve lifters, remove the front and rear access covers from the cylinder head. Guide the camshaft out of the cylinder head, being careful not to damage the bearings.

Before installing the camshaft, thoroughly lubricate the bearings and the shaft with motor oil. Support the shaft through the access holes while sliding it in. Install the valve lifters in their original position and close the access holes. Replace the cylinder head on the crankcase assembly.

PISTON AND CONNECTING ROD

The easiest way to remove the connecting rod assemblies from the engine is to remove the engine from the car. However, they can be serviced with the engine in the car by removing the front suspension and dropping the oil pan.

For instructions on the removal of the front suspension for the 1900 series, Opels with the 1.9 engine, and the Manta series see the paragraphs on "Timing Chain Cover Removal 1.9 Engine" in this chapter.

For instructions regarding the Opel with 1.1 engine, Chapter Eight will have the details.

The oil pan can be removed from the 1.9 engine installed in the GT by simply removing the front and rear crossmembers. This is also outlined in the "Timing Chain Cover Removal" paragraphs.

1. NOTCH IN PISTON HEAD FOR VALVES
2. RUBBER STAMPED ARROW POINTING TOWARD THE **FRONT**
3. NOTCH IN CONNECTING ROD CAP POINTING TOWARD THE **REAR**

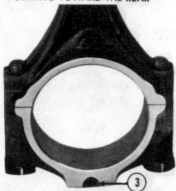

Locating marks of the piston and connecting rod showing proper installation in the 1.1 engine

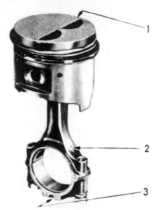

1. NOTCH IN PISTON HEAD POINTING TOWARD THE FRONT
2. OIL HOLE IN CONNECTING ROD POINTING TOWARD THE **RIGHT** (MANIFOLD SIDE)
3. NOTCH IN CONNECTING ROD CAP POINTING TOWARD THE REAR

Locating marks on 1.9 piston and rod

The following information on removal and installation of connecting rods and pistons applies to both engines in all series Opels.

Removal and Installation

1. Remove the oil pan and cylinder head.
2. Unbolt the connecting rod caps.
3. Push the piston and rod assemblies out of the block using a long thin piece of wood (such as a hammer handle).

CAUTION: *After removing the cylinder head, inspect the cylinder bore for a ridge. If a ridge exists in the wall, cut it out with a good ridge reamer before removing the pistons. Failure to do so will result in damage to the piston rings and the ring lands of the piston.*

4. Remove only one piston at a time and be certain to mark the piston so it can be installed in the same cylinder from which it was removed. After removal, assemble the connecting rod cap to its connecting rod.

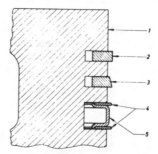

1. PISTON
2. NO. 1 COMPRESSION RING – INSTALLED WITH EITHER SIDE UP.
3. NO. 2 COMPRESSION RING – INSTALLED WITH "TOP" MARKING TOWARDS THE TOP.
4. UPPER AND LOWER STEEL BAND RING – INSTALLED WITH EITHER SIDE UP.
5. INTERMEDIATED RING – INSTALLED WITH EITHER SIDE UP.

Arrangement of piston rings

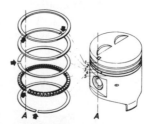

1. NO. 1 COMPRESSION – GAP IN FRONT
2. NO. 2 COMPRESSION – GAP IN REAR
3. UPPER STEEL BAND - 1 - 2 IN. TOWARDS THE LEFT OF INTERMEDIATE RING GAP
4. INTERMEDIATE RING – GAP IN FRONT
5. LOWER STEEL BAND - 1 - 2 IN. TOWARDS THE RIGHT OF INTERMEDIATE RING GAP
"A" VERTICAL LINE FOR PISTON AND RINGS, FRONT

Location of piston ring gaps

5. Measure the connecting rod journals of the crankshaft with an outside micrometer. If they are more than 0.002 in. out of round, the crankshaft should be reconditioned.

6. Carefully inspect all the journals, bearings, and connecting rods for damage.

7. Inspect the pistons and piston rings and, if necessary, replace the piston rings. Complete instructions follow at the end of this chapter on engine rebuilding.

To install the piston and rod assembly, rotate the crankshaft so that the journal for the rod you are replacing is at the top of its travel and centered in the cylinder bore. Remove the connecting rod cap and install two lengths of rubber hose on the connecting rod bolts. These will protect the journal and act as a guide for the installation. Slide the piston and rod into the cylinder bore until the piston rings stop the process. Install a piston ring compressor around the piston and rings so that the lower edge of the compressor is slightly seated in the cylinder bore. Using a hammer handle, drive the piston down until the connecting rod seats on the crankshaft journal. Install the connecting rod cap from below and tighten to specification.

Repeat the procedure for the other cylinders being careful to install each piston and connecting rod in the same cylinder from which it was removed. Thoroughly lubricate the cylinder wall and piston with engine oil prior to installation.

Engine Lubrication

OIL PAN

Removal and Installation

1900, MANTA MODELS, OPEL WITH 1.9 ENGINE

The details for this operation may be found in this chapter under "Timing Chain Cover Removal".

OPEL WITH 1.1 ENGINE

Information in Chapter Eight under "Front Suspension Removal".

GT

This procedure is found in the same section as the 1900 and Manta models.

Installing the rear main bearing oil seal on a 1.1 engine

REAR MAIN OIL SEAL

Removal and Installation

ALL ENGINES

1. Remove the transmission, bellhousing, and clutch assembly.

2. Remove the flywheel.

3. Use a punch to make a hole in the old oil seal. Then screw in a sheet metal screw and pull the seal out using pliers on the screw.

Removing the rear seal on a 1.9 engine

4. To ensure proper sealing, lubricate the new seal with protective grease and install it on tool J22928 (J21707-1 for 1.1 engine).

5. Tool J22928 is a tapered ring. Install the seal and ring on the crankshaft flange and move the lip of the seal over the end of the crankshaft.

CAUTION: *Do not tilt the seal.*

Installing the rear seal—1.9 engine

6. Drive in the seal with tool J22928-2 (tool J21707-1 for the 1.1 engine).

7. Install all removed components.

OIL PUMP

Removal and Installation

1.1 ENGINE

1. Remove the oil pan.

2. Using a serrated bit (J21736) remove the oil pump and gasket.

3. To replace the pump, fill the oil pump housing with engine oil and replace the star bolts using a new gasket between the oil pump and the block. Tighten to 15 ft lbs.

4. Install the oil pan with a new gasket.

Removing the oil pump—1.1 engine

1.9 ENGINE

The 1.9 engine does not have a conventional oil pump which is replaceable as a unit. The gears may be replaced however.

1. Remove the screws which attach the oil pump cover to the timing chain cover.

2. Remove the cover and the gears will slide out.

3. Wash the gears in solvent and replace any that are not serviceable.

4. Liberally lubricate the gear spindles

1.9 engine oil pan removed

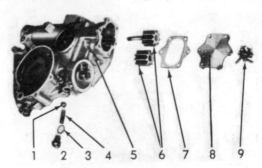

1.9 oil pump-disassembled

1. By-pass valve ball	6. Oil pump gears
2. Plug and by-pass valve	7. Cover gasket
3. Gasket	8. Cover
4. Spring	9. Cover attaching screws
5. Timing case	

and gear teeth. Replace the cover with a new gasket.

NOTE: *Discard the pump cover if it is scored by gear action; in extreme cases the distributor drive shaft bushing may be severely worn also necessitating complete replacement of the timing case cover. There are some production timing cases having 0.008 in. oversize bores for the pump gears and shafts. These can be identified by the number 0.2 stamped into the pump flange. When new gears are installed, you should check the end clearance in a dry pump housing with a straightedge and a feeler gauge. The gears must not protrude more than 0.004 in. over the pump housing.*

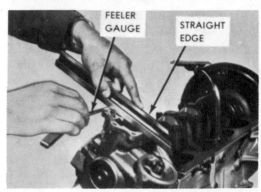

Checking the oil pump gear end clearance

Engine Cooling

RADIATOR

Removal and Installation—All Models

1. Loosen the radiator cap and then remove the lower radiator hose to drain the

coolant. If you plan to reuse the coolant, be sure it is collected in a clean container.

2. On vehicles with an automatic transmission, unscrew the oil lines from the connectors at the bottom of the radiator. Be certain that no dirt enters the lines as it will damage the transmission. On GT models, the lines will have to be disconnected at the coupling before they enter the tank in addition to their removal at the radiator. Use proper tools to hold the connectors on the bottom of the radiator so they will not be damaged.

3. Disconnect the upper hose and remove the lower attaching nut. The radiator can be removed by sliding it upward out of the engine compartment.

CAUTION: *It cannot be overemphasized that no dirt be allowed to enter the transmission cooling lines.*

4. Install by reversing the removal procedure, making all connections tight.

NOTE: *All Opels are provided with an initial radiator fill of antifreeze solution containing corrosion inhibitor. The antifreeze has either a glycol or glycerin base and protects the engine against freezing down to minus 22 degrees F. (minus 30 degrees C.). Before the start of the cold season, coolant must be checked with an antifreeze tester and, if necessary, brought to the necessary specific gravity by adding anti-freeze with a glycol or glycerin base. As the specific gravities of all anti-freeze solutions having a glycol or glycerin base are practically the same, the antifreeze tester can be used for all these types. Because of the tolerances of the antifreeze tester or slight differences in specific gravity, variations of plus or minus 5 degrees can be expected. Coolant must be checked at a temperature of plus 68 degrees F. (plus 20 degrees C.)*

WATER PUMP

Removal and Installation

1.1 ENGINE

Remove the lower radiator hose in order to drain the coolant. Loosen the generator

mounting bolts and remove the fan belt. Remove the fan mounting bolts and the fan, and all hoses from the water pump. Remove the water pump mounting bolts and remove the pump.

Install in the reverse order of removal.

1.9 ENGINE

Remove all radiator hoses, drain the coolant, and remove the radiator and shroud. Loosen the generator mounting bolts and remove the fan belt. Unbolt and remove the fan. If equipped with a clutch fan, remove it along with the fan. The clutch fan retaining bolt has a *left-hand* thread. Remove the pulleys from the water pump shaft and the crankshaft. Disconnect all hoses from the water pump, remove the mounting bolts, and remove the water pump and gasket.

Install in the reverse order of removal.

THERMOSTAT

Removal and Installation

1.1 ENGINE

The thermostat is located in the water pump housing and can be removed by partially draining the coolant to a level just below the upper hose. Remove the hose and the thermostat will be accessible.

1.9 ENGINE

1971–74

Partially drain the cooling system and remove the water outlet housing from the thermostat housing located on the right front side of the cylinder head.

1975

1. Partially drain the radiator, and remove the airflow meter and air cleaner. (See "Intake Manifold Removal and Installation").

2. Remove the throttle lever spring and the accelerator linkage springs.

3. Disconnect the EGR pipe and accelerator linkage at the throttle body housing.

4. Remove the thermostat.

Engine Rebuilding

This section describes, in detail, the procedures involved in rebuilding a typical engine. The procedures specifically refer to an inline engine, however, they are basically identical to those used in rebuilding engines of nearly all design and configurations. Procedures for servicing atypical engines (i.e., horizontally opposed) are described in the appropriate section, although in most cases, cylinder head reconditioning procedures described in this chapter will apply.

The section is divided into two sections. The first, Cylinder Head Reconditioning, assumes that the cylinder head is removed from the engine, all manifolds are removed, and the cylinder head is on a workbench. The camshaft should be removed from overhead cam cylinder heads. The second section, Cylinder Block Reconditioning, covers the block, pistons, connecting rods and crankshaft. It is assumed that the engine is mounted on a work stand, and the cylinder head and all accessories are removed.

Procedures are identified as follows:

Unmarked—Basic procedures that must be performed in order to successfully complete the rebuilding process.

Starred (*)—Procedures that should be performed to ensure maximum performance and engine life.

Double starred (**)—Procedures that may be performed to increase engine performance and reliability. These procedures are usually reserved for extremely heavy-duty or competition usage.

In many cases, a choice of methods is also provided. Methods are identified in the same manner as procedures. The choice of method for a procedure is at the discretion of the user.

The tools required for the basic rebuilding procedure should, with minor exceptions, be those

TORQUE (ft. lbs.)*

U.S.

Bolt Diameter (inches)	Bolt Grade (SAE)				Wrench Size (inches)	
	1 and 2	5	6	8	Bolt	Nut
1/4	5	7	10	10.5	3/8	7/16
5/16	9	14	19	22	1/2	9/16
3/8	15	25	34	37	9/16	5/8
7/16	24	40	55	60	5/8	3/4
1/2	37	60	85	92	3/4	13/16
9/16	53	88	120	132	7/8	7/8
5/8	74	120	167	180	15/16	1
3/4	120	200	280	296	1-1/8	1-1/8
7/8	190	302	440	473	1-5/16	1-5/16
1	282	466	660	714	1-1/2	1-1/2

Metric

Bolt Diameter (mm)	Bolt Grade				Wrench Size (mm) Bolt and Nut
	5D	8G	10K	12K	
6	5	6	8	10	10
8	10	16	22	27	14
10	19	31	40	49	17
12	34	54	70	86	19
14	55	89	117	137	22
16	83	132	175	208	24
18	111	182	236	283	27
22	182	284	394	464	32
24	261	419	570	689	36

*—Torque values are for lightly oiled bolts. CAUTION: Bolts threaded into aluminum require much less torque.

General Torque Specifications

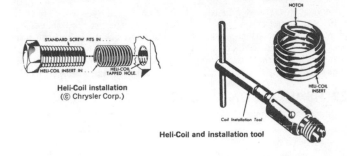

Heli-Coil installation
(© Chrysler Corp.)

Heli-Coil and installation tool

Heli-Coil Insert			Drill		Tap	Insert. Tool	Extracting Tool
Thread Size	Part No.	Insert Length (In.)	Size			Part No.	Part No.	Part No.
1/2 -20	1185-4	3/8	17/64(.266)		4 CPB	528-4N	1227-6
5/16-18	1185-5	15/32	Q(.332)		5 CPB	528-5N	1227-6
3/8 -16	1185-6	9/16	X(.397)		6 CPB	528-6N	1227-6
7/16-14	1185-7	21/32	29/64(.453)		7 CPB	528-7N	1227-16
1/2 -13	1185-8	3/4	33/64(.516)		8 CPB	528-8N	1227-16

Heli-Coil Specifications

included in a mechanic's tool kit. An accurate torque wrench, and a dial indicator (reading in thousandths) mounted on a universal base should be available. Bolts and nuts with no torque specification should be tightened according to size (see chart). Special tools, where required, all are readily available from the major tool suppliers (i.e., Craftsman, Snap-On, K-D). The services of a competent automotive machine shop must also be readily available.

When assembling the engine, any parts that will be in frictional contact must be pre-lubricated, to provide protection on initial start-up. Vortex Pre-Lube, STP, or any product specifically formulated for this purpose may be used. NOTE: *Do not use engine oil*. Where semi-permanent (locked but removable) installation of bolts or nuts is desired, threads should be cleaned and coated with Loctite. Studs may be permanently installed using Loctite Stud and Bearing Mount.

Aluminum has become increasingly popular for use in engines, due to its low weight and excellent heat transfer characteristics. The following precautions must be observed when handling aluminum engine parts:
—Never hot-tank aluminum parts.
—Remove all aluminum parts (identification tags, etc.) from engine parts before hot-tanking (otherwise they will be removed during the process).
—Always coat threads lightly with engine oil or anti-seize compounds before installation, to prevent seizure.
—Never over-torque bolts or spark plugs in aluminum threads. Should stripping occur, threads can be restored according to the following procedure, using Heli-Coil thread inserts:

Tap drill the hole with the stripped threads to the specified size (see chart). Using the specified tap (NOTE: *Heli-Coil tap sizes refer to the size thread being replaced, rather than the actual tap size*), tap the hole for the Heli-Coil. Place the insert on the proper installation tool (see chart). Apply pressure on the insert while winding it clockwise into the hole, until the top of the insert is one turn below the surface. Remove the installation tool, and break the installation tang from the bottom of the in-

sert by moving it up and down. If the Heli-Coil must be removed, tap the removal tool firmly into the hole, so that it engages the top thread, and turn the tool counter-clockwise to extract the insert.

Snapped bolts or studs may be removed, using a stud extractor (unthreaded) or Vise-Grip pliers (threaded). Penetrating oil (e.g., Liquid Wrench) will often aid in breaking frozen threads. In cases where the stud or bolt is flush with, or below the surface, proceed as follows:

Drill a hole in the broken stud or bolt, approximately 1/2 its diameter. Select a screw extractor (e.g., Easy-Out) of the proper size, and tap it into the stud or bolt. Turn the extractor counter-clockwise to remove the stud or bolt.

Magnaflux and Zyglo are inspection techniques used to locate material flaws, such as stress cracks. Magnafluxing coats the part with fine magnetic particles, and subjects the part to a magnetic field. Cracks cause breaks

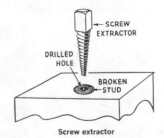

Screw extractor

in the magnetic field, which are outlined by the particles. Since Magnaflux is a magnetic process, it is applicable only to ferrous materials. The Zyglo process coats the material with a fluorescent dye penetrant, and then subjects it to blacklight inspection, under which cracks glow bright-

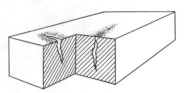

Magnaflux indication of cracks

ly. Parts made of any material may be tested using Zyglo. While Magnaflux and Zyglo are excellent for general inspection, and locating hidden defects, specific checks of suspected cracks may be made at lower cost and more readily using spot check dye. The dye is sprayed onto the suspected area, wiped off, and the area is then sprayed with a developer. Cracks then will show up brightly. Spot check dyes will only indicate surface cracks; therefore, structural cracks below the surface may escape detection. When questionable, the part should be tested using Magnaflux or Zyglo.

CYLINDER HEAD RECONDITIONING

Procedure	*Method*
Identify the valves:  **Valve identification** (© SAAB)	Invert the cylinder head, and number the valve faces front to rear, using a permanent felt-tip marker.
Remove the rocker arms:	Remove the rocker arms with shaft(s) or balls and nuts. Wire the sets of rockers, balls and nuts together, and identify according to the corresponding valve.
Remove the valves and springs:	Using an appropriate valve spring compressor (depending on the configuration of the cylinder head), compress the valve springs. Lift out the keepers with needlenose pliers, release the compressor, and remove the valve, spring, and spring retainer.
Check the valve stem-to-guide clearance:  **Checking the valve stem-to-guide clearance** (© American Motors Corp.)	Clean the valve stem with lacquer thinner or a similar solvent to remove all gum and varnish. Clean the valve guides using solvent and an expanding wire-type valve guide cleaner. Mount a dial indicator so that the stem is at 90° to the valve stem, as close to the valve guide as possible. Move the valve off its seat, and measure the valve guide-to-stem clearance by moving the stem back and forth to actuate the dial indicator. Measure the valve stems using a micrometer, and compare to specifications, to determine whether stem or guide wear is responsible for excessive clearance.
De-carbon the cylinder head and valves:  **Removing carbon from the cylinder head** (© Chevrolet Div. G.M. Corp.)	Chip carbon away from the valve heads, combustion chambers, and ports, using a chisel made of hardwood. Remove the remaining deposits with a stiff wire brush. NOTE: *Ensure that the deposits are actually removed, rather than burnished.*

Procedure	Method
Hot-tank the cylinder head:	Have the cylinder head hot-tanked to remove grease, corrosion, and scale from the water passages. NOTE: *In the case of overhead cam cylinder heads, consult the operator to determine whether the camshaft bearings will be damaged by the caustic solution.*
Degrease the remaining cylinder head parts:	Using solvent (i.e., Gunk), clean the rockers, rocker shaft(s) (where applicable), rocker balls and nuts, springs, spring retainers, and keepers. Do not remove the protective coating from the springs.
Check the cylinder head for warpage:  Checking the cylinder head for warpage (ⓒ Ford Motor Co.)	Place a straight-edge across the gasket surface of the cylinder head. Using feeler gauges, determine the clearance at the center of the straight-edge. Measure across both diagonals, along the longitudinal centerline, and across the cylinder head at several points. If warpage exceeds .003″ in a 6″ span, or .006″ over the total length, the cylinder head must be resurfaced. NOTE: *If warpage exceeds the manufacturers maximum tolerance for material removal, the cylinder head must be replaced.* When milling the cylinder heads of V-type engines, the intake manifold mounting position is altered, and must be corrected by milling the manifold flange a proportionate amount.
** Porting and gasket matching:  Marking the cylinder head for gasket matching (ⓒ Petersen Publishing Co.)  Port configuration before and after gasket matching (ⓒ Petersen Publishing Co.)	** Coat the manifold flanges of the cylinder head with Prussian blue dye. Glue intake and exhaust gaskets to the cylinder head in their installed position using rubber cement and scribe the outline of the ports on the manifold flanges. Remove the gaskets. Using a small cutter in a hand-held power tool (i.e., Dremel Moto-Tool), gradually taper the walls of the port out to the scribed outline of the gasket. Further enlargement of the ports should include the removal of sharp edges and radiusing of sharp corners. Do not alter the valve guides. NOTE: *The most efficient port configuration is determined only by extensive testing. Therefore, it is best to consult someone experienced with the head in question to determine the optimum alterations.*

Procedure	*Method*

** Polish the ports:

Relieved and polished ports
(© Petersen Publishing Co.)

Polished combustion chamber
(© Petersen Publishing Co.)

** Using a grinding stone with the above mentioned tool, polish the walls of the intake and exhaust ports, and combustion chamber. Use progressively finer stones until all surface imperfections are removed. NOTE: *Through testing, it has been determined that a smooth surface is more effective than a mirror polished surface in intake ports, and vice-versa in exhaust ports.*

---

* Knurling the valve guides:

Cut-away view of a knurled valve guide
(© Petersen Publishing Co.)

* Valve guides which are not excessively worn or distorted may, in some cases, be knurled rather than replaced. Knurling is a process in which metal is displaced and raised, thereby reducing clearance. Knurling also provides excellent oil control. The possibility of knurling rather than replacing valve guides should be discussed with a machinist.

Replacing the valve guides: NOTE: *Valve guides should only be replaced if damaged or if an oversize valve stem is not available.*

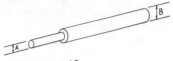

A-VALVE GUIDE I.D.
B-SLIGHTLY SMALLER THAN VALVE GUIDE O.D.

Valve guide removal tool

WASHERS

A-VALVE GUIDE I.D.
B-LARGER THAN THE VALVE GUIDE O.D.

Valve guide installation tool (with washers used during installation)

Depending on the type of cylinder head, valve guides may be pressed, hammered, or shrunk in. In cases where the guides are shrunk into the head, replacement should be left to an equipped machine shop. In other cases, the guides are replaced as follows: Press or tap the valve guides out of the head using a stepped drift (see illustration). Determine the height above the boss that the guide must extend, and obtain a stack of washers, their I.D. similar to the guide's O.D., of that height. Place the stack of washers on the guide, and insert the guide into the boss. NOTE: *Valve guides are often tapered or beveled for installation.* Using the stepped installation tool (see illustration), press or tap the guides into position. Ream the guides according to the size of the valve stem.

Procedure	Method
Replacing valve seat inserts:	Replacement of valve seat inserts which are worn beyond resurfacing or broken, if feasible, must be done by a machine shop.
Resurfacing (grinding) the valve face:  **Grinding a valve** (© Subaru) 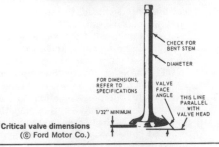 **Critical valve dimensions** (© Ford Motor Co.)	Using a valve grinder, resurface the valves according to specifications. CAUTION: *Valve face angle is not always identical to valve seat angle.* A minimum margin of 1/32" should remain after grinding the valve. The valve stem tip should also be squared and resurfaced, by placing the stem in the V-block of the grinder, and turning it while pressing lightly against the grinding wheel.
Resurfacing the valve seats using reamers:  **Reaming the valve seat** (© S.p.A. Fiat)  **Valve seat width and centering** (© Ford Motor Co.)	Select a reamer of the correct seat angle, slightly larger than the diameter of the valve seat, and assemble it with a pilot of the correct size. Install the pilot into the valve guide, and using steady pressure, turn the reamer clockwise. CAUTION: *Do not turn the reamer counter-clockwise.* Remove only as much material as necessary to clean the seat. Check the concentricity of the seat (see below). If the dye method is not used, coat the valve face with Prussian blue dye, install and rotate it on the valve seat. Using the dye marked area as a centering guide, center and narrow the valve seat to specifications with correction cutters. NOTE: *When no specifications are available, minimum seat width for exhaust valves should be 5/64", intake valves 1/16".* After making correction cuts, check the position of the valve seat on the valve face using Prussian blue dye.
* Resurfacing the valve seats using a grinder:  **Grinding a valve seat** (© Subaru)	Select a pilot of the correct size, and a coarse stone of the correct seat angle. Lubricate the pilot if necessary, and install the tool in the valve guide. Move the stone on and off the seat at approximately two cycles per second, until all flaws are removed from the seat. Install a fine stone, and finish the seat. Center and narrow the seat using correction stones, as described above.

Procedure	Method
Checking the valve seat concentricity:  Checking the valve seat concentricity using a dial gauge (© American Motors Corp.)	Coat the valve face with Prussian blue dye, install the valve, and rotate it on the valve seat. If the entire seat becomes coated, and the valve is known to be concentric, the seat is concentric.
	* Install the dial gauge pilot into the guide, and rest the arm on the valve seat. Zero the gauge, and rotate the arm around the seat. Run-out should not exceed .002″.
* Lapping the valves: NOTE: *Valve lapping is done to ensure efficient sealing of resurfaced valves and seats. Valve lapping alone is not recommended for use as a resurfacing procedure.* 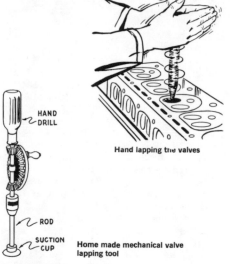 Hand lapping the valves HAND DRILL ROD SUCTION CUP Home made mechanical valve lapping tool	* Invert the cylinder head, lightly lubricate the valve stems, and install the valves in the head as numbered. Coat valve seats with fine grinding compound, and attach the lapping tool suction cup to a valve head (NOTE: *Moisten the suction cup*). Rotate the tool between the palms, changing position and lifting the tool often to prevent grooving. Lap the valve until a smooth, polished seat is evident. Remove the valve and tool, and rinse away all traces of grinding compound.
	** Fasten a suction cup to a piece of drill rod, and mount the rod in a hand drill. Proceed as above, using the hand drill as a lapping tool. CAUTION: *Due to the higher speeds involved when using the hand drill, care must be exercised to avoid grooving the seat.* Lift the tool and change direction of rotation often.
Check the valve springs: 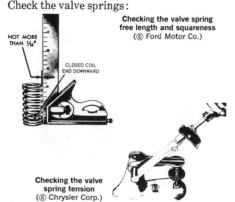 NOT MORE THAN 1/16″ CLOSED COIL END DOWNWARD Checking the valve spring free length and squareness (© Ford Motor Co.) Checking the valve spring tension (© Chrysler Corp.)	Place the spring on a flat surface next to a square. Measure the height of the spring, and rotate it against the edge of the square to measure distortion. If spring height varies (by comparison) by more than 1/16″ or if distortion exceeds 1/16″, replace the spring.
	** In addition to evaluating the spring as above, test the spring pressure at the installed and compressed (installed height minus valve lift) height using a valve spring tester. Springs used on small displacement engines (up to 3 liters) should be ± 1 lb. of all other springs in either position. A tolerance of ± 5 lbs. is permissible on larger engines.

Procedure	*Method*
* Install valve stem seals:  **Valve stem seal installation** (© Ford Motor Co.) SEAL	* Due to the pressure differential that exists at the ends of the intake valve guides (atmospheric pressure above, manifold vacuum below), oil is drawn through the valve guides into the intake port. This has been alleviated somewhat since the addition of positive crankcase ventilation, which lowers the pressure above the guides. Several types of valve stem seals are available to reduce blow-by. Certain seals simply slip over the stem and guide boss, while others require that the boss be machined. Recently, Teflon guide seals have become popular. Consult a parts supplier or machinist concerning availability and suggested usages. NOTE: *When installing seals, ensure that a small amount of oil is able to pass the seal to lubricate the valve guides; otherwise, excessive wear may result.*
Install the valves:	Lubricate the valve stems, and install the valves in the cylinder head as numbered. Lubricate and position the seals (if used, see above) and the valve springs. Install the spring retainers, compress the springs, and insert the keys using needlenose pliers or a tool designed for this purpose. NOTE: *Retain the keys with wheel bearing grease during installation.*
Checking valve spring installed height: 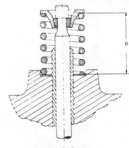  **Valve spring installed** **height dimension** (© Porsche) **Measuring valve spring** **installed height** (© Petersen Publishing Co.)	Measure the distance between the spring pad and the lower edge of the spring retainer, and compare to specifications. If the installed height is incorrect, add shim washers between the spring pad and the spring. CAUTION: *Use only washers designed for this purpose.*
** CC'ing the combustion chambers:	** Invert the cylinder head and place a bead of sealer around a combustion chamber. Install an apparatus designed for this purpose (burette mounted on a clear plate; see illustration) over the combustion chamber, and fill with the specified fluid to an even mark on the burette. Record the burette reading, and fill the combustion chamber with fluid. (NOTE: *A hole drilled in the plate will permit air to escape*). Subtract the burette reading, with the combustion chamber filled, from the previous reading, to determine combustion chamber volume in cc's. Duplicate this procedure in all combustion

Procedure	Method

CC'ing the combustion chamber
(© Petersen Publishing Co.)

chambers on the cylinder head, and compare the readings. The volume of all combustion chambers should be made equal to that of the largest. Combustion chamber volume may be increased in two ways. When only a small change is required (usually), a small cutter or coarse stone may be used to remove material from the combustion chamber. NOTE: *Check volume frequently.* Remove material over a wide area, so as not to change the configuration of the combustion chamber. When a larger change is required, the valve seat may be sunk (lowered into the head). NOTE: *When altering valve seat, remember to compensate for the change in spring installed height.*

Inspect the rocker arms, balls, studs, and nuts (where applicable):

 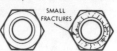

Stress cracks in rocker nuts
(© Ford Motor Co.)

Visually inspect the rocker arms, balls, studs, and nuts for cracks, galling, burning, scoring, or wear. If all parts are intact, liberally lubricate the rocker arms and balls, and install them on the cylinder head. If wear is noted on a rocker arm at the point of valve contact, grind it smooth and square, removing as little material as possible. Replace the rocker arm if excessively worn. If a rocker stud shows signs of wear, it must be replaced (see below). If a rocker nut shows stress cracks, replace it. If an exhaust ball is galled or burned, substitute the intake ball from the same cylinder (if it is intact), and install a new intake ball. NOTE: *Avoid using new rocker balls on exhaust valves.*

Replacing rocker studs:

Reaming the stud bore for oversize rocker studs
(© Buick Div. G.M. Corp.)

In order to remove a threaded stud, lock two nuts on the stud, and unscrew the stud using the lower nut. Coat the lower threads of the new stud with Loctite, and install.

Two alternative methods are available for replacing pressed in studs. Remove the damaged stud using a stack of washers and a nut (see illustration). In the first, the boss is reamed .005-.006″ oversize, and an oversize stud pressed in. Control the stud extension over the boss using washers, in the same manner as valve guides. Before installing the stud, coat it with white lead and grease. To retain the stud more positively, drill a hole through the stud and boss, and install a roll pin. In the second method, the boss is tapped, and a threaded stud installed. Retain the stud using Loctite Stud and Bearing Mount.

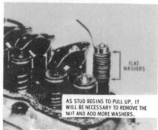

Extracting a pressed in rocker stud
(© Buick Div. G.M. Corp.)

AS STUD BEGINS TO PULL UP, IT WILL BE NECESSARY TO REMOVE THE NUT AND ADD MORE WASHERS.

Procedure	Method
Inspect the rocker shaft(s) and rocker arms (where applicable):  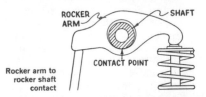 Disassembled rocker shaft parts arranged for inspection (© American Motors Corp.) Rocker arm to rocker shaft contact	Remove rocker arms, springs and washers from rocker shaft. NOTE: *Lay out parts in the order they are removed.* Inspect rocker arms for pitting or wear on the valve contact point, or excessive bushing wear. Bushings need only be replaced if wear is excessive, because the rocker arm normally contacts the shaft at one point only. Grind the valve contact point of rocker arm smooth if necessary, removing as little material as possible. If excessive material must be removed to smooth and square the arm, it should be replaced. Clean out all oil holes and passages in rocker shaft. If shaft is grooved or worn, replace it. Lubricate and assemble the rocker shaft.
Inspect the camshaft bushings and the camshaft (overhead cam engines):	See next section.
Inspect the pushrods:	Remove the pushrods, and, if hollow, clean out the oil passages using fine wire. Roll each pushrod over a piece of clean glass. If a distinct clicking sound is heard as the pushrod rolls, the rod is bent, and must be replaced.
	* The length of all pushrods must be equal. Measure the length of the pushrods, compare to specifications, and replace as necessary.
Inspect the valve lifters:  Check for Concave Wear on Face of Tappet Using Tappet for Straight Edge Checking the lifter face (© American Motors Corp.)	Remove lifters from their bores, and remove gum and varnish, using solvent. Clean walls of lifter bores. Check lifters for concave wear as illustrated. If face is worn concave, replace lifter, and carefully inspect the camshaft. Lightly lubricate lifter and insert it into its bore. If play is excessive, an oversize lifter must be installed (where possible). Consult a machinist concerning feasibility. If play is satisfactory, remove, lubricate, and reinstall the lifter.
* Testing hydraulic lifter leak down: 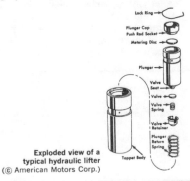 Lock Ring Plunger Cap Push Rod Socket Metering Disc Plunger Valve Seat Valve Valve Spring Valve Retainer Plunger Return Spring Tappet Body Exploded view of a typical hydraulic lifter (© American Motors Corp.)	Submerge lifter in a container of kerosene. Chuck a used pushrod or its equivalent into a drill press. Position container of kerosene so pushrod acts on the lifter plunger. Pump lifter with the drill press, until resistance increases. Pump several more times to bleed any air out of lifter. Apply very firm, constant pressure to the lifter, and observe rate at which fluid bleeds out of lifter. If the fluid bleeds very quickly (less than 15 seconds), lifter is defective. If the time exceeds 60 seconds, lifter is sticking. In either case, recondition or replace lifter. If lifter is operating properly (leak down time 15-60 seconds), lubricate and install it.

CYLINDER BLOCK RECONDITIONING

Procedure	*Method*
Checking the main bearing clearance :	Invert engine, and remove cap from the bearing to be checked. Using a clean, dry rag, thoroughly clean all oil from crankshaft journal and bearing insert. NOTE : *Plastigage is soluble in oil; therefore, oil on the journal or bearing could result in erroneous readings.* Place a piece of Plastigage along the full length of journal, reinstall cap, and torque to specifications. Remove bearing cap, and determine bearing clearance by comparing width of Plastigage to the scale on Plastigage envelope. Journal taper is determined by comparing width of the Plastigage strip near its ends. Rotate crankshaft 90° and retest, to determine journal eccentricity. NOTE : *Do not rotate crankshaft with Plastigage installed.* If bearing insert and journal appear intact, and are within tolerances, no further main bearing service is required. If bearing or journal appear defective, cause of failure should be determined before replacement.

Plastigage installed on main bearing journal
(© Chevrolet Div. G.M. Corp.)

Measuring Plastigage to determine
main bearing clearance
(© Chevrolet Div. G.M. Corp.)

Causes of bearing failure
(© Ford Motor Co.)

* Remove crankshaft from block (see below). Measure the main bearing journals at each end twice (90° apart) using a micrometer, to determine diameter, journal taper and eccentricity. If journals are within tolerances, reinstall bearing caps at their specified torque. Using a telescope gauge and micrometer, measure bearing I.D. parallel to piston axis and at 30° on each side of piston axis. Subtract journal O.D. from bearing I.D. to determine oil clearance. If crankshaft journals appear defective, or do not meet tolerances, there is no need to measure bearings; for the crankshaft will require grinding and/or undersize bearings will be required. If bearing appears defective, cause for failure should be determined prior to replacement.

Checking the connecting rod bearing clearance :	Connecting rod bearing clearance is checked in the same manner as main bearing clearance, using Plastigage. Before removing the crankshaft, connecting rod side clearance also should be measured and recorded.

Plastigage installed on connecting rod
bearing journal
(© Chevrolet Div. G.M. Corp.)

* Checking connecting rod bearing clearance, using a micrometer, is identical to checking main bearing clearance. If no other service

Procedure	Method

Measuring Plastigage to determine connecting rod bearing clearance
(© Chevrolet Div. G.M. Corp.)

is required, the piston and rod assemblies need not be removed.

Removing the crankshaft:

Connecting rod matching marks
(© Ford Motor Co.)

Using a punch, mark the corresponding main bearing caps and saddles according to position (i.e., one punch on the front main cap and saddle, two on the second, three on the third, etc.). Using number stamps, identify the corresponding connecting rods and caps, according to cylinder (if no numbers are present). Remove the main and connecting rod caps, and place sleeves of plastic tubing over the connecting rod bolts, to protect the journals as the crankshaft is removed. Lift the crankshaft out of the block.

Remove the ridge from the top of the cylinder:

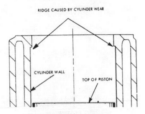

RIDGE CAUSED BY CYLINDER WEAR

CYLINDER WALL   TOP OF PISTON

Cylinder bore ridge
(© Pontiac Div. G.M. Corp.)

In order to facilitate removal of the piston and connecting rod, the ridge at the top of the cylinder (unworn area; see illustration) must be removed. Place the piston at the bottom of the bore, and cover it with a rag. Cut the ridge away using a ridge reamer, exercising extreme care to avoid cutting too deeply. Remove the rag, and remove cuttings that remain on the piston. CAUTION: *If the ridge is not removed, and new rings are installed, damage to rings will result.*

Removing the piston and connecting rod:

Removing the piston
(© SAAB)

Invert the engine, and push the pistons and connecting rods out of the cylinders. If necessary, tap the connecting rod boss with a wooden hammer handle, to force the piston out. CAUTION: *Do not attempt to force the piston past the cylinder ridge* (see above).

Procedure	Method
Service the crankshaft:	Ensure that all oil holes and passages in the crankshaft are open and free of sludge. If necessary, have the crankshaft ground to the largest possible undersize.
	** Have the crankshaft Magnafluxed, to locate stress cracks. Consult a machinist concerning additional service procedures, such as surface hardening (e.g., nitriding, Tuftriding) to improve wear characteristics, cross drilling and chamfering the oil holes to improve lubrication, and balancing.
Removing freeze plugs:	Drill a hole in the center of the freeze plugs, and pry them out using a screwdriver or drift.
Remove the oil gallery plugs:	Threaded plugs should be removed using an appropriate (usually square) wrench. To remove soft, pressed in plugs, drill a hole in the plug, and thread in a sheet metal screw. Pull the plug out by the screw using pliers.
Hot-tank the block:	Have the block hot-tanked to remove grease, corrosion, and scale from the water jackets. NOTE: *Consult the operator to determine whether the camshaft bearings will be damaged during the hot-tank process.*
Check the block for cracks:	Visually inspect the block for cracks or chips. The most common locations are as follows: Adjacent to freeze plugs. Between the cylinders and water jackets. Adjacent to the main bearing saddles. At the extreme bottom of the cylinders. Check only suspected cracks using spot check dye (see introduction). If a crack is located, consult a machinist concerning possible repairs.
	** Magnaflux the block to locate hidden cracks. If cracks are located, consult a machinist about feasibility of repair.
Install the oil gallery plugs and freeze plugs:	Coat freeze plugs with sealer and tap into position using a piece of pipe, slightly smaller than the plug, as a driver. To ensure retention, stake the edges of the plugs. Coat threaded oil gallery plugs with sealer and install. Drive replacement soft plugs into block using a large drift as a driver.
	* Rather than reinstalling lead plugs, drill and tap the holes, and install threaded plugs.

Procedure	*Method*

Check the bore diameter and surface:

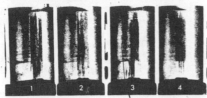

1, 2, 3 Piston skirt seizure resulted in this pattern. Engine must be rebored

4. Piston skirt and oil ring seizure caused this damage. Engine must be rebored

5, 6 Score marks caused by a split piston skirt. Damage is not serious enough to warrant reboring

7. Ring seized longitudinally, causing a score mark 1 3/16" wide, on the land side of the piston groove. The honing pattern is destroyed and the cylinder must be rebored

8. Result of oil ring seizure. Engine must be rebored

9. Oil ring seizure here was not serious enough to warrant reboring. The honing marks are still visible

Cylinder wall damage
(© Daimler-Benz A.G.)

Visually inspect the cylinder bores for roughness, scoring, or scuffing. If evident, the cylinder bore must be bored or honed oversize to eliminate imperfections, and the smallest possible oversize piston used. The new pistons should be given to the machinist with the block, so that the cylinders can be bored or honed exactly to the piston size (plus clearance). If no flaws are evident, measure the bore diameter using a telescope gauge and micrometer, or dial gauge, parallel and perpendicular to the engine centerline, at the top (below the ridge) and bottom of the bore. Subtract the bottom measurements from the top to determine taper, and the parallel to the centerline measurements from the perpendicular measurements to determine eccentricity. If the measurements are not within specifications, the cylinder must be bored or honed, and an oversize piston installed. If the measurements are within specifications the cylinder may be used as is, with only finish honing (see below). NOTE: *Prior to submitting the block for boring, perform the following operation(s).*

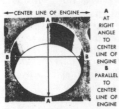

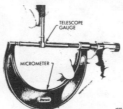

Cylinder bore measuring positions (© Ford Motor Co.)

Measuring the cylinder bore with a telescope gauge (© Buick Div. G.M. Corp.)

Determining the cylinder bore by measuring the telescope gauge with a micrometer (© Buick Div. G.M. Corp.)

Measuring the cylinder bore with a dial gauge (© Chevrolet Div. G.M. Corp.)

Procedure	Method
Check the block deck for warpage:	Using a straightedge and feeler gauges, check the block deck for warpage in the same manner that the cylinder head is checked (see Cylinder Head Reconditioning). If warpage exceeds specifications, have the deck resurfaced. NOTE: *In certain cases a specification for total material removal (Cylinder head and block deck) is provided. This specification must not be exceeded.*
* Check the deck height:	The deck height is the distance from the crankshaft centerline to the block deck. To measure, invert the engine, and install the crankshaft, retaining it with the center main cap. Measure the distance from the crankshaft journal to the block deck, parallel to the cylinder centerline. Measure the diameter of the end (front and rear) main journals, parallel to the centerline of the cylinders, divide the diameter in half, and subtract it from the previous measurement. The results of the front and rear measurements should be identical. If the difference exceeds .005″, the deck height should be corrected. NOTE: *Block deck height and warpage should be corrected concurrently.*
Check the cylinder block bearing alignment:  **Checking main bearing saddle alignment** (ⓒ Petersen Publishing Co.)	Remove the upper bearing inserts. Place a straightedge in the bearing saddles along the centerline of the crankshaft. If clearance exists between the straightedge and the center saddle, the block must be align-bored.
Clean and inspect the pistons and connecting rods: 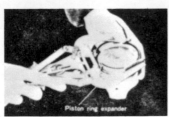 Piston ring expander **Removing the piston rings** (ⓒ Subaru)	Using a ring expander, remove the rings from the piston. Remove the retaining rings (if so equipped) and remove piston pin. NOTE: *If the piston pin must be pressed out, determine the proper method and use the proper tools; otherwise the piston will distort.* Clean the ring grooves using an appropriate tool, exercising care to avoid cutting too deeply. Thoroughly clean all carbon and varnish from the piston with solvent. CAUTION: *Do not use a wire brush or caustic solvent on pistons.* Inspect the pistons for scuffing, scoring, cracks, pitting, or excessive ring groove wear. If wear is evident, the piston must be replaced. Check the connecting rod length by measuring the rod from the inside of the large end to the inside of the small end using calipers (see

Procedure	Method

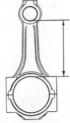

Cleaning the piston ring grooves
(© Ford Motor Co.)

Connecting rod
length checking
dimension

illustration). All connecting rods should be equal length. Replace any rod that differs from the others in the engine.

* Have the connecting rod alignment checked in an alignment fixture by a machinist. Replace any twisted or bent rods.

* Magnaflux the connecting rods to locate stress cracks. If cracks are found, replace the connecting rod.

Fit the pistons to the cylinders:

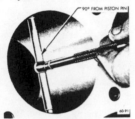

Measuring the cylinder
with a telescope gauge
for piston fitting
(© Buick Div.
G.M. Corp.)

Measuring the piston
for fitting
(© Buick Div.
G.M. Corp.)

Using a telescope gauge and micrometer, or a dial gauge, measure the cylinder bore diameter perpendicular to the piston pin, $2\frac{1}{2}''$ below the deck. Measure the piston perpendicular to its pin on the skirt. The difference between the two measurements is the piston clearance. If the clearance is within specifications or slightly below (after boring or honing), finish honing is all that is required. If the clearance is excessive, try to obtain a slightly larger piston to bring clearance within specifications. Where this is not possible, obtain the first oversize piston, and hone (or if necessary, bore) the cylinder to size.

Assemble the pistons and connecting rods:

Installing piston pin lock rings
(© Nissan Motor Co., Ltd.)

Inspect piston pin, connecting rod small end bushing, and piston bore for galling, scoring, or excessive wear. If evident, replace defective part(s). Measure the I.D. of the piston boss and connecting rod small end, and the O.D. of the piston pin. If within specifications, assemble piston pin and rod. CAUTION: *If piston pin must be pressed in, determine the proper method and use the proper tools; otherwise the piston will distort.* Install the lock rings; ensure that they seat properly. If the parts are not within specifications, determine the service method for the type of engine. In some cases, piston and pin are serviced as an assembly when either is defective. Others specify reaming the piston and connecting rods for an oversize pin. If the connecting rod bushing is worn, it may in many cases be replaced. Reaming the piston and replacing the rod bushing are machine shop operations.

Procedure	*Method*

Clean and inspect the camshaft:

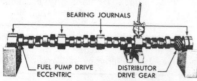

Checking the camshaft
for straightness
(© Chevrolet Motor
Div. G.M. Corp.)

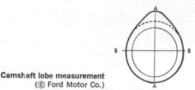

Camshaft lobe measurement
(© Ford Motor Co.)

Degrease the camshaft, using solvent, and clean out all oil holes. Visually inspect cam lobes and bearing journals for excessive wear. If a lobe is questionable, check all lobes as indicated below. If a journal or lobe is worn, the camshaft must be reground or replaced. NOTE: *If a journal is worn, there is a good chance that the bushings are worn.* If lobes and journals appear intact, place the front and rear journals in V-blocks, and rest a dial indicator on the center journal. Rotate the camshaft to check straightness. If deviation exceeds .001", replace the camshaft.

* Check the camshaft lobes with a micrometer, by measuring the lobes from the nose to base and again at 90° (see illustration). The lift is determined by subtracting the second measurement from the first. If all exhaust lobes and all intake lobes are not identical, the camshaft must be reground or replaced.

Replace the camshaft bearings:

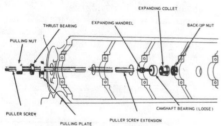

Camshaft removal and installation tool (typical)
(© Ford Motor Co.)

If excessive wear is indicated, or if the engine is being completely rebuilt, camshaft bearings should be replaced as follows: Drive the camshaft rear plug from the block. Assemble the removal puller with its shoulder on the bearing to be removed. Gradually tighten the puller nut until bearing is removed. Remove remaining bearings, leaving the front and rear for last. To remove front and rear bearings, reverse position of the tool, so as to pull the bearings in toward the center of the block. Leave the tool in this position, pilot the new front and rear bearings on the installer, and pull them into position. Return the tool to its original position and pull remaining bearings into position. NOTE: *Ensure that oil holes align when installing bearings.* Replace camshaft rear plug, and stake it into position to aid retention.

Finish hone the cylinders:

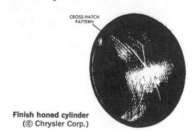

Finish honed cylinder
(© Chrysler Corp.)

Chuck a flexible drive hone into a power drill, and insert it into the cylinder. Start the hone, and move it up and down in the cylinder at a rate which will produce approximately a 60° cross-hatch pattern (see illustration). NOTE: *Do not extend the hone below the cylinder bore.* After developing the pattern, remove the hone and recheck piston fit. Wash the cylinders with a detergent and water solution to remove abrasive dust, dry, and wipe several times with a rag soaked in engine oil.

Procedure	*Method*
Check piston ring end-gap:  **Checking ring end-gap** (© Chevrolet Motor Div. G.M. Corp.)	Compress the piston rings to be used in a cylinder, one at a time, into that cylinder, and press them approximately 1″ below the deck with an inverted piston. Using feeler gauges, measure the ring end-gap, and compare to specifications. Pull the ring out of the cylinder and file the ends with a fine file to obtain proper clearance. CAUTION: *If inadequate ring end-gap is utilized, ring breakage will result.*
Install the piston rings: 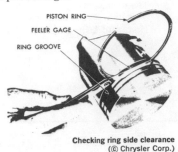 **Checking ring side clearance** (© Chrysler Corp.) 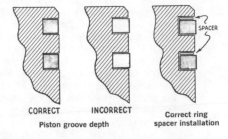 CORRECT INCORRECT Correct ring Piston groove depth spacer installation	Inspect the ring grooves in the piston for excessive wear or taper. If necessary, recut the groove(s) for use with an overwidth ring or a standard ring and spacer. If the groove is worn uniformly, overwidth rings, or standard rings and spacers may be installed without recutting. Roll the outside of the ring around the groove to check for burrs or deposits. If any are found, remove with a fine file. Hold the ring in the groove, and measure side clearance. If necessary, correct as indicated above. NOTE: *Always install any additional spacers above the piston ring.* The ring groove must be deep enough to allow the ring to seat below the lands (see illustration). In many cases, a "go-no-go" depth gauge will be provided with the piston rings. Shallow grooves may be corrected by recutting, while deep grooves require some type of filler or expander behind the piston. Consult the piston ring supplier concerning the suggested method. Install the rings on the piston, lowest ring first, using a ring expander. NOTE: *Position the ring markings as specified by the manufacturer (see car section).*
Install the camshaft:	Liberally lubricate the camshaft lobes and journals, and slide the camshaft into the block. CAUTION: *Exercise extreme care to avoid damaging the bearings when inserting the camshaft.* Install and tighten the camshaft thrust plate retaining bolts.
Check camshaft end-play:  Checking camshaft end-play with a feeler gauge (© Ford Motor Co.)	Using feeler gauges, determine whether the clearance between the camshaft boss (or gear) and backing plate is within specifications. Install shims behind the thrust plate, or reposition the camshaft gear and retest end-play.

Procedure	*Method*

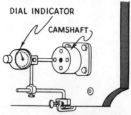

DIAL INDICATOR

CAMSHAFT

Checking camshaft end-play with a
dial indicator

* Mount a dial indicator stand so that the stem of the dial indicator rests on the nose of the camshaft, parallel to the camshaft axis. Push the camshaft as far in as possible and zero the gauge. Move the camshaft outward to determine the amount of camshaft end-play. If the end-play is not within tolerance, install shims behind the thrust plate, or re-position the camshaft gear and retest.

Install the rear main seal (where applic-able):

Seating the rear
main seal
(© Buick Div. G.M. Corp.)

Position the block with the bearing saddles facing upward. Lay the rear main seal in its groove and press it lightly into its seat. Place a piece of pipe the same diameter as the crankshaft journal into the saddle, and firmly seat the seal. Hold the pipe in posi-tion, and trim the ends of the seal flush if required.

Install the crankshaft:

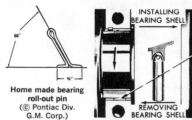

INSTALLING
BEARING SHELL

Home made bearing
roll-out pin
(© Pontiac Div.
G.M. Corp.)

REMOVING
BEARING SHELL

Removal and installation of upper
bearing insert using a roll-out pin
(© Buick Div. G.M. Corp.)

Thoroughly clean the main bearing saddles and caps. Place the upper halves of the bearing inserts on the saddles and press into posi-tion. NOTE: *Ensure that the oil holes align.* Press the corresponding bearing inserts into the main bearing caps. Lubricate the upper main bearings, and lay the crankshaft in position. Place a strip of Plastigage on each of the crankshaft journals, install the main caps, and torque to specifications. Remove the main caps, and compare the Plastigage to the scale on the Plastigage envelope. If clearances are within tolerances, remove the Plastigage, turn the crankshaft 90°, wipe off all oil and retest. If all clearances are correct, remove all Plastigage, thoroughly

PRY FORWARD

THRUST BEARING

PRY CRANKSHAFT FORWARD

HOLD
CRANKSHAFT
FORWARD

PRY CAP
BACKWARD

THRUST BEARING

PRY CAP BACKWARD

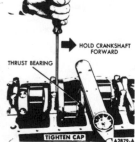

HOLD CRANKSHAFT
FORWARD

THRUST BEARING

TIGHTEN CAP

A2879-A

Aligning the thrust bearing
(© Ford Motor Co.)

Procedure	Method
	lubricate the main caps and bearing journals, and install the main caps. If clearances are not within tolerance, the upper bearing inserts may be removed, without removing the crankshaft, using a bearing roll out pin (see illustration). Roll in a bearing that will provide proper clearance, and retest. Torque all main caps, excluding the thrust bearing cap, to specifications. Tighten the thrust bearing cap finger tight. To properly align the thrust bearing, pry the crankshaft the extent of its axial travel several times, the last movement held toward the front of the engine, and torque the thrust bearing cap to specifications. Determine the crankshaft end-play (see below), and bring within tolerance with thrust washers.
Measure crankshaft end-play:  **Checking crankshaft end-play with a dial indicator** (© Ford Motor Co.) A 2908-A   **Checking crankshaft end-play with a feeler gauge** (© Chevrolet Div. (G.M. Corp.)	Mount a dial indicator stand on the front of the block, with the dial indicator stem resting on the nose of the crankshaft, parallel to the crankshaft axis. Pry the crankshaft the extent of its travel rearward, and zero the indicator. Pry the crankshaft forward and record crankshaft end-play. NOTE: *Crankshaft end-play also may be measured at the thrust bearing, using feeler gauges* (see illustration).
Install the pistons:	Press the upper connecting rod bearing halves into the connecting rods, and the lower halves into the connecting rod caps. Position the piston ring gaps according to specifications (see car section), and lubricate the pistons. Install a ring compresser on a piston, and press two long (8″) pieces of plastic tubing over the rod bolts. Using the plastic tubes as a guide, press the pistons into the bores and onto the crankshaft with a wooden hammer handle. After seating the rod on the crankshaft journal, remove the tubes and install the cap finger tight. Install the remaining pistons in the same man-

Procedure	*Method*

Tubing used as guide when installing
a piston
(© Oldsmobile Div. G.M. Corp.)

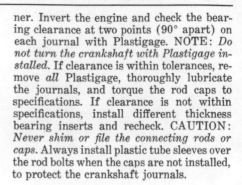

ner. Invert the engine and check the bearing clearance at two points (90° apart) on each journal with Plastigage. NOTE: *Do not turn the crankshaft with Plastigage installed.* If clearance is within tolerances, remove *all* Plastigage, thoroughly lubricate the journals, and torque the rod caps to specifications. If clearance is not within specifications, install different thickness bearing inserts and recheck. CAUTION: *Never shim or file the connecting rods or caps.* Always install plastic tube sleeves over the rod bolts when the caps are not installed, to protect the crankshaft journals.

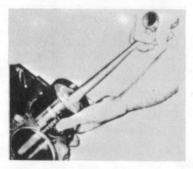

Installing a piston
(© Chevrolet Div. G.M. Corp.)

Check connecting rod side clearance:

Checking connecting rod side clearance
(© Chevrolet Div. G.M. Corp.)

Determine the clearance between the sides of the connecting rods and the crankshaft, using feeler gauges. If clearance is below the minimum tolerance, the rod may be machined to provide adequate clearance. If clearance is excessive, substitute an unworn rod, and recheck. If clearance is still outside specifications, the crankshaft must be welded and reground, or replaced.

Inspect the timing chain:

Visually inspect the timing chain for broken or loose links, and replace the chain if any are found. If the chain will flex sideways, it must be replaced. Install the timing chain as specified. NOTE: *If the original timing chain is to be reused, install it in its original position.*

Procedure	*Method*
Check timing gear backlash and runout:  Checking camshaft gear backlash (© Chevrolet Div. G.M. Corp.)  Checking camshaft gear runout (© Chevrolet Div. G.M. Corp.)	Mount a dial indicator with its stem resting on a tooth of the camshaft gear (as illustrated). Rotate the gear until all slack is removed, and zero the indicator. Rotate the gear in the opposite direction until slack is removed, and record gear backlash. Mount the indicator with its stem resting on the edge of the camshaft gear, parallel to the axis of the camshaft. Zero the indicator, and turn the camshaft gear one full turn, recording the runout. If either backlash or runout exceed specifications, replace the worn gear(s).

Completing the Rebuilding Process

Following the above procedures, complete the rebuilding process as follows:

Fill the oil pump with oil, to prevent cavitating (sucking air) on initial engine start up. Install the oil pump and the pickup tube on the engine. Coat the oil pan gasket as necessary, and install the gasket and the oil pan. Mount the flywheel and the crankshaft vibrational damper or pulley on the crankshaft. NOTE: *Always use new bolts when installing the flywheel.* Inspect the clutch shaft pilot bushing in the crankshaft. If the bushing is excessively worn, remove it with an expanding puller and a slide hammer, and tap a new bushing into place.

Position the engine, cylinder head side up. Lubricate the lifters, and install them into their bores. Install the cylinder head, and torque it as specified in the car section. Insert the pushrods (where applicable), and install the rocker shaft(s) (if so equipped) or position the rocker arms on the pushrods. If solid lifters are utilized, adjust the valves to the "cold" specifications.

Mount the intake and exhaust manifolds, the carburetor(s), the distributor and spark plugs. Adjust the point gap and the static ignition timing. Mount all accessories and install the engine in the car. Fill the radiator with coolant, and the crankcase with high quality engine oil.

Break-in Procedure

Start the engine, and allow it to run at low speed for a few minutes, while checking for leaks. Stop the engine, check the oil level, and fill as necessary. Restart the engine, and fill the cooling system to capacity. Check the point dwell angle and adjust the ignition timing and the valves. Run the engine at low to medium speed (800-2500 rpm) for approximately ½ hour, and retorque the cylinder head bolts. Road test the car, and check again for leaks.

Follow the manufacturer's recommended engine break-in procedure and maintenance schedule for new engines.

Emission Controls
and Fuel System

Emission Controls

Federal law specifies that each motor vehicle sold in the United States meet exacting standards regarding the quantities of pollutants emitted into the atmosphere. To meet these requirements, Opel has incorporated a number of emission control systems into their vehicles. These include a positive crankcase ventilation system, an evaporation control system, and the engine modifications which are collectively called the Opel Emission Control System.

PCV SYSTEM

The PCV (positive crankcase ventilation) system is a completely closed assembly which is sealed to the atmosphere. When the engine is idling or under a light load, fresh filtered air is supplied to the crankcase via a hose from the air cleaner. Intake manifold vacuum draws the crankcase vapors and fresh air through a hose into the intake manifold where they are combined with the fuel/air mixture and burned in the combustion chambers. The circular flow of gases is regulated by a metered orifice known as the PCV valve. Regular cleaning and replacement of this valve is a prerequisite for good performance and efficient combustion of crankcase emissions.

EVAPORATIVE CONTROL SYSTEM

Opels are equipped with an evaporative control system which is designed to minimize the escape of fuel vapors to the atmosphere. The system includes a special fuel tank, liquid-vapor separator, carbon canister, canister purge hoses, and carburetor modifications. Fuel vapors which would ordinarily escape into the atmosphere are directed into the carbon canister. The carbon absorbs the vapors and stores them.

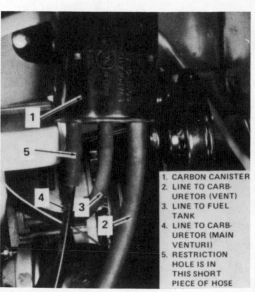

1. CARBON CANISTER
2. LINE TO CARBURETOR (VENT)
3. LINE TO FUEL TANK
4. LINE TO CARBURETOR (MAIN VENTURI)
5. RESTRICTION HOLE IS IN THIS SHORT PIECE OF HOSE

Evaporative control system carbon canister installed

The vapor is removed from the canister during periods of engine operation as manifold vacuum draws the vapors into the engine and burns them.

OPEL EMISSION CONTROL SYSTEM

The OECS (Opel Emission Control System) is designed to reduce pollutants in the exhaust by altering the combustion process. OECS features include a special air cleaner which thermostatically controls the temperature of the air fed to the engine, carburetor modifications, a specially calibrated distributor, and a modified combustion chamber design. Constant control of the intake air allows the engine to operate with a leaner fuel mixture. Complete effectiveness of this system can only be maintained by religious maintenence of the components. This includes a major tune-up at regular intervals with strict adherence to timing, dwell angle, and idle speed values as printed on the engine compartment sticker of your car.

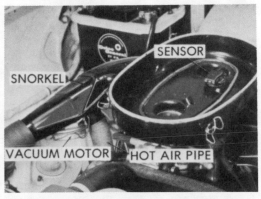

Heated air system—1.1 Engine

Heated air system—1.9 Engine

The principal component of the OECS is the heated air system. This unit has its activities centered in the air cleaner assembly and operates in the following way.

The exhaust manifold provides warm air for a stable intake temperature and accurate mixture by means of a stove mounted on the exhaust manifold. This heated air is drawn through the paper chimney pipe into the snorkel of the air cleaner. The temperature control air cleaner has a sensor that is designed to mix the heated air with colder outside air so the carburetor air inlet temperature averages about 115° F. This is done with the sensor, two doors in the air cleaner, and a vacuum motor. The motor operates the doors so that as one opens, the other closes mixing heated and cold air to keep the temperature constant. The doors are spring loaded so that when there is no vacuum from the engine, the cold air door is open. When the engine is running, the amount of vacuum delivered to the motor is regulated by the sensor and the amount of vacuum available from the engine. Thus, when under the hood temperatures rise above 135° F, the sensor allows no vacuum to the motor and the door for the heated air closes admitting only cold air. When accelerating hard, manifold vacuum drops and the motor gets no vacuum regardless of the temperature so again only the cold air door is open. When decelerating, the manifold vacuum is high and if the underhood temperature is less than 135°, the cold air door closes and only heated air is admitted. The hot air door opens fully at 9 in. of vacuum and the cold air door opens fully below 5 in. of vacuum.

Testing

VACUUM MOTOR

Before replacing any part of the OECS, certain tests should be performed to detect malfunctions. Set the timing, dwell angle, and idle speed to the exact specifications listed on your engine compartment sticker and test the system as follows:

To check the operation of the vacuum motor you must first make a visual inspection of the hoses for looseness, cracks, or other damage. With the ignition switched OFF, observe the damper door position through the snorkel opening. The damper door should be covering the heat stove passage and the snorkel passage should be open. If it is not, check the linkage for smooth operation. Disconnect the hose from the sensor unit to the vacuum motor and apply vacuum to the motor (this can be done by mouth). The damper door should close the snorkel air passage. Kink the hose to trap the vacuum and see that the door remains closed; if it doesn't, then the diaphragm assembly is leaking and should be replaced.

SENSOR

Test the sensor by seeing that it operates properly. When starting a cold engine, the air door should be closed. As soon as the engine is started, the air door should open. As the engine temperature rises, the air door should begin to close again and the air cleaner will be warm to the touch. If the system does not operate in this manner, you should perform a thermometer check of the sensor unit.

With the engine temperature at 85° or lower, remove the air cleaner cover and insert a suitable thermometer as close to the sensor as possible. The air door should begin to open as soon as the engine is started. After idling for several minutes, the air door will start to close again; at this point, remove the air cleaner cover again and read the temperature gauge. It must read 115° ± 20°. If the air door does not start to close at this temperature, the sensor is defective and must be replaced.

Removal and Installation

VACUUM MOTOR

There is a spring which holds the vacuum motor in place in the air cleaner assembly. To remove the motor, simply remove that spring and lift the motor while cocking it to one side to disengage the linkage at the control door. Install the new motor by reversing the process.

SENSOR

Carefully note the position of the sensor unit before removing. The new sensor must be replaced in the same position. Remove the retaining clips and the vacuum hoses and the sensor can be removed from the air cleaner.

When installing a new sensor, support the unit around the perimeter to protect

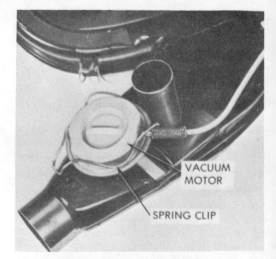

Replacing the vacuum motor assembly

Replacing the sensor assembly

the temperature sensing spring and be sure to relocate it in the same position as the one which was removed.

E.G.R. SYSTEM

To reduce emissions of nitrous oxides, all 1973 and later Opels are equipped with an exhaust gas recirculation system (E.G.R.). The 1973 system consists of a pipe connected to the center of the front exhaust pipe, an E.G.R. valve, a short pipe from the valve to the intake manifold, and a vacuum hose from the E.G.R. valve to the base of the carburetor. The California E.G.R. system is similar to the above except that an in-line shut off and regulating valve has been added. Testing is the same as the 1973 system. At idle speed the system does not receive sufficient vacuum to operate. When sufficient vacuum is present, the system permits regulated amounts

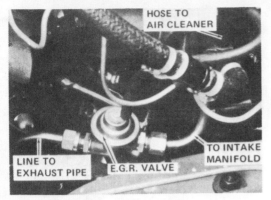

1973 exhaust gas recirculation valve

of exhaust gases to pass through the valve and into the intake manifold to be burned in the engine. The system requires annual maintenence and cleaning.

Testing

The testing procedure for the E.G.R. system is very simple and should be performed every 12,000 miles. There is no testing necessary on 1975 models.

With the engine at operating temperature, connect a tachometer and note the engine idle speed. Disconnect, at the intake manifold, the vacuum hose leading to the air cleaner. Disconnect the vacuum hose for the E.G.R. system from the throttle valve and connect that hose to the intake manifold where the other hose was removed. The engine speed should drop by 100–250 rpm (270–300 rpm for California models). If it drops by less than 100 rpm, the exhaust gas recirculation valve (shut-off valve on California models) and fitting should be removed and cleaned.

Removal and Installation

The valve and fitting are removed from the system by unscrewing the fittings on either side of the valve. Clean the valve with a piece of stiff wire to remove any exhaust deposits.

CAUTION: *Do not soak the valve in solvent. Thoroughly test the valve after installation and if it does not function properly, replace it.*

DASHPOT

1974 California Opels are equipped with a dashpot. Located on the carburetor, this device slows the closing of the throttle valve during deceleration which reduces

exhaust emissions. Before making any adjustments, check the operation of the dashpot. The stem of the dashpot should move in and out freely. With the engine idling at normal operating temperature, it should be possible to move the stem away from the throttle lever approximately $\frac{1}{16}$ in. When the throttle is opened, the stem should move out about $\frac{1}{8}$ in. If dashpot operation differs, proceed with the following adjustment.

Adjustment

1. With the engine idling at normal operating temperature, loosen the nut on the lower end of the dashpot and revolve the dashpot down until the stem comes free of the throttle lever.
2. Bring the dashpot up until the stem just touches the throttle lever. Turn the dashpot three turns against the throttle lever and tighten the nut on the bottom. Check dashpot operation. If it still does not function correctly, replace it.

1.1 ENGINE SYSTEM

1.1 engines use two carburetors. A lean idle is achieved through accurate fuel metering and good fuel distribution. An additional air/fuel mixture valve is attached to the balance tube on the intake manifold. This allows an additional air/fuel mixture to be drawn into the intake manifold when decelerating, which keeps combustion efficiency high and reduces emissions.

The deceleration control mechanism of the mixture valve unit consists of an electromagnetic valve, a diaphragm valve, and a deceleration mixture screw. The electromagnetic valve operates in relation to engine speed. Above 1,800 rpm, the valve is held open and below 1,800 rpm the valve is closed. The diaphragm valve is operated by intake manifold vacuum and can operate only above 1,800 rpm, when the electromagnetic valve is open. Therefore, at speeds over 1,800 rpm, when there is high engine vacuum (e.g., during deceleration), additional fuel-air mixture is supplied to the intake manifold to limit emission of pollutants.

The ignition timing of the 1.1 liter engine incorporates a combined advance-retard unit. At engine idle, high engine vacuum acts to retard the timing, as does the vacuum developed during deceleration, to a maximum of 10° ATDC. During acceleration, and other periods of low engine vacuum, the familiar advance mechanism takes over to advance the timing as usual.

CATALYTIC CONVERTER

All 1975 California Opels are equipped with a catalytic converter to control exhaust emissions. There is no scheduled maintenance for the converter, but it is a good idea to check it for exterior damage whenever the car is on a lift.

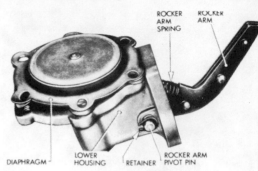

Rocker arm type fuel pump used on the 1.1 Engine

Fuel System

FUEL PUMP

There are three different types of fuel pumps used on all Opel engines. The fuel pump for the 1.1 engine is a conventional rocker arm type actuated by an eccentric on the camshaft. It is a single action pump attached to the front of the block with two star head bolts.

The 1971–74 1.9 engine uses a push-rod type fuel pump driven off of the distributor shaft. The push-rod is held in contact with the eccentric at all times by means of a push-rod spring.

Each time the push-rod is on the high part of the eccentric, the lighter diaphragm spring will push the diaphragm to replace any fuel used in the carburetor. The diaphragm seldom operates through a full stroke; under normal driving conditions the diaphragm moves only a few tenths of an inch.

All 1975 Opels are equipped with an electric fuel pump located directly in front of the fuel tank on the left-side.

Removal and Installation

1.1 ENGINE

To remove the fuel pump, disconnect the fuel lines and plug them. Remove the two star head bolts and take the fuel pump and gasket from the cylinder block.

NOTE: *The fuel tank is higher than the fuel pump; fuel will flow freely from the intake line when it is removed from the pump.*

Always install a new gasket when replacing the pump to avoid lubrication leaks.

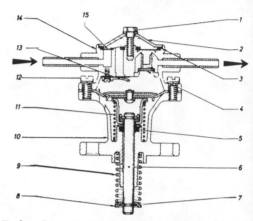

Push-rod type fuel pump—1.9 Engine

1. Pump cover attaching screw with seal ring
2. Pump cover
3. Gasket
4. Outlet valve
5. Oil seal ring
6. Push-rod
7. Retaining ring
8. Spring seat
9. Push-rod spring
10. Fuel pump lower housing
11. Diaphragm spring
12. Diaphragm
13. Leaf spring (inlet valve)
14. Fuel pump upper housing
15. Screen

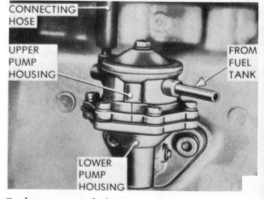

Rocker arm type fuel pump installed

1.9 ENGINE

The fuel pump is removed in the conventional manner by disconnecting the fuel

Fuel pump installation—1.9 Engine

lines, plugging them, and removing the pump. Upon replacement of the pump, be sure you properly install the asbestos spacer with a gasket on either side.

ELECTRIC FUEL PUMP

Removal and Installation

1. Disconnect the negative battery cable and raise the car.
2. Disconnect the fuel pump electrical connector. Using a 10 mm socket, remove the pump lower bracket bolt.
3. Open the bracket and remove the pump and insulator.
4. Loosen the hose clamps and remove the hoses. Some fuel will escape as the system is under pressure.
5. Remove the pump insulator. Replace the components in the reverse order of removal. The fuel pump is nonserviceable; it must be replaced if defective.

Testing

NOTE: *There are no internal replacement parts available for the fuel pump; therefore, if a pump is found to be defective, it must be replaced.*

The principal means of testing a fuel pump is by using a pressure gauge attached to the fuel pump outlet. These are readily available and are generally not expensive.

To begin the test it is first necessary to determine whether or not the fuel pump is getting fed through the supply system. Disconnect the fuel inlet at the carburetor and put a clear glass container under the line. Ground the distributor high tension lead so the engine cannot start and crank the engine for about 15 seconds. See that there is

fuel in the container and that it is free of dirt and water. If the presence of foreign material is noted, the supply lines and filter should be cleaned or replaced as necessary.

If the quantity of fuel discharged by the pump seems insufficient, the pump should be checked for suction with a vacuum gauge. Disconnect both the inlet and discharge lines from the fuel pump and attach a vacuum gauge to the inlet side with a length of rubber hose. Crank the engine until a stable reading is achieved. If the reading is not at least 15 in./Hg, the pump is faulty.

As a final testing procedure the fuel pump output pressure can be measured with a gauge. This test will measure the pump's ability to draw the fuel as well as discharge it. If the engine will run, it is best to connect all fuel and ignition lines and run the engine allowing the carburetor fuel bowl to fill. Then disconnect the fuel pump discharge and connect the gauge. Restart the engine and let it run at slow idle. If the engine will not run, the readings obtained at cranking speeds will indicate whether the pump is functioning. At 1950 rpm the Opel fuel pump pressure should be between 3.1 and 3.7 psi.

CARBURETORS—1971–74 MODELS

Opels use Solex carburetors of varying design on both the 1.1 and 1.9 engines. The 1.1 engine uses two Solex single barrel downdraft units linked together by a center unit. Both carburetors are factory adjusted and the individual adjustments should not be altered. In tune-up procedures the idle speed screw in the center unit and the mixture needle in the float bowl of the front carburetor are used for making adjustments. A bowden cable is used for choking the system manually.

The 1.9 engine uses a Solex two barrel carburetor with automatic choke. The secondary valve is vacuum operated except when the carburetor is installed on GT models. On the GT the secondary valve is mechanically operated from the primary throttle valve. The secondary throttle valve opens when the primary throttle valve is almost completely open.

Operation

All carburetors are similar in design having basic systems which enable them to

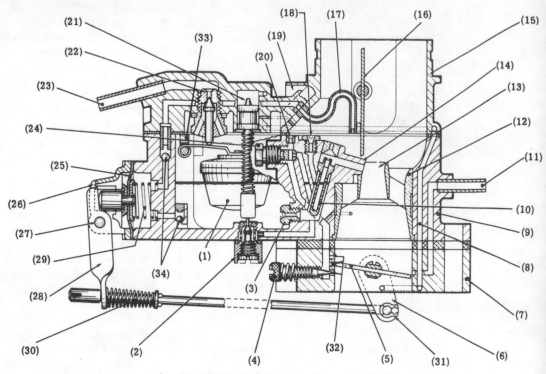

Solex 35 PDSI-2 carburetor used on 1.1 Engine

1. Float	12. Main venturi	24. Idle jet
2. Power valve	13. Boost venturi	25. Pump diaphragm
3. Main metering jet	14. Main nozzle	26. Pump cover
4. Idle mixture screw	15. Air horn	27. Pump lever shaft
5. Throttle valve	16. Choke	28. Diaphragm return spring
6. Throttle lever	17. Accelerator pump nozzle	29. Pump lever
7. Throttle body	18. High speed bleeder	30. Duration spring
8. Vacuum passage to power	19. Bowl vent	31. Clip
valve	20. Idle air bleed	32. Idle and off-idle ports
9. Float bowl	21. Vacuum piston	33. Leaf spring
10. Main well tube	22. Float needle valve	34. Check ball
11. Vacuum fitting	23. Fuel inlet	

perform their primary function of providing the correct fuel/air mixture for the engine.

These systems are float, starting, idle, progression, main feed, acceleration, and enrichment. Familiarity with these systems is helpful if not essential when overhauling carburetors. By understanding how a carburetor performs and what components are responsible for the various stages of operation, you will be better able to correct any malfunctions.

Float Circuit

The float mechanism maintains a constant fuel level so that atomization at all jets will be uniform under different vacuum conditions.

Operation of the circuit is simple. As the float drops, a needle valve is released which admits fuel from the supply (pump).

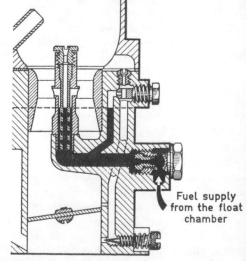

Fuel supply from the float chamber

The float mechanism keeps a constant fuel level for uniform atomization

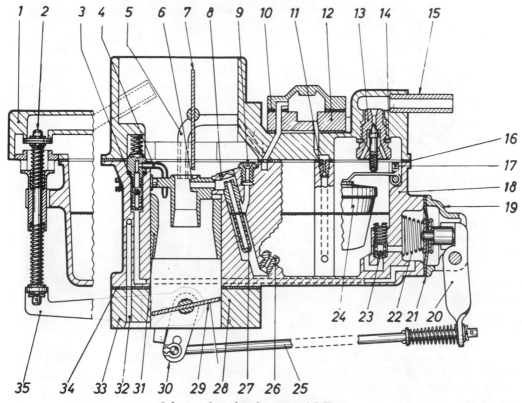

Solex two barrel carburetor—1.9 Engine

1. Carburetor	14. Float needle valve seal ring	27. Emulsion tube
2. Vent valve	15. Fuel line connecting tube	28. Vacuum passage for
3. Ball valve (pressure valve)	16. Carburetor cover gasket	enrichment
4. Injection tube	17. Leaf spring	29. Throttle valve
5. Primary venturi	18. Float chamber	30. Intermediate lever
6. Choke valve	19. Pump cover	31. Main venturi
7. Vent jet	20. Pump lever	32. Vacuum passage of
8. Air correction jet	21. Diaphragm	automatic choke
9. Diaphragm	22. Diaphragm spring	33. Throttle valve body
10. Thrust spring	23. Ball valve (suction valve)	34. Gasket
11. Enrichment jet	24. Float	35. Vent valve lever
12. Enrichment housing	25. Pump connecting rod	
13. Float needle valve	26. Metering jet	

The rising fuel level lifts the float to its former level, closing the valve. The assembly in the Solex carburetors is designed for a pumping pressure of approximately 2 psi. Needle valves which are operated by the float wear quickly and should be replaced during carburetor overhaul.

STARTING CIRCUIT

A choke is used to increase the vacuum of a starting engine. This causes a rich mixture of fuel and air to be drawn through all the jets to the carburetor throat. The rich mixture makes starting easier. The choke mechanism consists basically of a plate which covers the air intake of the carburetor and is operated either man-

ually as in the case of the 1.1 engine or by the action of a thermostatic spring as on the 1.9 engine.

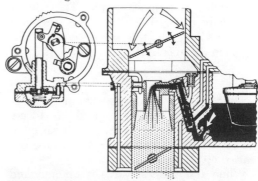

Automatic choke system as used on the 1.9 Engine

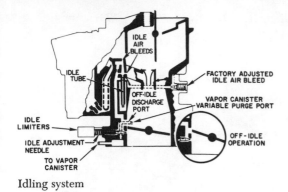

Idling system

IDLING CIRCUIT

The idling system provides fuel for the engine when the throttle plate is closed or barely open. The system provides a rich fuel air mixture below the throttle plate by providing a passage for fuel to enter and mix with the small quantity of air which can pass through the throttle valve. In the Solex carburetor the fuel for the idle circuit is taken after it passes through the main jet. It ceases to draw fuel after the main jet is activated by open throttle conditions. The idle speed adjustment screw located below the level of the throttle plate provides the fuel metering device for the idle circuit.

PROGRESSION OR SECOND IDLE CIRCUIT

As the throttle valve is opened, vacuum at the idle adjustment orifice is lessened because more air is passing around the throttle plate. With lower vacuum, less mixture is drawn into the throat at the moment when more air is passing into the manifold. To provide more fuel, one or more orifices are drilled into the carburetor idle passage at points which are in line with the angled throttle plate. These holes composing the progression circuit ensure a smooth transfer from idling to main jet circuits. These holes are easily clogged if dirt enters the carburetor. Clogging of the circuit creates "flat spots" in the acceleration.

MAIN JET CIRCUIT

The main jet circuit consists of the venturi, the main jet, high speed air bleed, and main vent tube. This circuit supplies the fuel/air mixture for normal engine operation.

When the throttle valve is opened and the vacuum present in the air horn is sufficient to draw fuel from the main jet cen-

tered in the venturi, then this circuit is in full operation.

ACCELERATION CIRCUIT

The longer the intake manifold the greater the need for acceleration pumps to inject emulsified fuel quickly (mixed with air) into the carburetor as the throttle valve is quickly snapped open.

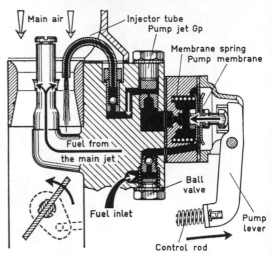

The Solex accelerator pump uses a diaphragm to push extra fuel into the air horn; a spring on the control rod absorbs the initial thrust and lengthens the duration of the injection

As the pump plunger moves upward, fuel is drawn into the plunger chamber through the strainer and the inlet check valve. When the throttle plate is opened, the accelerator plunger is pushed downward discharging fuel through the accelerator jet and into the carburetor. The size of the accelerator jet determines the duration of the injection.

Both the amount of fuel injected and the duration of the injection are adjustable on the Solex carburetors. Fuel quantity is changed by adjusting the length of the control rod. Duration is dependent on the size of the acceleration jet and the compression of the pump spring.

Solex has three basic types of accelerator pumps. Neutral pumps have identification numbers ending in "2" and are used for feeding regular four cylinder engines. Numbers ending in "3" identify rich pumps and are used on sport models or other high performance applications.

Pumps with a final digit "4" are lean and are used on carburetors which are feeding only one or two cylinders such as the mul-

Side view of Solex PDSI 2 barrel carburetor

Inside view of PDSI with float cover off

Inside view of PDSI float cover

A Automatic choke cover (water temp)
B Choke adjustment screws
C Cover of choke control mechanism
D Float chamber vent tube
E Enrichment diaphragm chamber
F Fuel inlet
G Float cover screws
H Idle jet
I Accelerator pump screws
J Vacuum pipe for distributor advance
K Idle air (speed) adjusting screw
L Accelerator pump adjustment
M Connection for A.I.R.
N Idle mixture (volume) adjustment
O Throttle stop screw
P Throttle lever
Q Choke-throttle connecting rod

R Venturi set screw
S Secondary throttle control rod
T Hot water hose connections
U Enrichment air jet
V Check valve carrier for accelerator pump
W Injection nozzle for accelerator pump
X Main nozzle bleed (emulsion tube underneath)
Y Primary venturi (choke tube)
AA Air channel of progression circuit for secondary venturi
BB Control arm for outside ventilation channel to float bowl
CC High speed air bleed (main air jet)
DD Primary main metering jet (secondary main metering jet not visible)
EE Fuel inlet to check valve
FF Enrichment fuel inlet
GG Control rod for the inside-outside ventilator for the float bowl
HH Enrichment tube
II Secondary-throttle diaphragm chamber
JJ Vacuum-choke diaphragm chamber
KK Choke valve
LL Vacuum passage to enrichment chamber
MM Needle valve carrier
NN Float bowl ventilation passage

tiple carburetor arrangement on the 1.1 Litre engine.

POWER CIRCUIT

This circuit is used to enrich the fuel/air mixture automatically when great volumes of air are being drawn into the engine intake manifold. This condition arises under heavy load or high speed situations. When the vacuum in the air horn is low, a vacuum piston is released which allows fuel from the float bowl to by-pass the main jet and raise the level in the main well of the carburetor. This allows a richer fuel/air mixture to be drawn into the venturi.

NOTE: *When you are having poor performance and you have isolated the carburetor as the source of the power loss, consider these various systems in order to better determine the proper corrective measures.*

Removal and Installation

1.1 ENGINE

1. Remove the air cleaner assembly.
2. Pull the fuel and vacuum hoses off of the carburetor fittings.
3. Loosen the choke control cable clamp and set-screw and disconnect it.
4. Unhook the throttle linkage by removing the cotter pin and two washers.
5. Remove the nuts and lockwashers which attach the carburetors to the intake manifold and remove the carburetors.

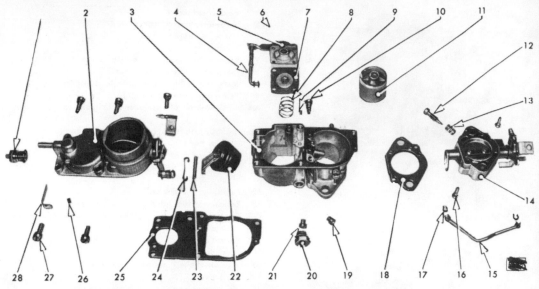

1.1 carburetor disassembled

1. Float needle valve incl. needle with seal ring
2. Air horn
3. Float bowl
4. Pump rod
5. Pump cover
6. Pump cover attaching screws (4)
7. Pump diaphragm
8. Diaphragm return spring
9. Plug for power by-pass passage
10. Idle jet
11. Venturi
12. Idle adjustment screw
13. Thrust spring for idle adjustment screw
14. Throttle body
15. Fast idle rod
16. Throttle body to float bowl attaching screw (2)
17. Snap ring
18. Insulating flange gasket
19. High speed bleeder
20. Plug with seal ring for main jet
21. Main jet
22. Float
23. Float pivot
24. Leaf spring
25. Air horn gasket
26. Accelerator pump channel plug
27. Carburetor cover attaching screw lockwasher (5)
28. Identification plate

6. The installation procedure is the reverse of removal. Pay special attention to the following items.

a. Be sure to firmly seat the rubber rings in the intake manifold.

b. When attaching the choke control cable, be sure the choke is completely open when the dash knob is pushed in.

1.9 ENGINE

1. Remove the air cleaner assembly.

2. Remove the fuel and vacuum hoses from the carburetor fittings.

3. Remove the choke wire.

4. Disconnect the throttle linkage by removing the lockpin and unsnapping the ball socket from the ball on the end of the throttle shaft.

5. Remove the four nuts and lockwashers which secure the carburetor to the intake manifold.

Prior to the installation of the carbu-retor, place new gaskets on the intake manifold. Make certain that the choke housing is set on the index and that the choke valve is nearly closed at room temperature.

Overhaul

Carburetors are relatively complex devices. Proper performance depends upon the cleanliness and correct adjustment of all the internal and external components. In addition to the adjustment made at the regular tune up intervals, it will eventually become necessary to remove, disassemble, and overhaul your carburetor. To overhaul the carburetor you must first purchase the proper rebuilding kit to supply you with the parts needed. Be prepared when you go out to buy the kit by knowing the exact year and model of your carburetor and by making note of any identifying numbers on the casting. This will make it easier for you to get the right parts. Read the re-

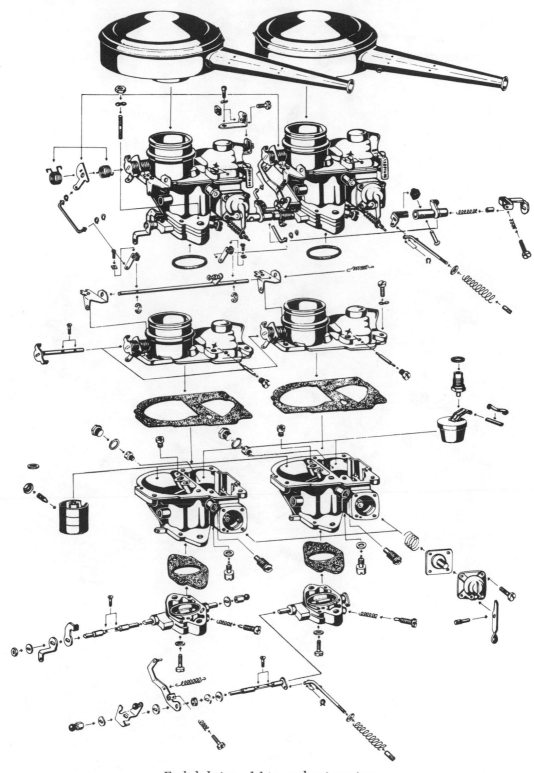

Exploded view—1.1 two carburetor system

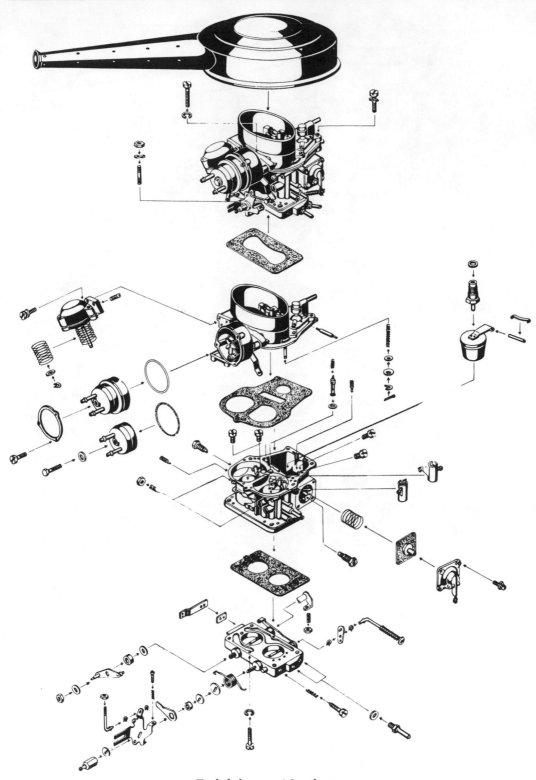

Exploded view—1.9 carburetor

building instructions carefully and study the exploded drawings. Then proceed to remove the carburetors and disassemble.

The following information is basic and should be used in conjunction with the instructions in the rebuilding kit.

ALL TYPES

Efficient carburetion depends greatly on careful cleaning and inspection during overhaul since dirt, gum, water, or varnish in or on the carburetor parts are often responsible for poor performance.

Overhaul your carburetor in a clean, dust-free area. Carefully disassemble the carburetor, referring often to the exploded views. Keep all similar and look-alike parts segregated during disassembly and cleaning to avoid accidental interchange during assembly. Make a note of all jet sizes.

When the carburetor is disassembled, wash all parts (except diaphragms, electric choke units, pump plunger, and any other plastic, leather, fiber, or rubber parts) in clean carburetor solvent. Do not leave parts in the solvent any longer than is necessary to sufficiently loosen the deposits. Excessive cleaning may remove the special finish from the float bowl and choke valve bodies, leaving these parts unfit for service. Rinse all parts in clean solvent and blow them dry with compressed air or allow them to air dry. Wipe clean all cork, plastic, leather, and fiber parts with a clean, lint-free cloth.

Blow out all passages and jets with compressed air and be sure that there are no restrictions or blockages. Never use wire or similar tools to clean jets, fuel passages, or air bleeds. Clean all jets and valves separately to avoid accidental interchange.

Check all parts for wear or damage. If wear or damage is found, replace the defective parts. Especially check the following:

1. Check the float needle and seat for wear. If wear is found, replace the complete assembly.

2. Check the float hinge pin for wear and the float(s) for dents or distortion. Replace the float if fuel has leaked into it.

3. Check the throttle and choke shaft bores for wear or an out-of-round condition. Damage or wear to the throttle arm, shaft, or shaft bore will often require replacement of the throttle body. These parts require a close tolerance of fit; wear may allow air leakage, which could affect starting and idling.

NOTE: *Throttle shafts and bushings are not included in overhaul kits. They can be purchased separately.*

4. Inspect the idle mixture adjusting needles for burrs or grooves. Any such condition requires replacement of the needle, since you will not be able to obtain a satisfactory idle.

5. Test the accelerator pump check valves. They should pass air one way but not the other. Test for proper seating by blowing and sucking on the valve. Replace the valve if necessary. If the valve is satisfactory, wash the valve again to remove breath moisture.

6. Check the bowl cover for warped surfaces with a straightedge.

7. Closely inspect the valves and seats for wear and damage, replacing as necessary.

8. After the carburetor is assembled, check the choke valve for freedom of operation.

Carburetor overhaul kits are recommended for each overhaul. These kits contain all gaskets and new parts to replace those that deteriorate most rapidly. Failure to replace all parts supplied with the kit (especially gaskets) can result in poor performance later.

Some carburetor manufacturers supply overhaul kits of three basic types: minor repair; major repair; and gasket kits. Basically, they contain the following:

Minor Repair Kits:
    All gaskets
    Float needle valve
    Volume control screw
    All diaphragms
    Spring for the pump diaphragm
Major Repair Kits:
    All jets and gaskets
    All diaphragms
    Float needle valve
    Volume control screw
    Pump ball valve
    Main jet carrier
    Float
    Complete intermediate rod
    Intermediate pump lever
    Complete injector tube
    Some cover hold-down screws and washers

Gasket Kits:

All gaskets

After cleaning and checking all components, reassemble the carburetor, using new parts and referring to the exploded view. When reassembling, make sure that all screws and jets are tight in their seats, but do not overtighten, as the tips will be distorted. Tighten all screws gradually, in rotation. Do not tighten needle valves into their seats; uneven jetting will result. Always use new gaskets. Be sure to adjust the float level when reassembling.

Throttle Linkage Adjustment

1970–72 Opels, All GT Models

To determine whether or not adjustment is necessary, have a helper depress the accelerator pedal to the floor and see if the throttle valves are completely open. If they are not and adjustment is necessary, proceed in this manner:

1. Unhook the accelerator pedal return spring.

2. Remove the lock spring at the upper end of the vertical control rod and detach the rod.

3. Lengthen or shorten the control rod so that wide open throttle is obtained when the accelerator pedal is about ¼ in. from the floor.

4. Reinstall the control rod, lock spring, and pedal return spring.

Opel 1900 and Manta Series

The carburetor bowden control wire is properly adjusted when the ball of the carburetor bowden control wire (A) rests against the accelerator pedal lever and the accelerator pedal is at an angle of 25° to the vertical plane with the engine at operating temperature at idle speed. Adjustment is as follows:

1. The accelerator pedal must be positioned at an angle of 25°. To do this, loosen the lock nut of the adjusting bolt and unscrew the bolt a few turns. Push a wood block measuring about 1⅜ in. between the accelerator pedal and the dash panel. Screw in the adjusting bolt until the accelerator pedal lever releases the wood block; then tighten the lock nut.

2. Adjust the engine idle speed.

3. Adjust the bowden wire at the adjuster located in the engine compartment.

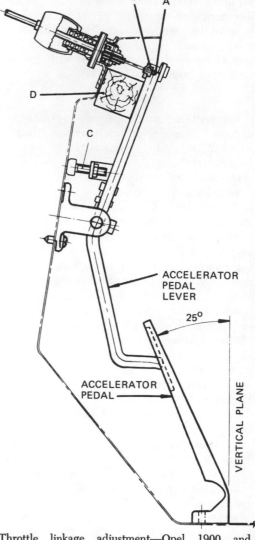

Throttle linkage adjustment—Opel 1900 and Manta

A. Ball end of cable   C. Adjusting bolt and locknut
B. Plastic bushing   D. 1⅜ wood block

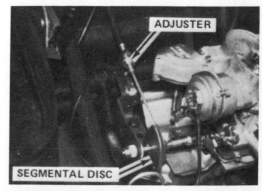

Bowden control wire adjuster and segmental disc —1.9 engine

Set the bowden wire so that the ball rests against the accelerator pedal lever and the wire core between the adjuster bracket and the segmental disc on the carburetor is not sagging.

4. Depress the accelerator pedal to the floorboard and check to see that the throttle valves are completely open.

Throttle Linkage Removal

ALL OPEL 1900 AND MANTA SERIES

At some point it may become necessary to replace the throttle cable; however, the replacement is fairly simple.

1. Remove the control wire from the bracket in the engine compartment and unhook it from the segmental disc at the carburetor.

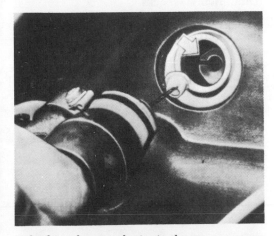

Unhooking the control wire in the passenger compartment—1900 and Manta

Positioning the plastic bushing

2. In the passenger compartment unhook the control wire, with the ball and plastic bushing, from the accelerator pedal lever.

3. From the engine compartment pull the bowden control wire out of the bracket on the dash panel.

4. To reinstall, simply feed the new control wire through the hole in the dash panel from the engine compartment and hook it in the accelerator pedal lever. Seat the plastic bushing firmly in the lever and hook the other end in the segmental disc. Attach the cable to the bracket and adjust.

Float Level Adjustment

The float level is fixed and there is no provision for adjustment. The float level is established by the thickness of the copper seal ring on the float needle valve. The correct seal ring thickness for the 1.1 engine Solex carburetor is 0.06. If any other thickness gasket is used, the float level will be changed.

The same applies to the Solex two barrel carburetor used on the 1.9 engine with the exception of the seal ring thickness. The correct gasket thickness for this carburetor is 0.08.

Fast Idle Speed Adjustment

1.9 ENGINE SOLEX 2V

It is best to perform this operation when the engine has been run to operating temperature. The actual adjustment should be made initially with the engine OFF.

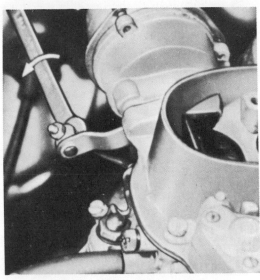

Increasing fast idle speed—2 barrel carburetor

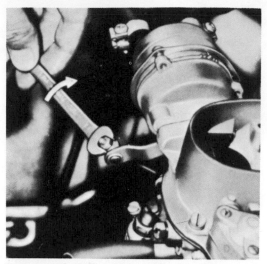

Decreasing fast idle speed—2 barrel carburetor

1. Operate the throttle linkage by hand until the throttle valve is half open. With your other hand, completely close the choke valve. Release the throttle valve first and then the choke valve.

2. By performing this operation the abutment lever in the automatic choke body has come to rest on the highest step of the fast idle cam and the throttle valve is partially open.

3. Start the engine but do not touch the accelerator pedal. The slightest touch will release the position of the fast idle mechanism.

4. With a tachometer connected to the engine, check the fast idle speed. It should be within 200 rpm of the specified speed.

5. Adjustments to the fast idle speed are made by lengthening or shortening the throttle connecting link.

6. Shorten the rod to decrease engine speed by loosening the lower nut and tightening the upper.

7. Lengthen the rod to increase engine speed by loosening the upper nut and tightening the lower.

ELECTRIC FUEL INJECTION

All 1975 Opels use electronic fuel injection to meter fuel to the cylinders. Information is fed to the control unit (the "brain" of the system), from various engine sources; the control unit constantly computes the proper fuel and air mixture for all operating conditions. The computer also controls the pulse time of the injectors so that the right mixture can be achieved.

Most testing operations involve specialized testing equipment and should be left to a qualified dealer, but there are some checks that you can make.

1. First, make sure that the ignition system is in good working order.

2. Vacuum leaks in the manifold system, or between the airflow meter and the combustion chambers can cause misfiring, a rough idle, hard starting, or stalling. If a leak is suspected, correctly torque the intake manifold bolts, then check all vacuum hoses for condition and poor connections.

3. Disconnect the brake booster hose at the intake manifold and apply a soapy water solution around all fittings and gaskets. Apply about 5 psi of air to the hose. Air leaks will produce bubbles.

Dual Relay Checks

The dual relay is made up of two relays which control current to the entire fuel injection system. One relay provides current to the control unit and pre-resistors; the other provides current to the electric fuel pump.

Dual relay with terminal plugs "A" and "B"

1. Disconnect plug "A" from the dual relay, and hook up a test light.

2. Insert the probe into terminal 88Z. If the plug does not light, there is a short between the plug and the battery.

3. Insert the probe into terminal 88Y. If it does not light, the fuel pump fuse is blown. The fuel pump is in its own holder next to the fuse box.

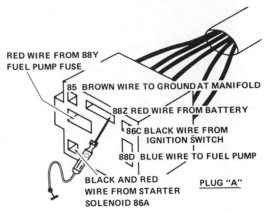

RED WIRE FROM 88Y
FUEL PUMP FUSE

85 BROWN WIRE TO GROUND AT MANIFOLD

88Z RED WIRE FROM BATTERY

86C BLACK WIRE FROM
     IGNITION SWITCH

88D BLUE WIRE TO FUEL PUMP

BLACK AND RED   PLUG "A"
WIRE FROM STARTER
SOLENOID 86A

Terminal plug "A' with leads shown

4. Turn the ignition switch on; insert the probe into terminal 86C. If it does not light, there is a short between the plug and the ignition switch.

5. With the ignition switch on, insert the probe into terminal 86A and crank the starter. If the light does not come on, check the black and red wire connected to the starter solenoid.

6. With an ohmmeter, check for continuity between terminal 85 and ground. If there is no continuity, the brown wire between the terminal plug and intake manifold is broken.

Fuel Supply Checks

1. Install a fuel pressure gauge to the fuel feed line of the cold start injector. Take readings while cranking and with the engine running; the pressure should be between 31–44 psi.

Fuel pressure gauge installed

2. If there is no pressure, check the fuse. If it is OK, remove the "A" plug from the dual relay and connect a jumper between terminals 88D and 88Y of the plug. If the pump does not run, check for current at the fuel pump. If you are getting current and the ground is good, and the pump still will not work, replace the pump. If the pump works with the jumper wire installed, replace the dual relay. If the problem still exists with the new relay, repeat the dual relay checks.

3. If you get normal fuel pressure readings while cranking, but it drops off when the engine is running, the airflow meter circuit has to be checked. Remove the electronic fuel injection wiring harness plug and connect a jumper between terminals 36 and 39 of the plug. Turn the ignition switch on; if the pump operates, the wiring harness and dual relay are OK, and the problem is in the airflow meter.

Jumper wire on the airflow meter terminal plug

Connect an ohmmeter to terminals 36 and 39 of the airflow meter. Disconnect the hose at the front of the airflow meter and operate the baffle plate by hand. You must register continuity when the baffle plate is moved from the closed position.

4. If the fuel pump is operating, but you are reading no pressure, check for obstruction and restrictions in the fuel lines.

5. If you are registering pressure, and it is over 44 psi, check for a restricted fuel return line from the pressure regulator valve to the fuel tank. If it is not restricted,

the pressure regulator valve is faulty. If the pressure does not vary with intake manifold vacuum, either the pressure regulator valve is not receiving vacuum or the valve itself is bad. If the pressure you are registering is low, check the pressure regulator valve, the fuel pump, and the fuel lines.

6. If you are not getting enough fuel flow, remove the fuel line from the cold start injector. Run a hose from the line to a container and insert a jumper wire between terminals 88D and 88Y on terminal plug "A." If the volume pumped is not at least 1.5 qts in a minute, check the lines for restrictions; if there are none, replace the fuel pump.

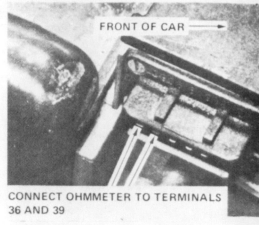

CONNECT OHMMETER TO TERMINALS 36 AND 39

Airflow meter ohmmeter connections

Idle Speed Adjustment

1. Connect a tachometer to the engine.
2. Loosen the locknut and turn the idle air adjustment screw in or out as necessary to set the correct idle speed. The idle air adjustment screw is located on the throttle valve housing.
3. Have the exhaust emission level checked with the proper equipment.

THROTTLE VALVE HOUSING

IDLE AIR ADJUSTMENT SCREW

Adjusting the idle speed—1975 Opel

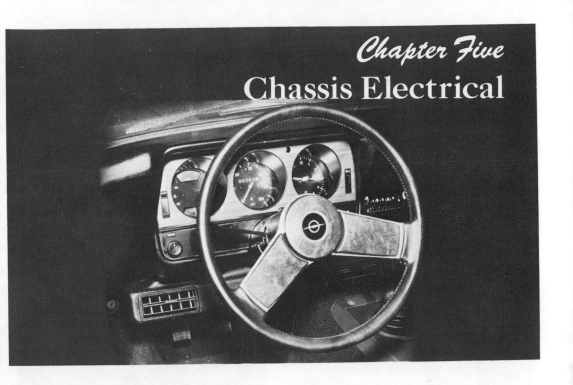

Heater

The function of the heater is obvious and with the exception of component placement, the various models are similar. Basi-cally a heater system incorporates a thermostatic control valve (generally manually operated), an air intake route, a distribution housing, and a heater core similar to a radiator. The distributor housing is fitted with manual controls to direct the heated air in the desired direction. Additionally

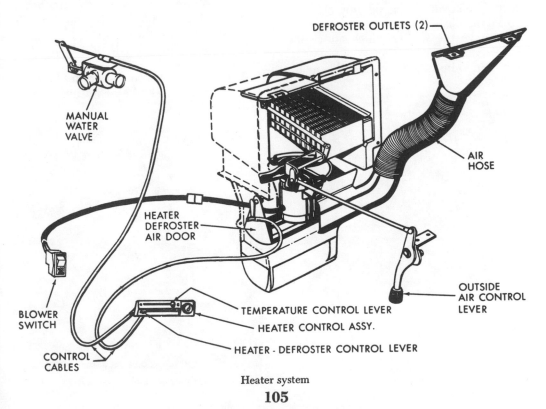

Heater system

most systems have an electric fan to force the heated air into the car.

Fresh air is drawn through openings in the cowl or hood into the air distributor housing and from there is directed to either the passenger compartment or the defroster outlets, depending on the position of the controls. A two-speed blower motor is positioned in the heater housing above the heater core. The blower draws air entering the housing and blows it through the heater core to outlets designated by the position of the doors in the housing.

The heater valve regulates the flow of coolant through the heater core thus varying the temperature of the air forced past it.

BLOWER

Removal and Installation

OPEL (EXCEPT 1900 AND GT)

1. Disconnect the wire leading to the blower from the blower switch.
2. Disconnect the control cable from the distributor door.
3. Remove the screws which secure the air distributor housing to the dash and partially remove the housing from the dash.
4. Remove both the air hoses and complete the removal of the distributor housing from the dash.
5. Remove the screws which attach the blower motor to the housing.
6. When reinstalling, replace the motor

Heater distributor housing—Opel

1. Sheet metal screws
2. Heater-defroster control wire
3. Air distribution housing
4. Wire to blower switch
5. Hose to defroster

in the housing and make electrical and control connections prior to installing the unit in the dash.

1900 AND MANTA

1. From the engine compartment remove the five screws on the heater shroud cover.
2. Remove the cover.
3. Pull the water hose off of the windshield wiper jet.

Heater shroud—1900 series

4. Disconnect the wires to the heater motor; this is done by disconnecting the plug on the left of the shroud.
5. Remove the three bolts which secure the motor.
6. Install in the reverse order, remembering to connect the windshield wiper water jet.

Heater blower motor attaching screws

GT

NOTE: *The GT models have a heater system which must be removed as a unit. In order to do this, it is necessary to first remove the instrument panel.*

1. Remove the lower radiator hose and drain the coolant.

2. Detach the hoses from the heater core inlet and outlet in the engine compartment.

3. From the engine compartment, remove the hood lock control clip and cable from the lock bar.

4. Remove the console shift cover between the seats by removing the ash tray and the two screws under it. Remove the retaining screw in the headlamp lever handle and remove the handle. There are four push-button type studs holding the

GT heater and defroster duct hoses

cover in place and they can be undone by prying the cover up. Slowly work the cover upward over the shift lever and the boot.

5. Remove the instrument panel as outlined in this chapter.

Location of heater blower case bolt and screws

6. Unscrew the heater controls and the support bracket.

7. Remove one bolt at the top of the heater blower case and two nuts from the bottom of the case. The entire assembly may now be removed.

CORE

Removal and Installation

OPEL, 1900, MANTA

1. From the engine compartment, unscrew the heater housing cover from the dash panel.

2. Drain the cooling system.

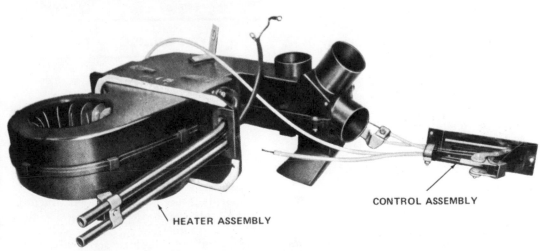

CONTROL ASSEMBLY

HEATER ASSEMBLY

GT heater system

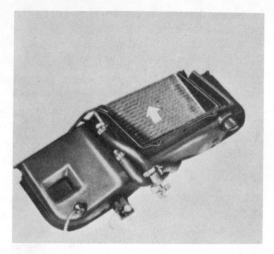

1900 heater core

Radio support bracket

3. Remove the heater hoses from their connections on the core.

4. The windshield washer hose may interfere with removal on some models. If it does, simply remove the hose from the jet.

5. Remove the housing and core.

6. Upon installation it is necessary to use a sealer on the housing before attaching to the dash panel.

GT

As has been mentioned, the GT heater is a one piece assembly. Follow the instructions above for complete removal procedures.

Radio

Removal and Installation

OPEL AND 1900 EXCEPT RALLYE

1. Disconnect the battery ground cable.

2. Remove the radio knobs and undo the mounting nuts underneath.

3. Remove the receiver bracket lower screw from the receiver and loosen the upper bolt about three turns.

4. The radio can be tilted and lowered out of the dash.

NOTE: *When installing the radio the antenna trimmer should be adjusted as follows: extend the antenna to a height of 31 in., tune the radio to a barely audible station around 1400 KC, and turn the*

trimmer screw (on the bottom of the receiver) until maximum volume is obtained.

RALLYE

The procedure is the same as for the 1900 except that the glove box and right defroster duct must be removed and the radio removed and installed through the glove box opening.

GT

To remove the radio the entire instrument panel must be removed; there are instructions in this chapter covering this procedure. Once the panel is removed, the job is simple: just remove the mounting nuts, knobs, and connections, and remove the radio.

Windshield Wipers

MOTOR

Removal and Installation

ALL OPEL, 1900, AND MANTA

1. Remove the crank arm nut and crank arm from the wiper motor driveshaft located above the clutch and brake pedals inside the car.

2. Unbolt the three nuts which attach the motor and drive to the firewall and remove the wiper motor.

3. Install by loosely attaching the motor to the firewall and then installing the crank

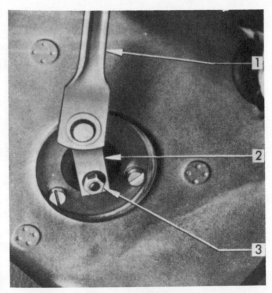

Crank arm attachment to motor

1. Connecting rod to   2. Crank arm
    left wiper transmission   3. Hex nut and lockwasher

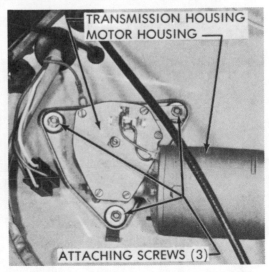

Wiper motor installed

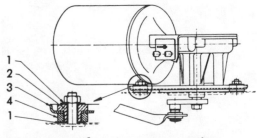

Components used in wiper motor mounting

1. Sleeve   3. Mounting plate
2. Damper bushing   4. Damper ring

arm and nut. When all the parts are properly positioned, tighten securely.

GT

1. Unbolt the retaining nuts and remove the wiper arms.

2. Remove the three bolts which retain the wiper posts to the deflector panels and allow the posts to drop out of the panels.

3. Unscrew the left and center deflector panels and remove the left panel, including the motor and linkage.

4. Remove the crank arm nut from the wiper drive and separate the linkage from the motor.

5. Unbolt the three retaining nuts and remove the motor from the deflector panel.

6. Install in the reverse order of removal.

NOTE: *When installing the wiper arms, ensure that they are in the proper position at rest.*

Instrument Cluster

Removal and Installation

OPEL EXCEPT GT AND 1900

1. Disconnect the battery ground cable.

2. Disconnect the speedometer cable at the speedometer housing.

3. Reach under the dash and apply equal pressure on the instrument housing, compressing the four retaining clamps. Tilt the instrument housing out of the instrument panel toward the rear of the car.

4. Disconnect the wires from the terminals.

5. To install, attach the wires and line housing clips with the holes in the panel. Push in until the clips lock in the panel.

1900 AND MANTA

NOTE: *Disconnect the battery ground cable before beginning the procedure.*

1. Remove the headlight switch by depressing the retaining clip on the shaft and pulling back on the switch knob.

2. Remove the two plugs on the cluster panel.

3. Remove the two screws behind the plugs.

4. Pull off the heater control knobs.

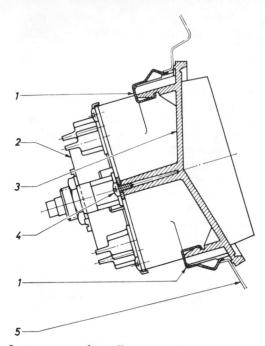

Instrument panel installation—Opel

1. Retaining clamp   4. Sheet metal screw
2. Speedometer   5. Instrument panel
3. Instrument housing

Removing the plugs in the dashboard—1900

5. Carefully pull the instrument cover toward the steering wheel and remove it.

6. Remove the lower attaching screws.

7. Disconnect the speedometer cable.

8. Pull the right and left cluster sides partially out and disconnect the wires from the back of the cluster.

9. The installation is simply the reverse of this procedure with no special problems.

Lower housing attaching screws—1900

GT

CAUTION: *The removal of the instrument cluster and panel involves lowering the steering column. As this is a collapsible column, it is imperative that the column receive no shock or other rough treatment which could cause it to become inoperative.*

Right access cover and screw—GT

Left access cover and screw—GT

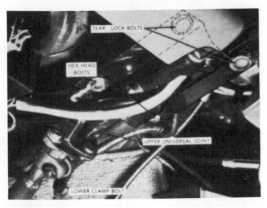

Steering column bolts—GT

Removing the instrument cluster—GT

NOTE: *Disconnect the battery ground cable before beginning the removal procedure.*

1. Remove the right access cover and underlying screw.

2. Remove the left access cover and concealed screw.

3. Remove the flasher unit.

4. Position the steering so that the front wheels are straight.

5. Two of the bolts in the support for the steering column are shear bolts. To remove them, drill a ³⁄₁₆ in. pilot hole and use a stud extractor (sometimes called an Easy-Out®) to remove the bolts.

6. Disconnect the electrical plugs to the steering column.

7. Support the steering column and remove the remaining hex head bolts.

8. Drop the steering column to the floor.

9. Disconnect the speedometer cable.

10. Remove the six screws on the instrument cluster.

Instrument cluster screws—GT

11. Pull back on the instrument cluster from the top to remove.

CAUTION: *Replacement of the shear bolts is critical to the safety and performance of the car. They must be re-*placed with bolts having the exact specifications. When replacing the steering column, tighten the hex head bolts to 14 ft lbs. Tighten the shear bolts until the head of the bolt is sheared off completely.

12. Replace all components in the reverse order of removal.

NOTE: *This procedure applies to work done on the radio, heater, or instruments within the cluster.*

Headlights

Removal and Installation

OPEL EXCEPT GT, 1900, AND MANTA

Remove the three screws which hold the headlight door in place. The two small screws on the retaining ring hold the sealed beam in place. Remove the connector plug and replace the beam.

CAUTION: *Do not touch the headlight adjuster screws.*

1900 BODY STYLE 51, 53, 54

The sealed beam is held in place by two screws on the headlight ring and four screws which hold the retainer to the body. Remove these screws and the wire connector and remove the sealed beam from the engine compartment.

1900 BODY STYLE 57, 57R

The headlight retainer screws are inside the engine compartment. Remove the screws and the wire connector to replace the sealed beam.

GT

Rotate the headlights to the open position and remove the headlight retaining ring, the wire connector, and the sealed beam.

NOTE: *Any time the headlight is replaced, the adjusting screws must not be moved. If they are disturbed, the headlights will have to be reaimed.*

DISABLING THE STARTER INTERLOCK SYSTEM

1. Disconnect the negative battery cable. Locate the logic module, which is a small metal box located behind the instrument panel to the left of the steering column.
2. Remove the two terminal connectors (identified by three black and red wires), and connect two of these wires together.
3. Find the buzzer unit which is located to the left of the logic module.
4. Cut the black and white wire going to it and tape the ends to prevent grounding.
5. Connect the negative battery cable and check system operation.

Light Bulb Recommendation Chart

Location	Opel	GT	1900
Headlight	6012	6012	6012
Tail light	1034	1034	1034
Stop light	1034	1034	1034
Turn signal	1034	1073	1034
License plate	97	97	67
Back-up light	1073	2098180	1073
Marker lights	97	97	67
Dome light	57	57	2098176

NOTE: *The seven digit number is an Opel part number.*

Fuse Recommendations Opel

Fuse Position	Amperage	Buick-Opel Part No.	Description
1	8	2096601	Horn, windshield wiper, parking brake warning light
2	5	1238300	Direction signal, stop lamp, back-up lamp, brake system warning light
3	8	2096601	Heater, cigar lighter
4	5	1238300	Interior lamp, electric clock, hazard warning flasher, rear side marker lights
5	5	1238300	Left parking and tail lamp
6	5	1238300	Right parking and tail lamp; license plate lamp, instrument light, glove box light, front side marker lights
In relay switch in engine compartment	16	1286925	Electrically heated back window

Fuse Recommendations GT

Fuse Position	Amperage	Buick-Opel Part No.	Description
1	8	2096601	Horn, back-up light, windshield wiper, windshield washer
2	5	1238300	Turn signal and indicator, brake warning indicator, stop lamp, radio
3	8	2096601	Cigar lighter, heater
4	5	1238300	Electric clock, hazard warning flasher
5	5	1238300	Left parking lamp (front), left tail lamp (rear), left side marker light (rear)
6	5	1238300	Right parking lamp (front), right tail lamp (rear), right side marker light (rear)
7	5	1238300	Instrument lights, license plate lights, shift quadrant lights

Fuse Recommendations 1900

Fuse Position	Amperage	Description
1	5	Left parking light, left tail light, left side marker lights
2	5	Right parking light, right tail light, right side marker lights, instrument lights
3	8	Warning buzzer, trunk light, hazard warning light, passing signal, courtesy light
4	15	Back-up lights, blower motor, cigar lighter, radio
5	15	Wiper motor, horn
6	8	Signal system, stop lights, tachometer and oil pressure gauge (Opel Rallye), indicator lights, temperature gauge, fuel gauge

The fuse for the heated glass back window is located in relay switch.

CAUTION: *Do not use fuses of higher amperage rating than those specified.*

Wiring Diagrams

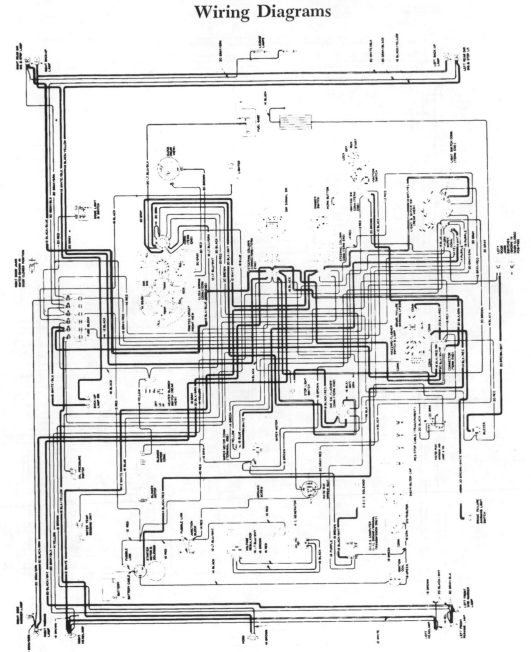

1971 1900 Opel Sedan

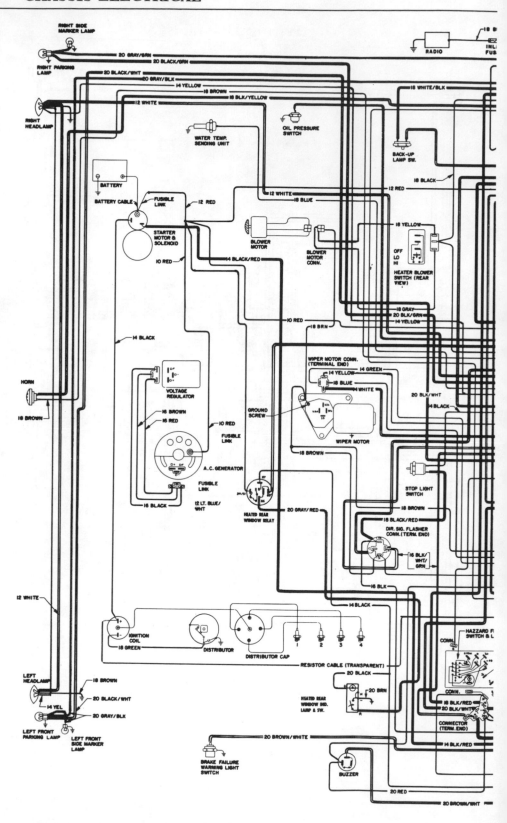

1972 1900 Opel Sedan

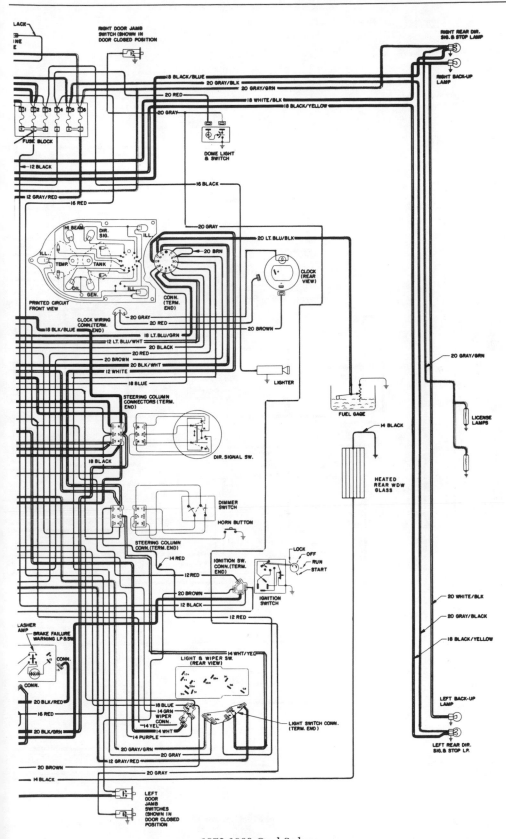

1972 1900 Opel Sedan

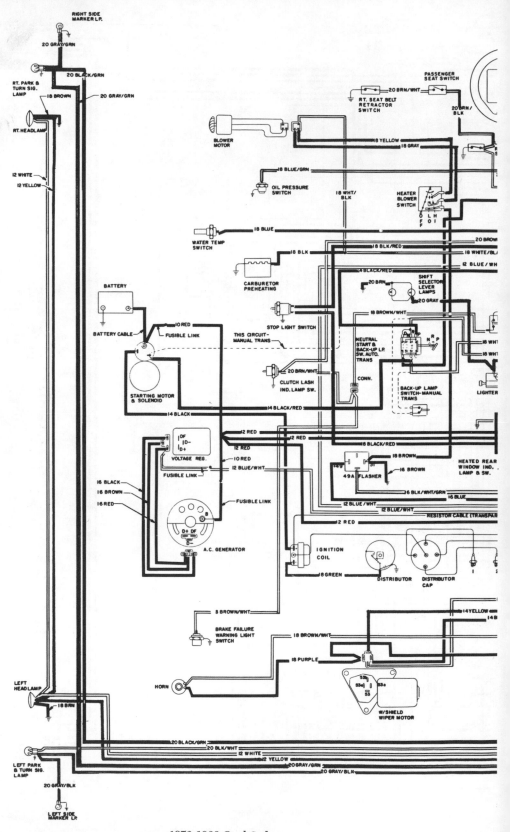

1973 1900 Opel Sedan

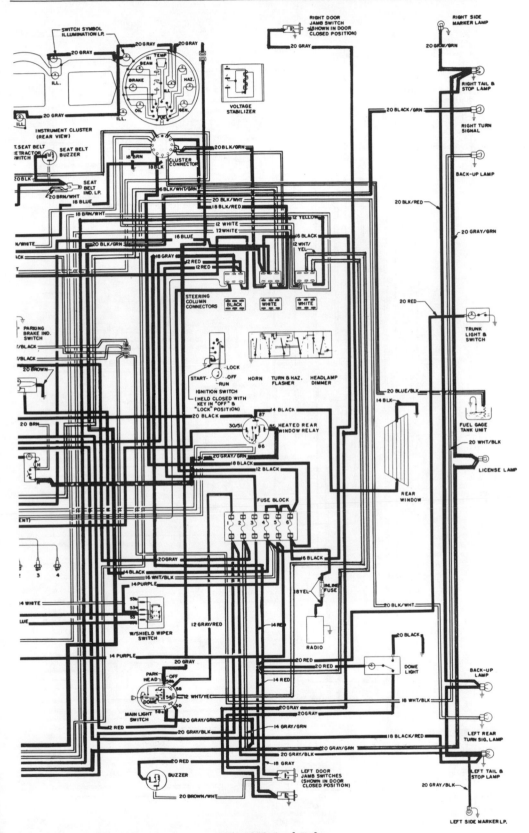

1973 1900 Opel Sedan

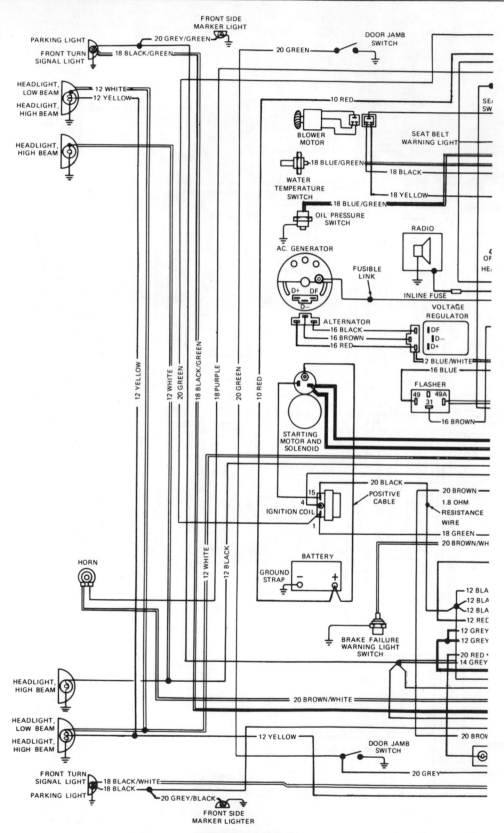

1975 1900 Opel Sedan

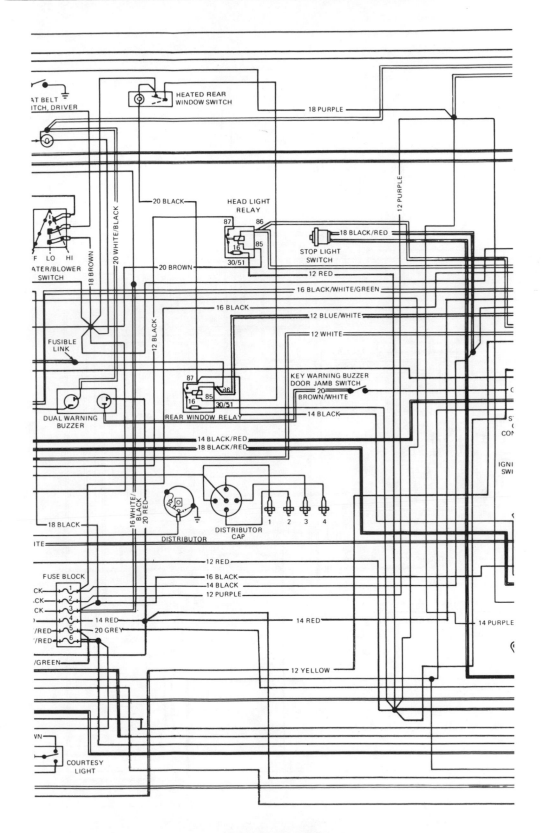

1975 1900 Opel Sedan

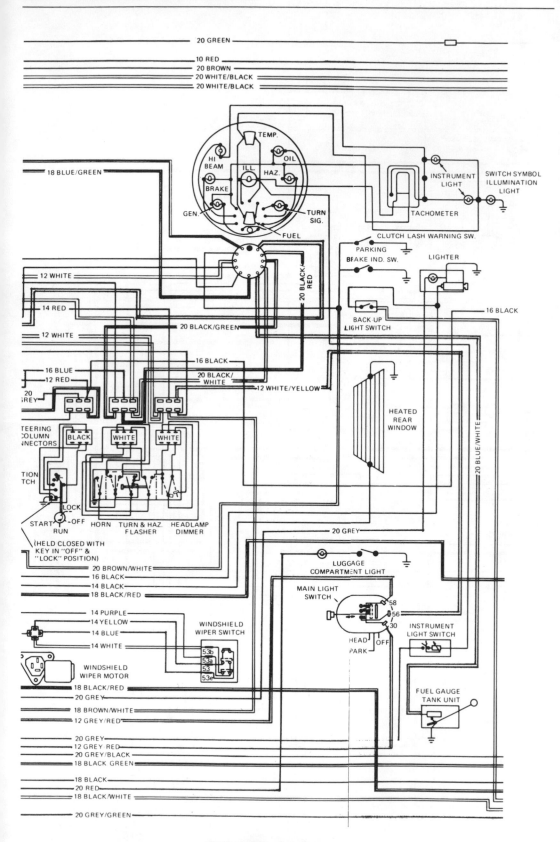

1975 1900 Opel Sedan

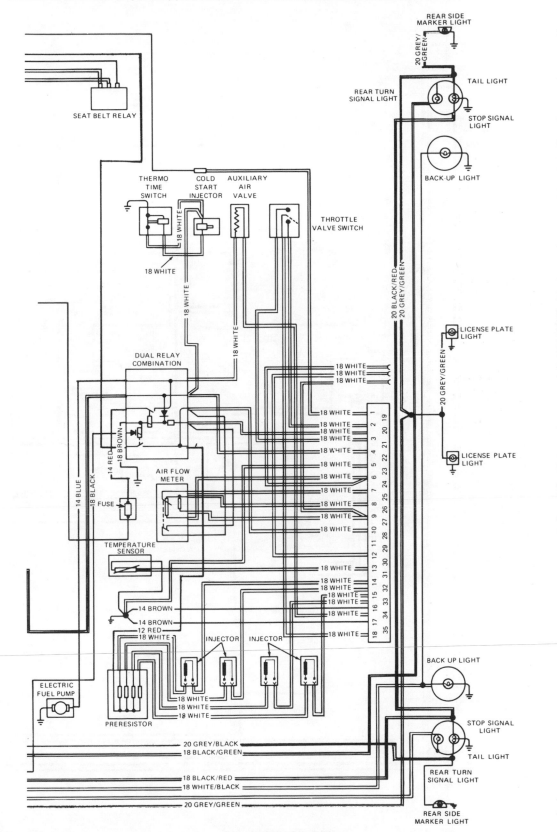

1975 1900 Opel Sedan

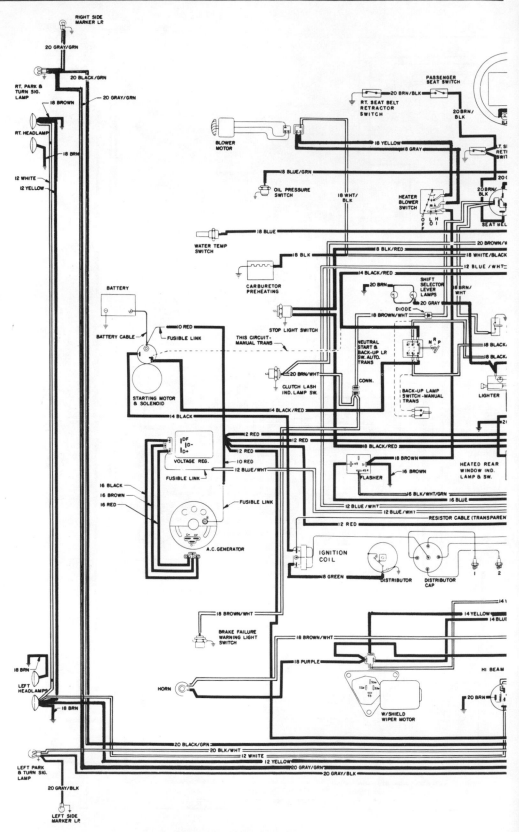

1971–73 1900—Manta

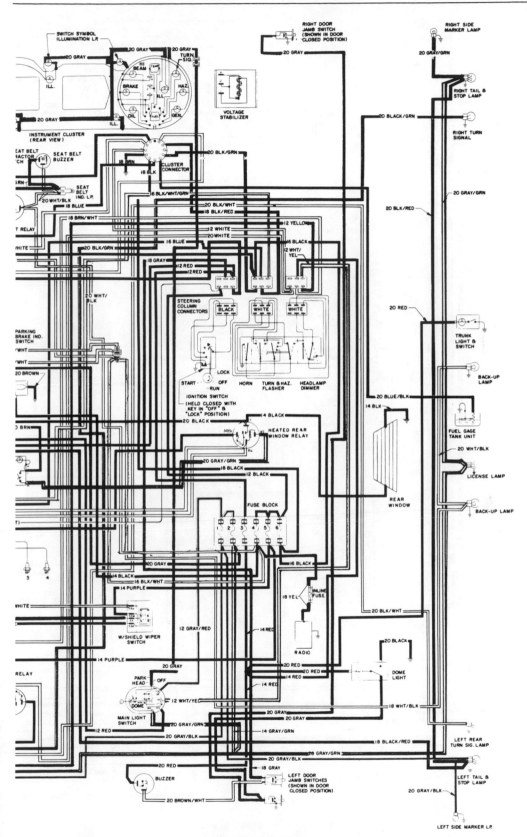

1971-73 1900—Manta

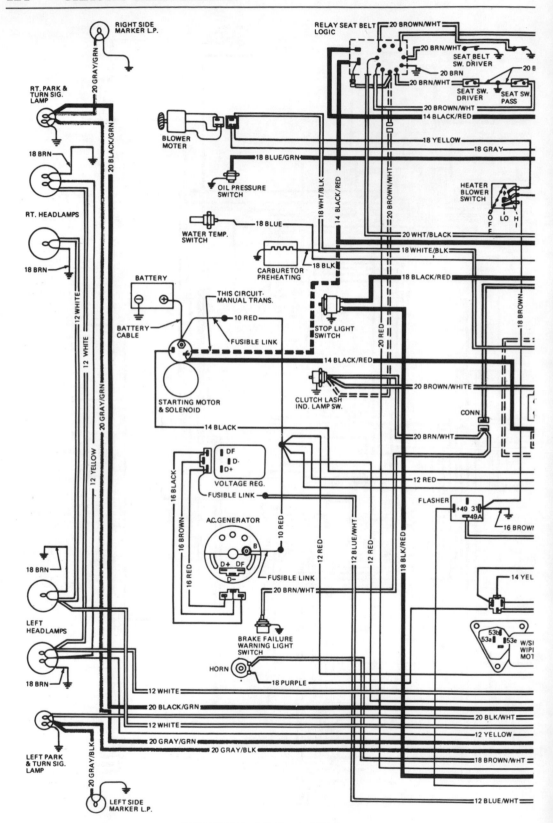

1974 1900 Opel Sedan and Manta

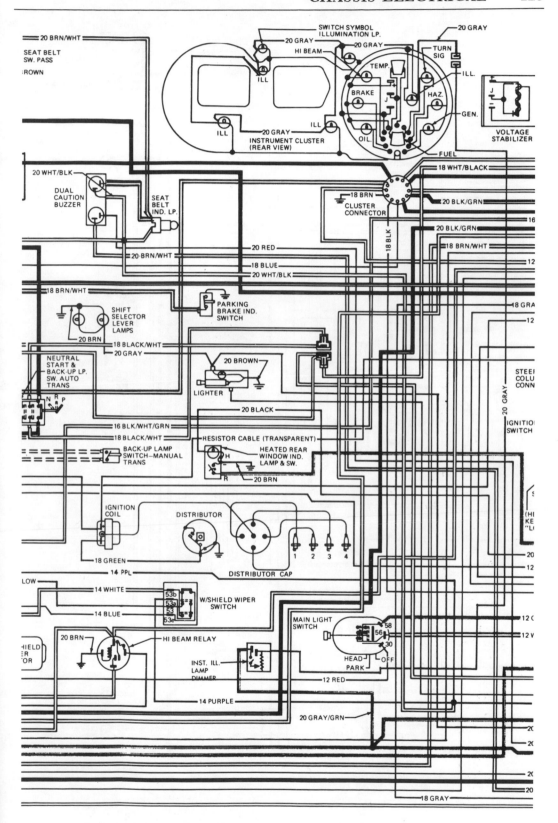

1974 1900 Opel Sedan and Manta

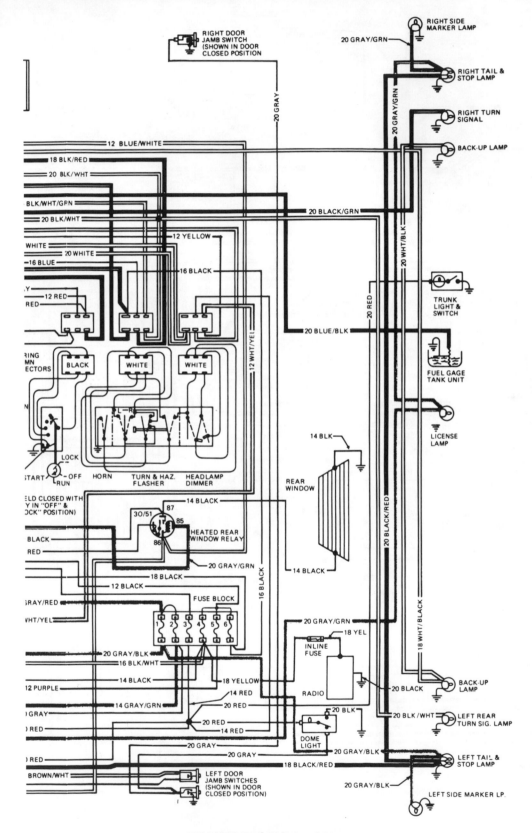

1974 1900 Opel Sedan and Manta

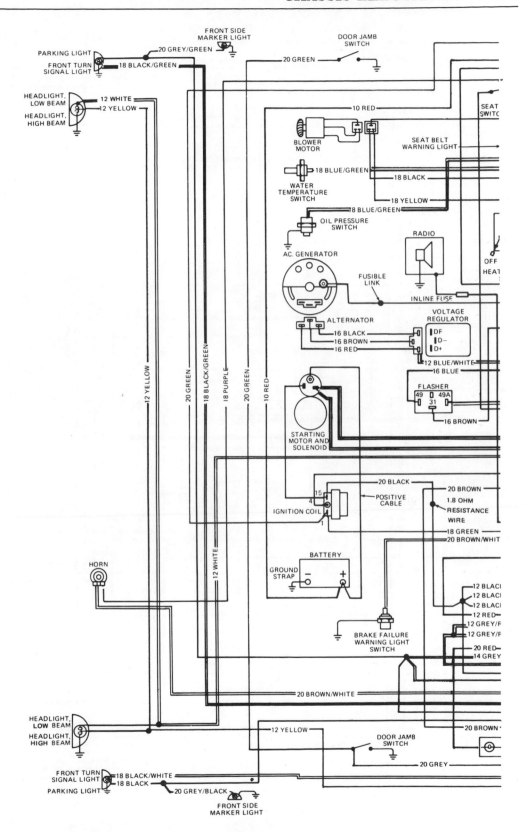

1975 Manta

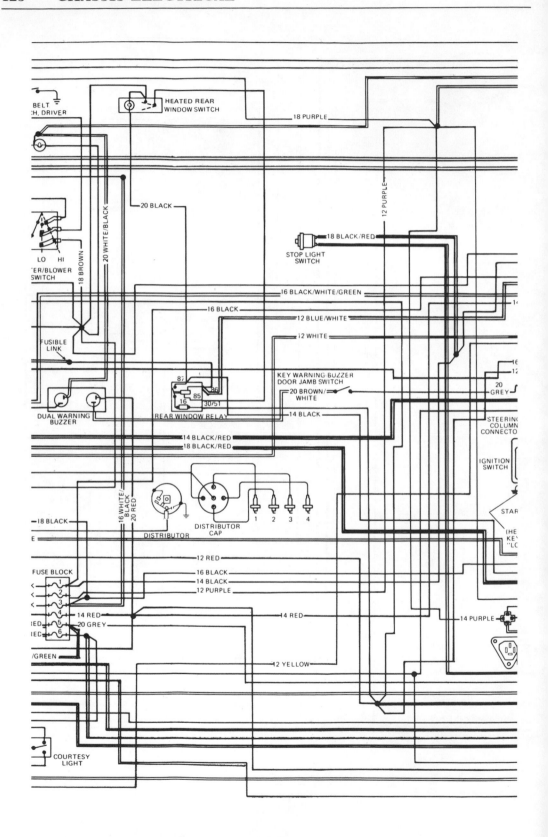

1975 Manta

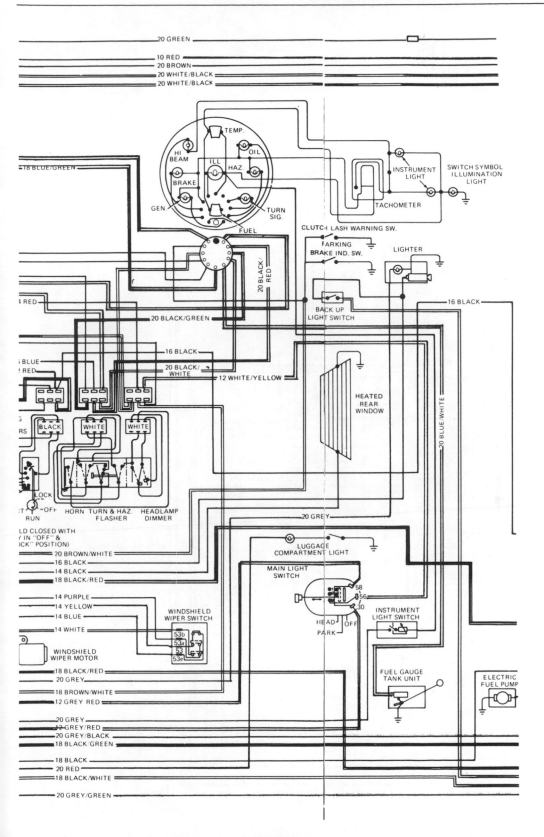

1975 Manta

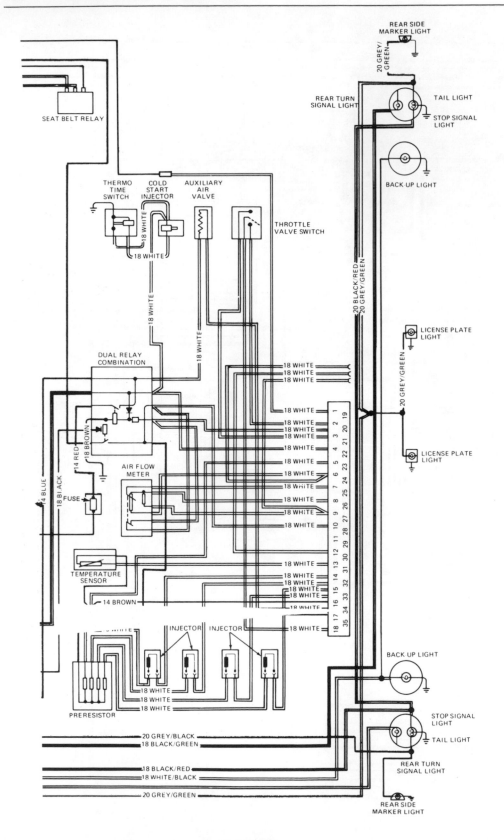

1975 Manta

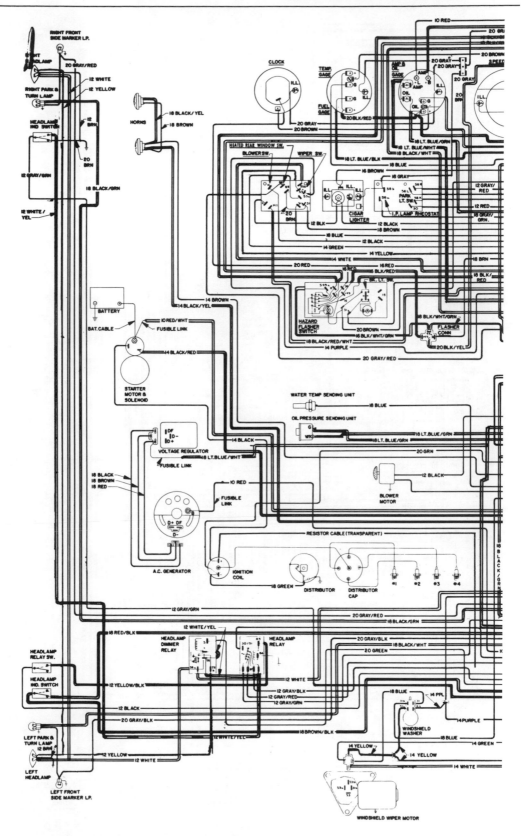

1971 Opel GT

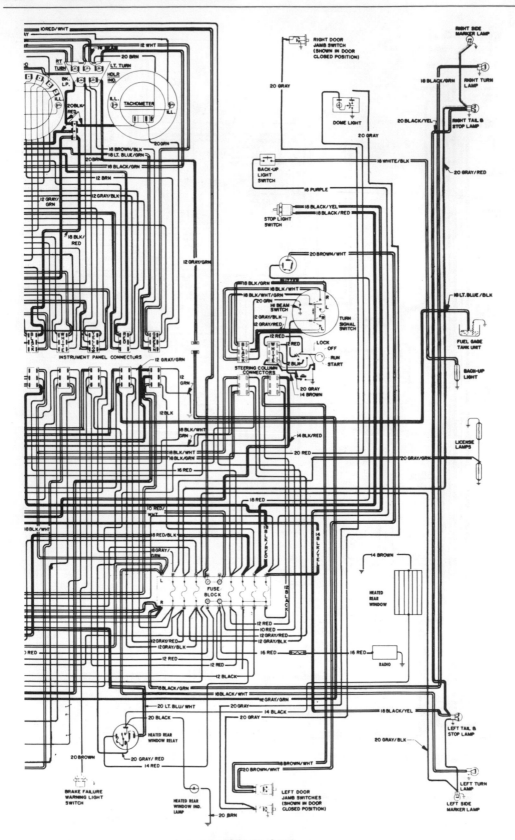

1971 Opel GT

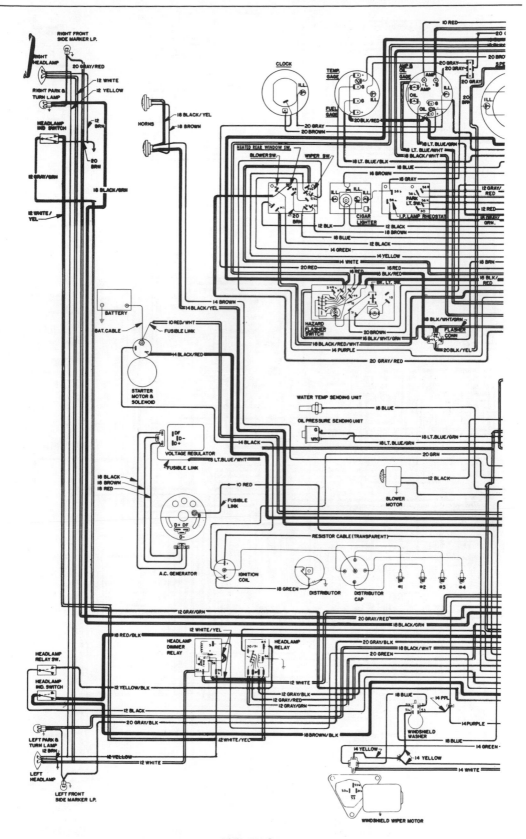

1972 Opel GT

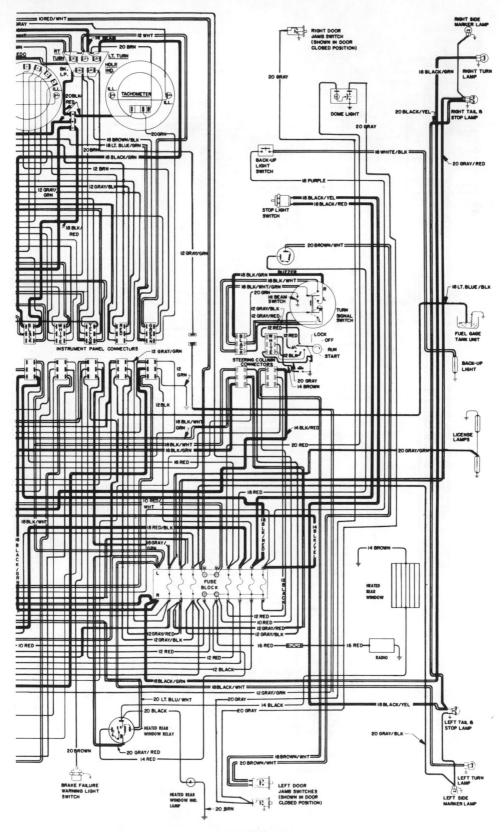

1972 Opel GT

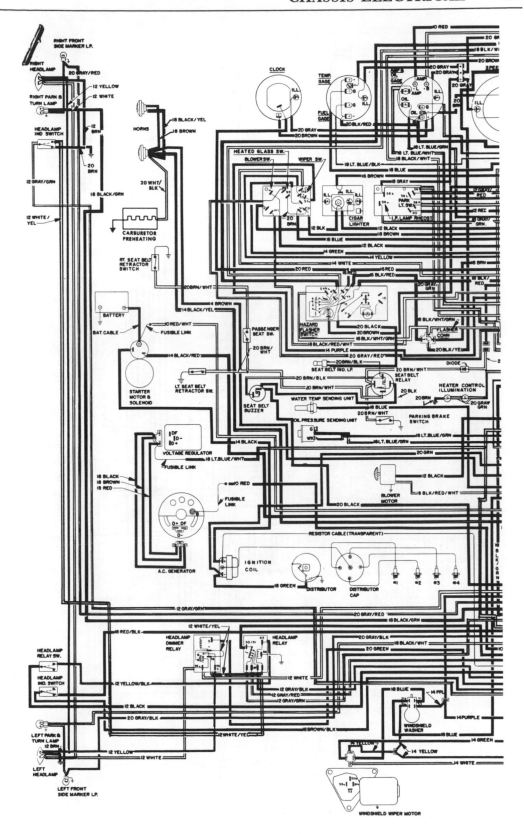

1973 Opel GT

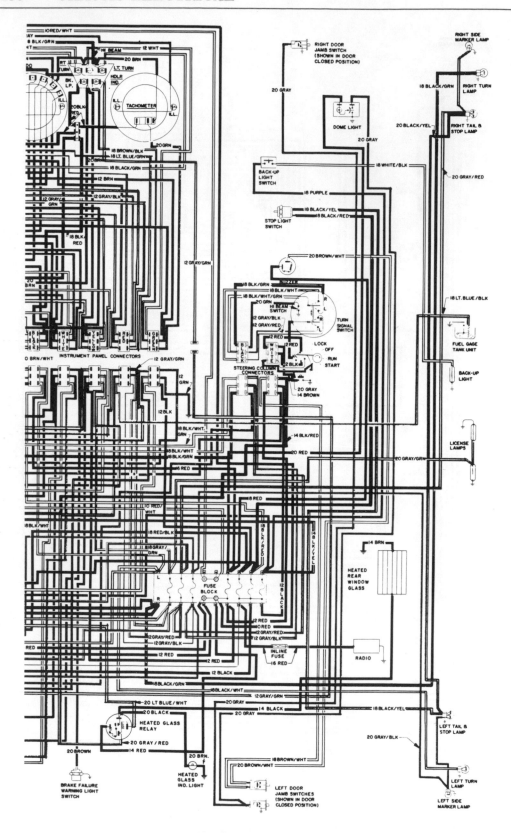

1973 Opel GT

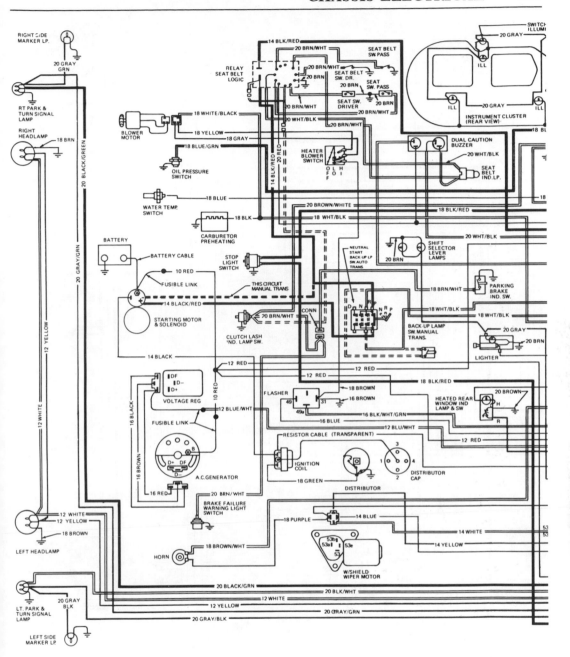

1974 Sport Wagon

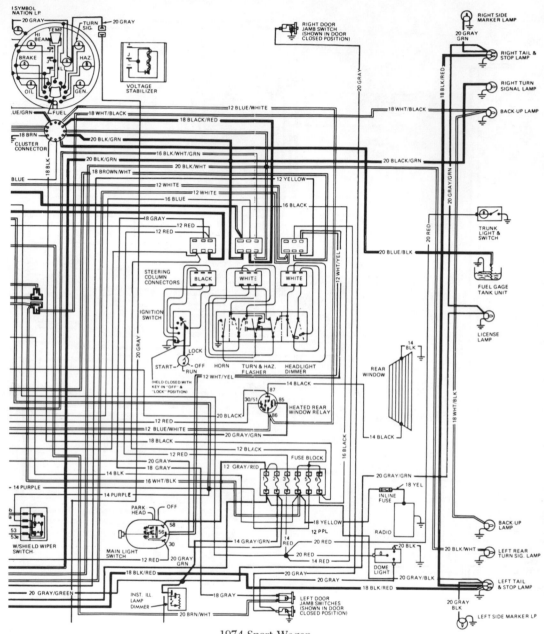

1974 Sport Wagon

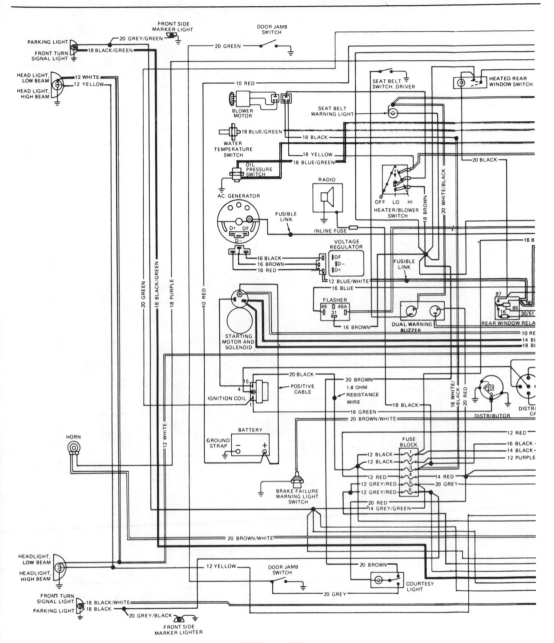

1975 Sport Wagon

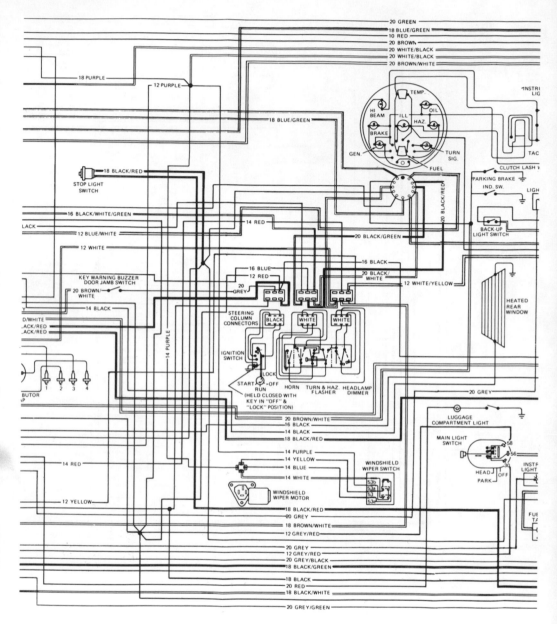

1975 Sport Wagon

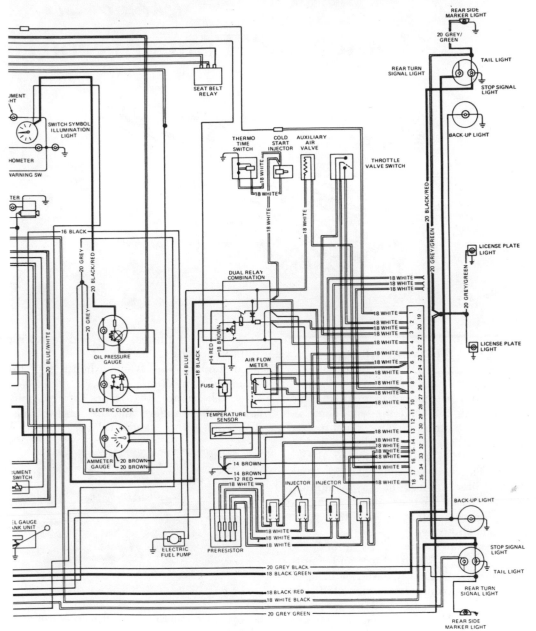

1975 Sport Wagon

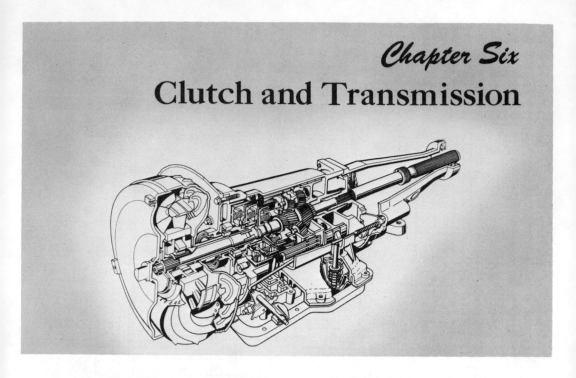

Clutch and Transmission

Manual Transmission

There are two types of manual transmissions used in all Opel models. They are both four speed transmissions, synchronized in all forward speeds, and differentiated by their application and bellhousing configuration. The transmission used in Opels with 1.1 liter engines has a bellhousing which is part of the transmission case. The 1.9 engine uses a transmission that has a separate bellhousing.

The gears are changed by a first and second speed yoke, a third and fourth speed yoke and a reverse shifter cam, all operated by a transmission mounted floor lever on the 1.1 model and by externally mounted gearshift linkage on the 1.9 version.

Removal and Installation

ALL MODELS

The transmission may be removed without removing the engine.

CAUTION: *Use safe equipment to support the car while working underneath. Do not rely on cinder blocks or bumper jacks.*

1. Remove the air cleaner. Remove the throttle rod from the carburetor and the rear support.

2. Support the car front and rear with suitable supports.

3. Loosen the front exhaust pipe-to-manifold connection.

4. There are two types of gearshift levers—the standard and the sport models. To remove the standard lever, a special

Removing the standard gearshift lever—Opel with 1.1 engine

Removing the sport shifter

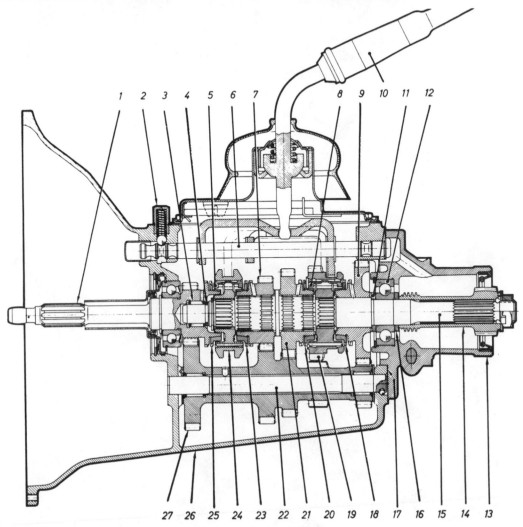

A sectional view of the manual transmission used with the 1.1 engine

1. Clutch gear
2. Lock ball and spring plug
3. Neede bearing assy.
4. Thrust ring
5. Key for 3rd-and-4th-speed clutch sleeve (3)
6. 1st-and-2nd-speed shifter shaft
7. 3rd-speed gear
8. Key for 1st-and-2nd-speed clutch sleeve (3)
9. 1st-speed gear
10. Gearshift lever
11. Spacer between 1st-speed gear and ball bearing
12. Ball bearing
13. Speedometer drive housing (bearing retainer)
14. Mainshaft sleeve
15. Mainshaft
16. Spacer between ball bearing and mainshaft sleeve
17. Gasket between speedometer drive housing and transmission case
18. 1st-speed synchronizer ring
19. 1st-and-2nd-speed sliding gear
20. 2nd-speed synchronizer ring
21. 2nd-speed gear
22. Countergear shaft
23. 3rd-speed synchronizer ring
24. 3rd-and-4th-speed clutch sleeve
25. 4th-speed synchronizer ring
26. Transmission case
27. Countergear

tool (# J21709) is required. Lift the boot and place the tool around the bottom of the shift lever. Turn counterclockwise until the lock plate loosens. The sport lever removal requires that the three screws which hold the cover plate in place be removed and that the snap-ring which retains the lever be taken off with standard snap-ring pliers.

NOTE: *For removal of later model shifters, refer to "Shifter Service 1900, Manta, GT" under "Shifter Overhaul."*

5. Remove the clutch cable-to-fork lock nut and adjusting nut. Remove the cable from the transmission being careful not to twist the cable.

6. Disconnect the wires to the back-up light switch at the transmission.

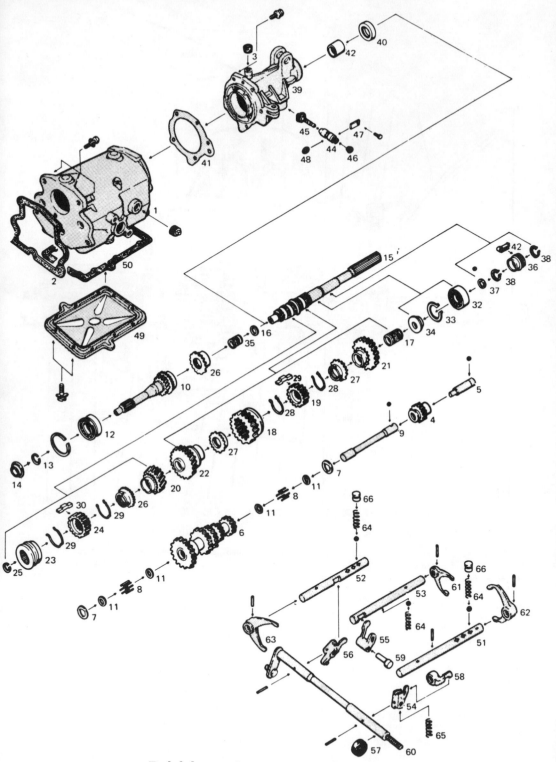

Exploded view of 1.9 engine manual transmission

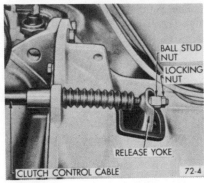

Clutch cable attaching parts—typical

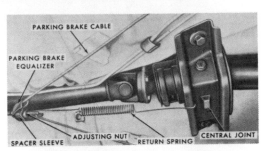

Parking brake equalizer and return spring

7. Remove the three cap screws from the flywheel cover plate between the transmission and the oil pan. Remove the cover.

8. Disconnect the speedometer cable from the gear housing.

9. Unhook the parking brake cable return spring and remove the cable adjusting nut, equalizer, and spacer.

10. Remove one of the bolts which holds the speedometer gear housing and rear of the transmission to the underbody. Just loosen the other bolt.

NOTE: *The one bolt must remain in place to prevent damage to the heater by the throttle rod when the engine and transmission are tilted downward in the rear.*

11. Disconnect the drive shaft at the central joint. Remove the shaft as follows:

 a. Raise the rear of the car and support it properly on jackstands.

 b. Mark the mating parts of the U-joint and the drive pinion extension shaft flange.

 c. Loosen the bolt locks and remove the bolts.

1. Transmission case
2. Trans. case-to-clutch housing gasket
3. Ventilator cap
4. Reverse idler gear w/bushings
5. Reverse idler gear shaft
6. Countershaft cluster gear
7. Counter gear thrust washer trans.
8. Counter gear bearing roller trans.
9. Cluster gear countershaft
10. Main drive gear
11. Trans. counter gear bearing roller spacer ring
12. Trans. main shaft pilot bearing
13. Trans. main drive gear ball bearing lock ring
14. Main drive gear to clutch seal ring
15. Main shaft
16. Trans. main shaft snap—front ring
17. 1st speed gear on main shaft needle bearing
18. 1st and 2nd speed sliding gear
19. 1st and 2nd speeding sliding gear guide unit
20. 3rd speed gear
21. 1st speed gear
22. 2nd speed gear
23. Trans. gear shifter sleeve
24. Trans. gear shifter sleeve carrier
25. Trans. gear shifter sleeve snap ring
26. Trans. 3rd and 4th speed synchronizer cone
27. Trans. 1st and 2nd speed synchronizer cone
28. Synchronizer (1st and 2nd speed) spring
29. Synchronizer spring
30. 1st and 2nd speed shifter shoe
31. 3rd and 4th speed shifter shoe
32. Trans. main shaft—r.r. bearing
33. Trans. main shaft ball bearings snap ring
34. Main shaft—between inner ball bearing and 1st speed gear washer

35. Trans. main shaft needle—right bearing
36. Speedometer drive gear
37. Speedo—drive gear washer
38. Speedo—drive gear snap ring
39. R.r. bearing retainer
40. Trans. r.r. oil seal
41. R.r. bearing retainer gasket
42. Trans. main shaft—r.r. bushing
43. Speedo—gear clip
44. Speedo—drive guide
45. Speedo—driven gear
46. Speedo—shaft sleeve seal
47. Speedo and guide on trans. bracket
48. Speedo drive guide seal ring
49. Trans. case cover
50. Trans. case cover gasket
51. 1st and 2nd speed shifter shaft
52. 3rd and 4th speed shifter shaft
53. Reverse speed shifter shaft
54. 1st and 2nd speed shifter intermediate lever
55. Reverse shifter intermediate lever
56. Intermediate 3rd, 4th and reverse lever
57. Shifter shaft oil in trans. seal
58. Cam. on shifter shaft
59. Intermediate lever reverse shifter shaft
60. W/lever and bolt, in trans. shaft
61. Reverse speed shifter fork (yoke)
62. Trans. shifter (1st and reverse) yoke
63. Trans. 2nd and 3rd speed fork (yoke)
64. Trans. gearshift interlock thrust spring
65. Reverse speed gearshift interlock detent spring
66. Gearshift interlock detent plug

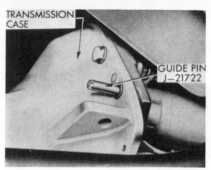

Guide pins installed—Opel with 1.1 engine shown

d. Work the propeller shaft forward, lower the rear end of the shaft, and slide the assembly rearward. Remove the thrust spring.

e. Put a plug in the rear end of the transmission to prevent loss of fluid. (Stuffing a heavy rag in will do.)

12. Remove the lower bolt on each side of the transmission-to-crankcase union and, to avoid warping the clutch disc, install guide pins (J21722).

NOTE: *If guide pins are not available, cut the heads off of two bolts that will thread into the crankcase.*

13. Place a jack under the front generator-to-block mount. Remove the right engine mount-to-crossmember bracket bolts. Raise the engine slightly with the jack which will in turn lower the transmission to provide the necessary clearance for removal.

NOTE: *On later model Opels and 1900 series cars as well as the Manta and GT, remove the rear engine mount bolts and let the transmission down as far as possible to gain the clearance required for removal.*

14. Remove the remaining transmission-to-crankcase bolts. Slide the transmission back off of the guide pins and clutch spline.

NOTE: *It may be necessary to rotate the transmission case slightly.*

The replacement of the transmission is a straightforward reversal of the removal procedures. Pay special attention to the following items.

a. Make certain that the main drive gears are clean and dry and be certain the transmission is in Neutral before you attempt to install.

b. Use a clutch aligning tool to properly position the clutch disc if it has been moved.

c. When reassembling the drive shaft, tighten the U-joint flange-to-pinion flange bolts to 18 ft lbs.

d. After the installation has been completed, fill the 1.1 transmission with 1½ pints of SAE 90 gear oil. Fill the 1.9 engine with 2½ pints of SAE 80 or 80-90 multi-purpose gear oil.

Shifter Service 1900, Manta, and GT

Adjusting Reverse Blocker

1. Engage Second gear.

2. Adjust the selector ring so that the ball on the lower end of the shift finger has an equal clearance on both sides when seated into the transmission case extension bolt hole.

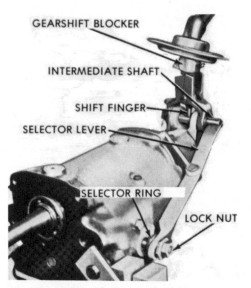

Reverse gearshift blocker adjustment

3. Back off the selector ring an additional ¼ turn and tighten the locknut.

Overhauling the Shift Lever

1. Remove the shifter by unscrewing the console, removing the shifter boot from the cover plate, and unbuttoning the intermediate shift lever protective cap. Unhook the tension spring of the gearshift lever and, after removing the retaining washer, push the pivot pin out of the intermediate shift lever.

2. Grease the support and the spherical end of the shift finger.

3. Replace any worn parts and reas-

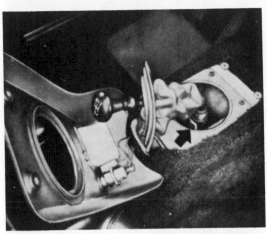

Position of the intermediate shift lever pin—1900, Manta, and GT

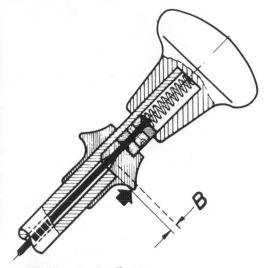

Travel distance of pull-ring

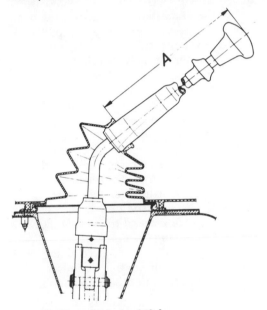

Assembled length of gearshift lever

THREADED PIN

Threaded pin for Bowden control wire connection

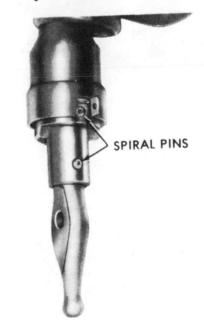

SPIRAL PINS

Spiral pins at the lower end of the gearshift lever

semble. The assembly should measure 8.07 in. as is represented in the drawing by "A."

4. When assembled, the pull ring should travel about 0.04–0.08 in. and the stop sleeve should still rest on the intermediate shift lever. If this is not the case, loosen the threaded pin for the Bowden control wire attachment and adjust the free travel by lifting the pull ring and tightening the threaded pin.

REPLACING THE BOWDEN CONTROL WIRE

1. Remove the gearshift lever.
2. Knock off the gearshift lever knob and loosen the threaded pin for the control wire attachment.

3. Drive the spiral pin and clamping sleeve out of the the shift finger tube and stop sleeve.

4. Remove the shift finger and pull the control cable and thrust spring out of the gearshift lever.

5. Oil the sliding surface of the stop sleeve on the shift finger tube with a thin lubricant.

6. Install the thrust spring and install a new control wire with the clamping sleeve. When doing this, the cutout on the stop sleeve should be on the left of the shift lever. The spiral pins must not protrude.

7. Clamp the control wire tightly with the threaded pin. The pull ring must rest on the gearshift lever tube and the clamping block on the pull ring.

8. Heat a new gearshift lever knob in boiling water and push it onto the lever tube. Be sure to maintain a distance (as shown in the illustration) of 0.3 in.

NOTE: *Due to the design of the shift lever, the old knob cannot be reused.*

9. Attach the shift finger with spiral pin and install the gearshift lever.

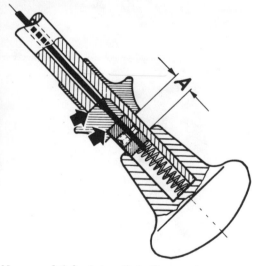

New gearshift knob installed; distance A represents 0.3 in. clearance between the bottom of the knob and the top of the pull-ring.

Clutch

Removal and Installation

1.1. ENGINE

1. Remove the transmission as outlined in this chapter.

2. Look at the clutch assembly in the car to see if there are any existing alignment marks. If you intend to reinstall the old pressure plate, you should scribe or paint alignment marks on the plate and on the flywheel.

3. Remove the four clutch cover retaining bolts by loosening them alternately. This will prevent distortion of the clutch parts.

4. Remove the pressure plate and the disc.

5. Inspect the flywheel for deep scoring or grease. Any minor imperfections can be removed with crocus cloth and some hard rubbing.

6. Check the pilot bearing for free rotation. (The pilot bearing is located in the end of the crankshaft.) If the bearing needs replacement, you will need a puller designed to hold this size bearing and a slide hammer. A new bearing can be installed by using a soft drift and a light hammer.

NOTE: *Do not soak the throwout bearing in solvent to clean it.*

7. Install the clutch by holding the complete assembly against the flywheel and inserting a clutch aligning tool. In the absence of such a tool, the main shaft of a disassembled transmission will work.

NOTE: *Be sure the disc is positioned so that the side marked to face the flywheel is indeed facing the flywheel.*

Loosely install the four retaining bolts and tighten in alternating sequence without removing the pilot tool (15 ft lbs).

1.9 ENGINE

1. Remove the transmission.

2. Remove the bolts from the engine support brackets.

3. Remove the flywheel cover pan.

4. Remove the bellhousing-to-engine attaching bolts and pry the housing from the locating pins.

5. Remove the release bearing from the clutch fork by sliding off the ball stud against the spring action. Remove the ball stud locknut and remove the stud from the housing.

6. Loosen the pressure plate-to-flywheel attaching bolts one at a time until spring pressure is released.

7. Support the pressure plate while re-

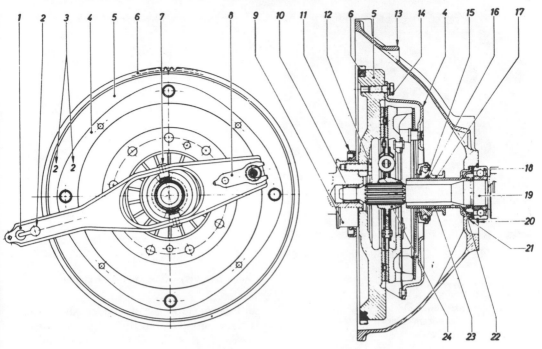

Arrangement of clutch—1.9 engine

1. Clutch release lever
2. Slot in lever for control cable ball end
3. Assembly marks
4. Clutch assembly
5. Flywheel
6. Flywheel ring gear
7. Thrust pin
8. Retaining spring
9. Crankshaft
10. Clutch gear pilot bushing
11. Oil seal
12. Flywheel bolt
13. Clutch housing
14. Clutch assy. bolt and lockwasher
15. Hollow space under felt ring filled with molybdenum disulfide paste
16. Felt ring
17. Clutch release bearing
18. Clutch gear ball bearing
19. Clutch gear
20. Snap-ring
21. Paper gasket
22. Clutch gear oil seal
23. Clutch release bearing sleeve
24. Clutch disc with long end of hub facing rearward

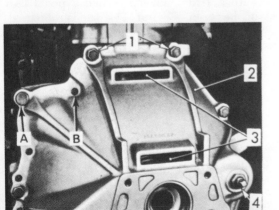

Rear view of 1.9 engine

moving the last bolt and then remove the plate and disc from the flywheel.

8. Make a thorough inspection of all clutch parts to determine which parts are to be replaced. Clean the flywheel surface with crocus cloth.

9. To install the assembly, place the pressure plate and disc against the flywheel and insert a pilot tool through both parts and into the crankshaft.

NOTE: *Be sure the clutch disc is positioned so that the long end of the*

1. Upper attaching bolts
2. Flywheel housing
3. Vent holes
4. Clutch release lever ball stud and lock nut
5. Recess in flywheel housing
6. Clutch release bearing sleeve
7. Clutch release lever and boot

Aligning the clutch before final tightening of the clutch cover bolts

1. Flywheel
2. Clutch assembly
3. Assembly marks
4. Clutch aligning arbor j-22934

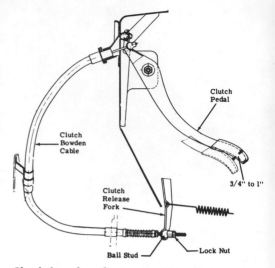

Clutch free-play adjustment—1.1 engine

splined hub is facing forward toward the flywheel.

10. Install the retaining bolts through the pressure plate and tighten them slowly in rotation so that even force is distributed on the unit.

11. Tighten the bolts in several stages to 36 ft lbs.

12. Install the release bearing.

13. Install the bellhousing tightening bolts to 36 ft lbs.

14. Install the bellhousing lower cover.

15. Install the clutch return spring and control cable.

16. Install the transmission. (See preceding section)

17. Use the instructions in this chapter to adjust the clutch control cable.

Clutch Release Yoke and Bearing Removal and Installation

1.1 Engine

1. Disconnect the clutch return spring at the transmission and remove the yoke boot from the transmission case.

2. Slip the yoke from the ball stud and bearing flange; slide both forward over the spline shaft.

3. If the release bearing is dry or rough, replace it. Do not wash the bearing in solvent.

4. Before reassembling, pack the inner

and outer grooves of the release bearing with a small quantity of wheel bearing grease. Lightly lubricate the ball stud with graphite grease.

5. Install the yoke and bearing assembly.

6. Install the yoke boot and connect the return spring.

Clutch Control Cable Adjustment

1.1. Engine

Adjust the ball stud on the clutch release fork. Hold the hexagon end of the cable with a 7 mm wrench. When a pedal lash of between ¾ and 1¼ in. is obtained, tighten the locknut which secures the ball stud nut.

GT with 1.9 Engine

NOTE: *It is recommended that this operation be performed only when a new clutch disc or clutch control cable is installed.*

1. Adjust the ball stud so that the outer end protrudes about ¾ in. out of the clutch housing.

2. Adjust the distance between the release lever and the clutch housing face at the eyelet for the control cable to about 4¼ in. Holding the cable in this position, place the E-ring two grooves ahead of the washer on the rubber grommet. The clutch pedal free travel is now between ¾ and 1¼ in. and the release bearing has the proper clearance from the pressure plate.

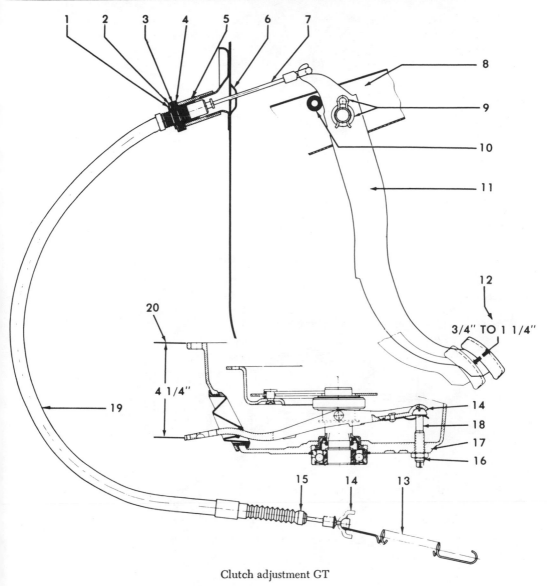

Clutch adjustment GT

1. E-ring	9. Washer, hairpin clip	16. Ball stud lock nut
2. Washer	10. Rubber stop	17. Clutch housing
3. Rubber grommet	11. Clutch pedal	18. Ball stud
4. Washer	12. Clutch pedal free travel—¾ to	19. Bowden control cable
5. Sleeve	1¼ in.	20. Distance between release lever and
6. Dash panel	13. Return spring	clutch housing
7. Bowden control cable	14. Release lever	
8. Bracket	15. Rubber bellows	

OPEL 1900 AND MANTA

1. Adjust the ball stud on the clutch housing to the basic ¾ in. dimension. With the lower end of the control cable unhooked, push the clutch release lever toward the front so that the clutch release bearing rests against the clutch spring. Now, adjust the ball stud so that the dimen-sion between the clutch housing contacting surface and the clutch release lever amounts in the rear to 4¼ in.

2. Pull the bowden cable out of the dash panel until the clutch pedal rests against the clutch wear indication switch.

3. In this position, install a lockwasher at the upper control wire attachment three grooves toward the front. The cable is now

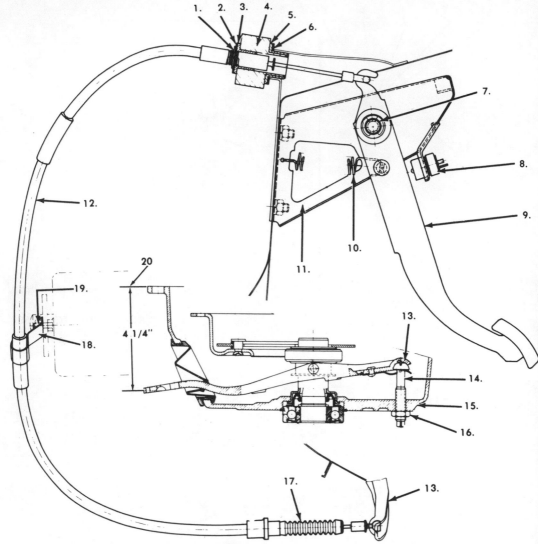

Clutch adjustments—all models with 1.9 engine except GT

1. E-ring	8. Adjustment switch	15. Clutch housing
2. Washer	9. Clutch pedal	16. Ball stud lock nut
3. Rubber grommet	10. Return spring	17. Rubber bellows
4. Clutch operating damper	11. Bracket	18. Cable support bracket
5. Grommet	12. Cable	19. Nut, cable support bracket
6. Washer	13. Release lever	20. Distance between release lever
7. E-ring	14. Ball stud	and clutch housing

properly adjusted and the pedal is also adjusted properly. The clutch on this model operates with no pedal free travel.

NOTE: *The only time a clutch adjustment of any sort is required is when the indicator lamp for this purpose is lit on on the dashboard. This lamp serves also as the parking brake warning light. If it is lit when operating the car, first release the emergency brake and (if it stays lit)* *then suspect that a clutch adjustment is necessary.*

Free-play Adjustment

1.1 ENGINE

Pedal lash or free-play must be adjusted occasionally to compensate for normal wear of the clutch facings. As the driven plate wears thinner, pedal free-play decreases.

1. Loosen the locknut on the ball stud end of the clutch control cable.

2. Adjust the ball stud to obtain ¾–1¼ in. of free-play in the pedal.

3. Tighten the lock nut to secure the ball stud nut.

GT with 1.9 Engine

NOTE: *When adjusting the pedal lash, do not in the process change the length of the control cable.*

1. Loosen the lock nut on the ball stud end located to the right of the transmission on the bellhousing. Position the ball stud so that the outer end protrudes ¾ in. out of the housing and finger tighten the locknut.

2. Adjust the ball stud while pivoting the clutch release fork until the required ¾–1¼ in. free-play is obtained.

Opel 1900 and Manta

The clutch mechanism operates with no pedal free-play. The only time adjustment is necessary is when the indicator lamp on the dashboard is lit.

NOTE: *The indicator lamp for clutch wear also indicates that the emergency brake is applied. If the lamp is lit when the brake is off, then the adjustment should be performed.*

Carry out the adjustment with the ball stud on the clutch housing only. Adjust the distance from the clutch housing contacting surface and the clutch release lever to 4¼ in. measured to the rear.

Automatic Transmission

Opels use a three speed fully automatic transmission of their own design. The power transmission is achieved with a torque converter, a Ravigneaux planetary gear set, three multiple disc clutches, and a single band providing three forward speeds and reverse. Automatic shifting is controlled by road speed, engine vacuum, and a mechanical connection from the accelerator pedal to the transmission.

It is unlikely that you will ever disassemble the automatic transmission but there are a number of minor service operations which you will certainly want to carry out on your own. There are also a number of minor problems which will make the transmission behave poorly; if you are aware of these things, you will probably avoid some unnecessary trips to the repair shop.

Before any major repair is anticipated, you should understand the correct oil checking procedures. Many times a malfunctioning transmission will be traced to low oil level, improper reading of the dipstick, or poor oil condition.

Checking and Adding Fluid

The Opel three speed automatic is designed to operate at the FULL mark on the dipstick at normal operating temperature (180°). The fluid should always be checked when the engine is at this temperature and never any other. Normal operating temperature is achieved in the transmission after about 15 miles of highway driving or 10 miles of stop-and-go city driving. There is a one pint difference between the FULL and ADD marks on the dipstick.

Place the car on level ground and with the transmission at operating temperature move the selector through all ranges. Do not race the engine! Immediately check the fluid level and see that it is even with the FULL mark.

Look at the oil closely to see that it is devoid of bubbles. Oil with air bubbles indicates an air leak in one of the internal suction lines. Look for traces of water in the oil. Water will make the fluid appear milky pink. Change the transmission oil if any discoloration or foreign matter is evident.

Pan Removal and Installation

1. Raise the car and drain the oil.

2. Remove the twelve bolts which hold the oil pan to the transmission.

3. Remove the oil pan and gasket.

4. Installation is the reverse of removal.

NOTE: *Always replace the old gasket and be careful not to over-tighten the pan bolts.*

Filter or Strainer Service

1. Raise the car and support it safely.

2. Drain all fluid from the oil pan.

3. Remove the oil pan and gasket. Discard the old gasket.

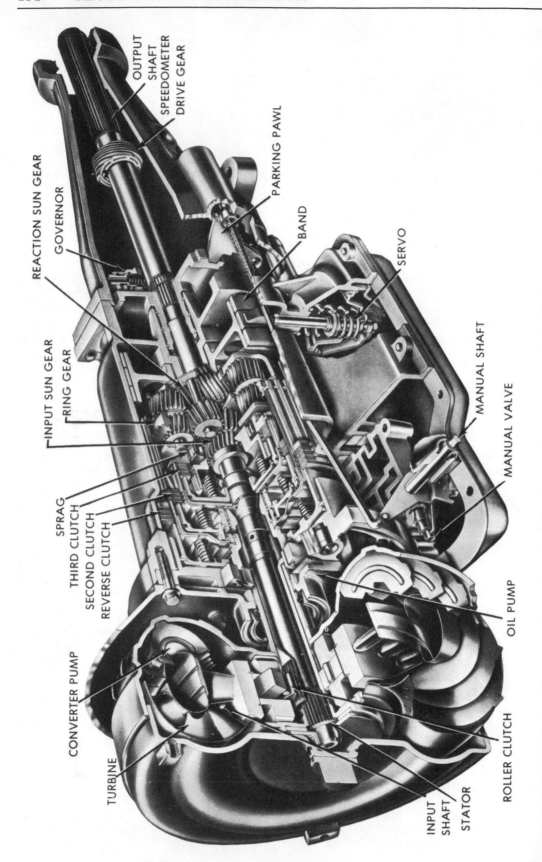

OUTPUT SHAFT SPEEDOMETER DRIVE GEAR

PARKING PAWL

REACTION SUN GEAR

GOVERNOR

BAND

SERVO

INPUT SUN GEAR

RING GEAR

MANUAL SHAFT

MANUAL VALVE

SPRAG

THIRD CLUTCH

SECOND CLUTCH

REVERSE CLUTCH

OIL PUMP

CONVERTER PUMP

TURBINE

INPUT SHAFT

STATOR

ROLLER CLUTCH

Removing the oil pan

4. Remove the strainer assembly and strainer gasket and discard the gasket.

5. Install a new oil strainer gasket. Install a new strainer assembly.

6. Install a new gasket on the oil pan and install the pan. Tighten the attaching bolts to 7–10 ft lbs.

7. Lower the car and add approximately three (3) pints of transmission fluid through the filler tube.

8. With the manual control lever in the Park position, start the engine. DO NOT RACE THE ENGINE. Move the manual control lever through each range.

9. Immediately check the fluid level with the selector lever in Neutral, engine running, and vehicle on a level surface.

10. Add additional fluid to bring the level to ¼ in. below the ADD mark on the dipstick. Do not overfill.

Detent Cable Replacement and Adjustment

The function of the detent valve in the transmission is to provide a controlled downshift for additional performance when the accelerator is pressed to the floorboard. This is sometimes incorrectly called "passing gear". It is not an individual gear mode of the transmission but rather a downshift. The detent valve is connected mechanically to the throttle linkage by means of a bowden control cable. The reliability of the entire system is wholly dependent on the correct adjustment of the control cable.

It is important to remember that the free end of the wire not become kinked during installation as the end will fray and individual strands of the cable will separate. The cable flexes during operation and these frayed wires will break causing malfunction of the downshift mechanism.

Although replacement and adjustment procedures are identical for all models, the location of the upper (throttle) end will vary.

1. To remove the old cable, detach the retainer at the detent cable connection to the accelerator linkage.

Detent cable connection at the accelerator

2. Loosen the rear transmission crossmember from the body and remove the right side bolt.

3. Insert a block of wood between the floor pan and the right rear corner of the transmission to expose the detent cable bracket at the transmission.

Wood block installed between the floor pan and transmission

4. Unscrew the detent cable connecting retainer from the transmission and pull the cable out of the transmission.

5. Unhook the cable from the detent valve.

Detent cable attachment to detent valve

6. Pry the detent cable out of the retainers.

7. Unscrew the upper and lower adjuster nuts and remove the detent cable. NOTE: *On Manta models loosen the lock nut and screw adjuster out of the bulkhead (top right of engine firewall).*

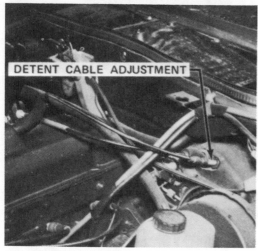

Detent cable adjuster nut

8. The first step in installing a new cable is to route the cable smoothly from the throttle end to the transmission, being careful not to kink the cable.

9. Place the cable in the upper bracket and install the upper and lower adjuster nuts and retainers. NOTE: *On Manta models screw the adjuster into the bulkhead.*

10. Hook the detent cable to the detent valve in the transmission and install the retainer.

11. After the cable is installed it must be adjusted in the following manner.

NOTE: *Before adjusting the detent cable, it is essential that the throttle control linkage be adjusted correctly so that full throttle opening is achieved. The instructions for said adjustment may be found in Chapter Four.*

a. Position the accelerator to full throttle.

NOTE: *The pedal is not fully depressed at full throttle.*

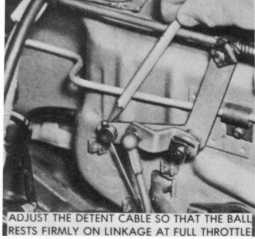

All models

b. Loosen and tighten the upper and lower adjusting nuts until the ball end of the cable rests firmly against the lever. NOTE: *On Manta models simply turn the adjuster.*

c. At this point measure the length of the exposed inner cable. Depress the

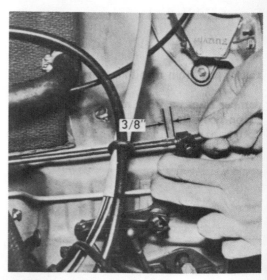

Checking installed cable operation

accelerator pedal fully and again measure the inner cable. If the cable is correctly adjusted, the detent cable should move about ⅜ in.

Automatic Transmission Linkage Adjustment

Remove the lock clip which holds the control rod to the selector lever. Remove the control rod from the selector lever and place both the selector lever and the transmission shift lever in the Drive position. Adjust the control rod by turning, until it slides freely over the pin on the selector lever, and install the lock clip.

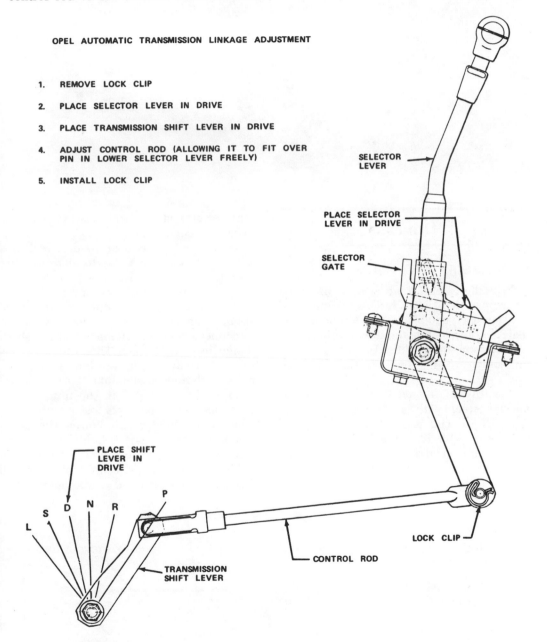

OPEL AUTOMATIC TRANSMISSION LINKAGE ADJUSTMENT

1. REMOVE LOCK CLIP

2. PLACE SELECTOR LEVER IN DRIVE

3. PLACE TRANSMISSION SHIFT LEVER IN DRIVE

4. ADJUST CONTROL ROD (ALLOWING IT TO FIT OVER PIN IN LOWER SELECTOR LEVER FREELY)

5. INSTALL LOCK CLIP

SELECTOR LEVER

PLACE SELECTOR LEVER IN DRIVE

SELECTOR GATE

PLACE SHIFT LEVER IN DRIVE

L   S   D   N   R   P

LOCK CLIP

CONTROL ROD

TRANSMISSION SHIFT LEVER

Driveline

DRIVESHAFT AND U-JOINTS

Driveshafts of various lengths are used in conjunction with various engine and transmission combinations. Although the shafts vary in length, the service procedures are the same because the U-joints and central joints are of essentially the same design.

The driveshaft used with 1.1 engines is tubular steel with a slip spline at the transmission end and a flanged universal joint at the differential end. Four bolts attach the universal joint flange to the pinion extension flange. On manual transmission models a thrust spring is used between the output shaft of the transmission and the driveshaft connection.

The driveshaft used on models with the 1.9 engine is stronger due to increased engine torque and it also uses two universal joints. The front universal joint is attached to the transmission output shaft by a splined slip joint. The rear universal joint is connected to the pinion extension shaft flange by two U-bolts. The splines of the two driveshaft sections are internally lubricated with transmission lubricant.

There is an oil seal in the transmission extension which prevents loss of lubricant. The torque tube which houses the drive pinion extension shaft is bolted to the differential housing. The torque tube rides in rubber elements of the central joint support bracket which is bolted to the floor panel.

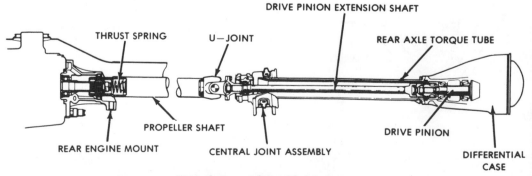

Driveshaft—models with 1.1 engine

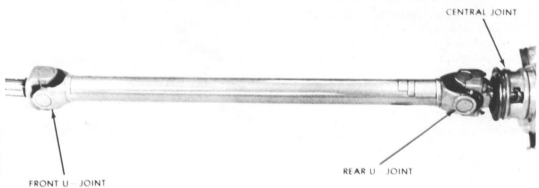

CENTRAL JOINT

REAR U JOINT

FRONT U JOINT

Driveshaft—models with 1.9 engine

There is also a bearing in the central joint which supports the shaft and provides for vibration free operation.

Removal and Installation

1. Using suitable equipment, raise and support the rear of the car at the jacking brackets.

2. Disconnect the parking brake equalizer from the rod.

3. On 1900 and Manta models, unhook the parking brake cable from the floor panel.

4. On models with 1.1 engines, loosen the rear engine mount bolts and remove one of them.

NOTE: *One bolt must remain loosely installed.*

5. Mark the mating parts of the U-joint and the drive pinion extension shaft flange.

6. Loosen the bolt locks and remove the bolts.

7. Work the driveshaft forward, lower the rear end of the shaft, and slide the assembly rearward. Remove the thrust spring.

8. To prevent loss of fluid from the transmission, plug the extension housing.

NOTE: *When the word "driveshaft" is used, it applies only to that shaft which goes from the transmission output to the center joint assembly.*

9. When assembling on 1.1 engine models, put the thrust spring on the end of the transmission output shaft and slide the drive shaft through the oil seal and onto the barrel spline. (On 1.9 engine models slide the shaft through the oil seal and onto the transmission output shaft.)

10. Align the rear universal joint and pinion flange locating marks and replace the bolts.

CAUTION: *Do not substitute fasteners*

in this location. Use bolts of the same quality and strength.

11. Tighten the bolts to 18 ft lbs on 1.1 models and 11 ft lbs on 1.9 models.

12. If you removed the rear engine mount bolts, replace them.

13. Connect the parking brake hardware.

NOTE: *Always check the condition of the oil seal in the transmission extension housing before reassembly.*

CENTRAL JOINT

Removal, Installation, and Service

1. Raise and support the car under the rear axle tubes.

2. Release the brake line bracket from the rear of the torque tube.

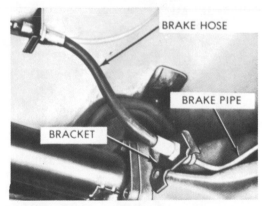

BRAKE HOSE

BRAKE PIPE

BRACKET

Brake hose bracket released

3. Disconnect the parking brake equalizer and the return spring from the brake rod.

4. Mark the universal joint and flange. Disconnect the driveshaft from the flange and support it out of the way.

5. Use a jack to gently support the torque tube.

6. Remove the center joint bracket-to-underbody attaching bolts.

7. Lower the torque tube.

8. Disconnect the torque tube from the differential carrier by removing the attaching bolts.

9. The self-locking pinion flange nut must be removed in order to remove the drive pinion extension shaft from the torque tube. In order to do this, the pinion flange must be held tight to remove the nut. At Opel service facilities this is done with tool #J-8614. In the absence of this tool, another method will have to be improvised. Any approach will work so long as the flange is not damaged. Remove the pinion flange nut and the pinion flange. Remove the drive pinion extension shaft from the torque tube.

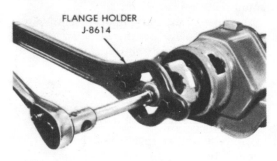

Holding the pinion flange with a tool

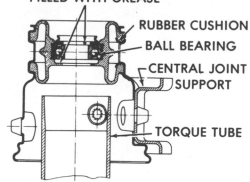

GAP BETWEEN BALL BEARING AND SHEET METAL CASING FILLED WITH GREASE

Installed torque tube bearing

10. Remove the ball bearing from the cushion.

11. Place the torque tube in a vise and remove the support bracket and central joint.

12. Check the condition of the central joint support cushions and if new parts

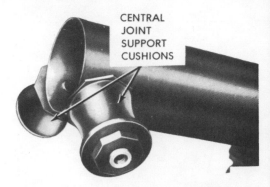

Support cushions installed on the torque tube

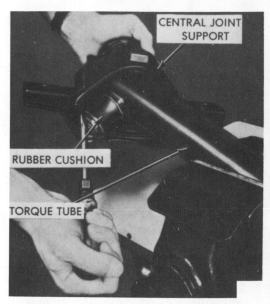

Installing the central joint support bracket on the torque tube

are required, install them and tighten to 29 ft lbs.

13. Install the ball bearing into the rubber cushion and pack the area in front of the bearing with grease.

NOTE: *The flange must face the front of the car.*

14. Install the support bracket onto to torque tube. Place the support on the tube so that one of the cushions is properly seated and then use a screwdriver to pry the other one into position. Tighten the attaching bolts to 15 ft lbs.

15. Install the drive pinion extension shaft using a soft mallet.

NOTE: *Installation is easier from the rear of the tube.*

16. Install the flange. Tap it onto the shaft with a soft mallet just far enough for

the nut to engage firmly then draw it into position with the nut.

17. Hold the flange (tool #J-8614) and tighten the nut to 73 ft lbs on 1.1 cars and 87 ft lbs on 1.9 cars.

18. Install the torque tube in the car.

19. Tighten the central joint support bracket-to-underbody bolts to 36 ft lbs.

AXLE SHAFT ASSEMBLY

Removal and Installation

1. Raise and support the rear of the car.
2. Remove the wheel and brake drum from the side to be removed.

Removing the axle shaft retaining nuts

3. Unscrew the axle shaft retaining plate and pull the axle from the housing.
4. Installation is the reverse of removal.

Overhaul

1. Check the radial runout (0.002 in.) and lateral runout (0.004 in.) of the axle shaft. If these tolerances are exceeded, the shaft must be replaced.

2. Press a new bearing onto the shaft so that the oil seal groove faces the shaft splines.

NOTE: *When replacing a bearing, always replace the outer race which is located in the housing.*

3. Check the axle shaft end-play.

   a. Measure the depth of the axle bearing seat in the housing.

   b. Measure the width of the bearing

outer race. The maximum end-play is 0.002–0.006 in.

REAR AXLE AND DIFFERENTIAL HOUSING ASSEMBLY

Removal and Installation

1. Raise the rear of the vehicle and support it with jackstands at the jack brackets.

Removing rear axle assembly

2. Remove both rear wheels and one rear brake drum.

3. Disconnect the parking brake rod from the equalizer and the cable from the actuating lever on the side with the drum removed.

4. Separate the cable from the lower control arm brackets and hang the free end over the exhaust pipe.

5. Unbolt the shock absorbers, the track rod, and (if so equipped) the stabilizer shackles, from the rear axle brackets.

6. Mark the mating parts of the drive-shaft-to-pinion extension flange, separate the flange, and tie the driveshaft out of the way.

7. Disconnect and cap the brake hoses at the differential.

8. Lower the axle enough to remove load from the springs and remove the springs.

9. Unbolt the central joint bracket from the under pan and the lower control arms from the axle brackets and roll the axle out from under the vehicle.

10. Install in the reverse order of removal.

NOTE: *When installing the central joint to the underpan, place a load of approximately 350 lbs in the trunk.*

11. Support the vehicle by the differential housing (raise off of the jackstands), and torque the bolts to 33 ft lbs.

NOTE: *Following installation of the axle, the brake system must be bled.*

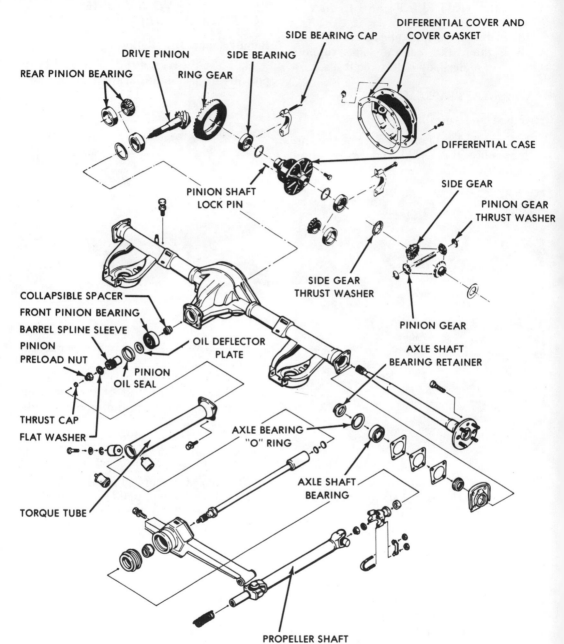

Rear axle assembly for 1.9 engine exploded

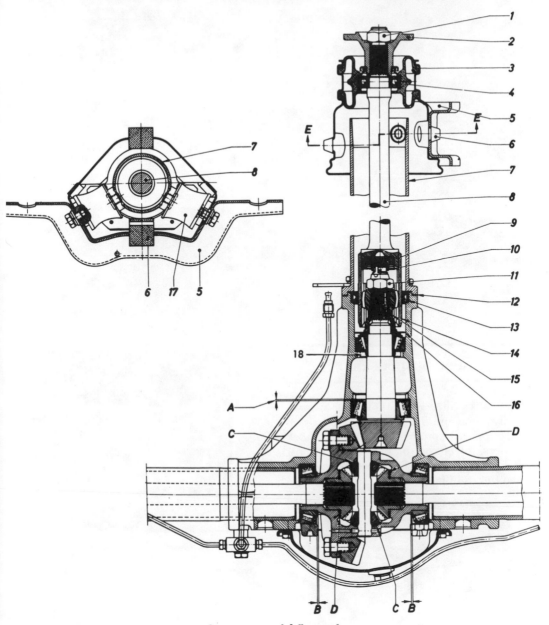

Cross-section of differential

1. Self-locking nut
2. Drive-pinion-shaft extension flange
3. Rubber cushion
4. Ball bearing with sheet metal casing
5. Central joint support
6. Rubber cushion on central joint support
7. Torque tube
8. Drive pinion extension
9. Hard rubber disc
10. Thrust cap
11. Hex. nut
12. Paper gasket
13. Oil seal
14. Slip joint
15. Splined sleeve
16. Oil deflector
17. Rubber cushion
18. Collapsible spacer
   (a) Shims for drive-pinion height adjustment
   (b) Shims for ring gear and pinion backlash adjustment
   (c) Spherical washer
   (d) Shim for differential side gears

Chapter Eight

Suspension and Steering

Rear Suspension

All Opels utilize a three link rear suspension arrangement. This type of suspension consists of coil springs, a track rod, shock absorbers, lower control arms and, on most models, a stabilizer bar. The GT does not utilize the stabilizer bar.

Underside of Opel showing rear suspension

The track rod controls the lateral stability of the rear axle assembly. The track rod is of tubular construction and is bolted to a frame side member and to the rear axle assembly.

The lower control rods are also tubular and are attached to the frame via side rails welded there for that purpose. They attach to the rear axle assembly through the front portion of the spring seat bracket. The

Coil spring installed

lower control arms act as two links of the three link system and control the fore and aft movement of the rear axle assembly.

The third link of the system is the torque tube which is connected to the differential carrier and to the underbody through rubber bushings in the central joint support bracket. The torque tube works in unison with the lower control arms to absorb acceleration and braking torque.

SHOCK ABSORBERS

Removal and Installation

NOTE: *The trim panel under the spare tire must be removed on the GT to gain access to the attaching nuts.*

1. Remove the upper attaching nut.

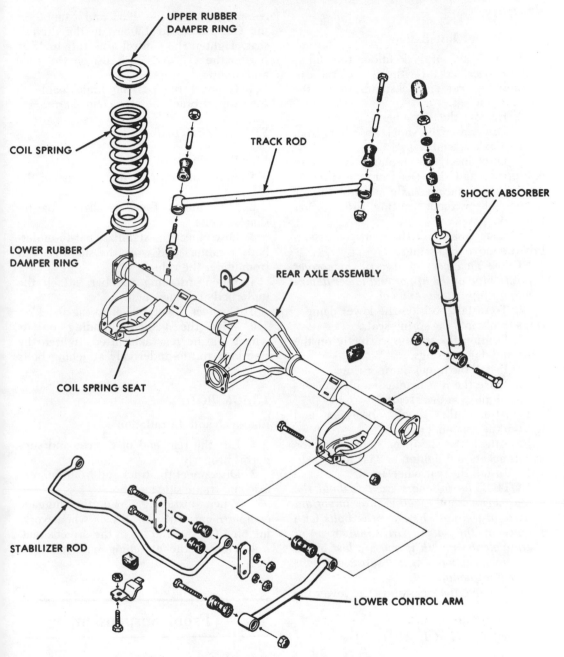

UPPER RUBBER
DAMPER RING

COIL SPRING

TRACK ROD

SHOCK ABSORBER

LOWER RUBBER
DAMPER RING

REAR AXLE ASSEMBLY

COIL SPRING SEAT

STABILIZER ROD

LOWER CONTROL ARM

Opel rear suspension components—1900 and Manta shown

2. Remove the lower attaching nut and rubber grommet retainer; compress the shock absorber and remove it from the lower mounting pin.

3. Replace the upper and lower grommets before installing a new shock absorber.

4. Extend the shock absorber and position it in the car. Attach the lower end first and torque the attaching nut to 15 ft lbs on the GT and 47 ft lbs on the 1900 and Manta.

5. Install the rubber grommet, retainer, and self-locking nut at the top of the shock absorber. Tighten to 10 ft lbs.

NOTE: *Always use new self-locking nuts.*

SPRINGS

Removal and Installation

1. Place a floor jack under the differential carrier and raise the rear of the car. Support the car on jackstands under the jacking brackets.

2. Remove the rear wheels.

3. Disconnect the shock absorbers from the rear axle assembly.

4. Disconnect the stabilizer bar (if so equipped) and shackles from the frame.

5. Lower the rear axle assembly as far as possible without putting pressure on the brake hoses.

6. If necessary, tilt the rear axle assembly to remove the springs.

NOTE: *Take care to observe the correct positioning of the upper and lower dampening rings before removal.*

7. To install, position the lower damper rings firmly into the spring seats.

8. Position the springs correctly on the seats and damper rings.

9. Install the upper damper rings.

10. Raise the rear axle assembly to compress the rings in their seats.

11. Attach the shock absorbers and tighten the retaining nuts.

12. Attach the stabilizer shackles to the axle brackets and tighten to 25 ft lbs.

13. Install the rear wheels.

NOTE: *The fasteners used to hold the rear suspension together are important parts of the unit. Replace the bolts with bolts of the same part number or of equivalent strength if any are lost in the repair operation. Do not substitute bolts of lesser quality.*

14. Remove the jackstands and lower the car.

LOWER CONTROL ARM

Removal and Installation

NOTE: *This operation may be performed with the vehicle at curb height or elevated.*

1. Disconnect the parking brake cable from the support bracket on the control arm.

2. Loosen and remove the front and rear control arm attaching nuts and remove the control arm.

3. When reinstalling the control arm, place a load of about 350 lbs in the luggage compartment of the 1900 and Manta; in the GT put about 150 lbs in the driver's seat. Tighten the control arm nuts to 18 ft lbs on the GT and 23 ft lbs on the 1900 and Manta.

4. Connect the parking brake cable to the support bracket on the control arm.

STABILIZER BAR

Removal and Installation

1. Raise and support the rear end of the car.

2. Disconnect the stabilizer bar-to-shackle bolts.

3. Disconnect the stabilizer bar-to-underbody retainers and work the stabilizer out from under the vehicle.

4. When installing the bar, attach the underbody retainers first.

5. Connect the stabilizer to the shackles.

6. With the vehicle standing on its wheels or the rear axle lifted, tighten the stabilizer rod-to-underbody attaching bolts to 15 ft lbs.

TRACK ROD

Removal and Installation

1. Lift the rear end of the car and support it properly.

2. Disconnect the track rod from the rear axle and frame side member.

3. When installing, load the luggage compartment with 350 lbs or when working on a GT put 150 lbs in the driver's seat.

4. Tighten the attaching bolts to 40 ft lbs.

Front Suspension

1971–72 Opel and 1971–73 GT

These models use an independent front suspension featuring unequal length control arms and a transverse leaf spring. Opels with 1.1 engines use a two-leaf spring and, when equipped with the 1.9 engine, a three-leaf spring. All GT models use the three-leaf unit. The entire front suspension can be removed from its mounting on the crossmember as a unit if desired. Ball joints are used as pivoting points between the control arms and the steering knuckles

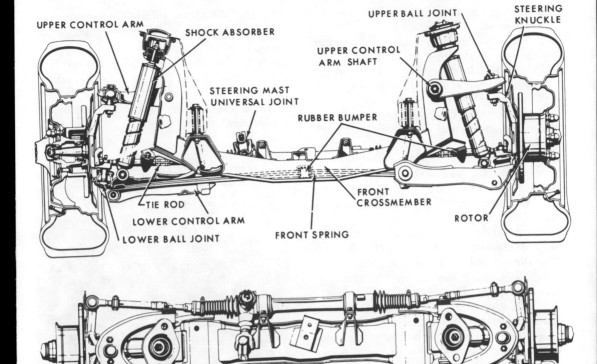

UPPER CONTROL ARM   SHOCK ABSORBER   UPPER BALL JOINT   STEERING KNUCKLE   UPPER CONTROL ARM SHAFT   STEERING MAST UNIVERSAL JOINT   RUBBER BUMPER   TIE ROD   LOWER CONTROL ARM   LOWER BALL JOINT   FRONT SPRING   FRONT CROSSMEMBER   ROTOR

1970–71 Opel and 1970–73 GT front suspension with disc brakes

in the conventional manner. All moving parts in the front end are permanently lubricated and require no maintenance.

1971–75 Opel 1900 and Manta

These models use coil springs and unequal length control arms. A stabilizer is used as a tie strut, its end supported in a rubber bushing located in a piece of tubing welded into the longer control arm. To minimize brake torque, the horizontal

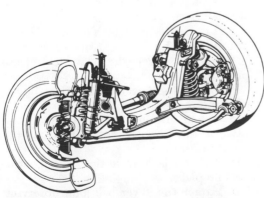

1971–74 Opel 1900 and Manta front suspension

shafts of the upper and lower control arms are non-parallel. The front suspension is mounted as a unit to the underbody in four places to facilitate removal. As with earlier Kadett and GT units, all the moving parts are permanently lubricated.

SPRINGS

Removal and Installation

1971–72 OPEL AND 1971–73 GT

The factory recommended procedures for removing the front transverse leaf spring on Opels and GT models require the use of special tools which in all probability are not available to you. Therefore, an alternative method will be put forth here which is used on other makes of cars utilizing a similar suspension. It should be noted that this procedure is difficult without the factory special tools and would best be left to an authorized dealer.

CAUTION: *The leaf spring in its installed position is tensioned against the rest of the suspension. Do not position yourself in such a way as to be caught* by the spring's recoil should there be any difficulty in removing it.

1. Raise the front of the car and support it at the rear of the front frame rails.

CAUTION: *It is imperative that the car be stationary and solidly supported.*

2. Remove the front wheels.

3. Remove the cotter pin from the castle nut on the lower ball joint studs and back off the castle nut two turns.

NOTE: *Do not remove the castle nut!*

4. Strike the ball stud sharply with a hammer to separate it.

5. On one side of the car place a jack under the lower control arm and leaf spring as far from center as possible. Raise the jack enough to take the spring tension off of the control arm attaching nuts.

6. Disconnect the shock absorbers at their lower mounting.

7. Remove the lower control arm-to-crossmember nuts and bolts.

8. Remove the lower ball joint stud nut. In this way the lower control arm is released from the crossmember and steering knuckle.

9. Lower the jack and allow the spring to hang with the lower control arm attached.

CAUTION: *If you are going to experience difficulty, it will be at this point. Be extremely careful when lowering the jack.*

10. Repeat the procedure on the opposite side of the car.

11. With the assembly on the ground, remove the control arm-to-spring attaching nuts and bolts.

12. To install the spring, assemble the lower control arms to the spring and position one side in the car.

13. Attach the lower control arm to the crossmember and the steering knuckle.

14. After firmly attaching one side, position a jack on the other side and line the control arm up to the crossmember and attach it. Attach the ball joint.

NOTE: *If any nuts or bolts are ruined in the operation, be sure to replace them with bolts of equal or greater capacity.*

TORQUE VALUES FOR
FRONT END COMPONENTS *

Control arm-to-spring	18
Ball joint castle nut	54
Shock absorber	30

* All readings in ft lbs.

1971–74 OPEL 1900 AND MANTA

Front coil spring removal on these vehicles is not a recommended procedure unless adequate equipment is available. It is advised that if spring replacement is necessary and special tools not available, the vehicle be taken to an authorized repair establishment.

Coil spring holding device

1. Install the upper control arm hooks (Opel part number J-23697).

NOTE: *The procedure can be effected without these units.*

2. Raise the car and support it on jackstands. A jack should be positioned under the lower control arm to maintain pressure on that component.

3. Remove the front wheel.

4. Detach both the front stabilizer bar supports from the crossmember.

5. Remove the shock absorber.

6. Remove the cotter pin and castle nut from the lower ball joint.

7. Using a suitable tool, separate the ball joint from the steering knuckle.

8. Loosen the nut which holds the lower control arm to the front crossmember.

9. Slowly lower the jack to release spring tension.

10. Swing the lower control arm downward and remove the spring.

11. When installing, position the spring between the lower control arm and the crossmember.

12. Using a jack, raise the lower control arm into place.

13. Attach the lower ball joint observing the correct torque values.

14. Tighten the control arm-to-cross-

Lower control arm attachment

member bolts. Again be careful to observe the torque values.

15. Replace the stabilizer bar.
16. Install the shock absorber.
17. Replace the wheel.

TORQUE VALUES FOR FRONT END COMPONENTS *

Ball joint-to-steering knuckle   54
Control arm-to-crossmember   43
Shock absorber   30

All readings in ft lbs.

SHOCK ABSORBERS

The function of the shock absorber is to minimize harsh spring movement and to provide a system to dissipate the motion of the wheels so that the shocks incurred at the wheel are not transmitted totally to the frame and body. As the wheels move up and down, the shock absorber shortens and lengthens and imposes a restraint on the movement by hydraulic action. A simple way to see if your shock absorbers are functioning properly is to push down firmly on a corner of the car. This will compress the spring on that corner of the car as well as the shock absorbers. If the shock absorber is functioning properly, it will control the spring's tendency to remain in motion. Thus the car will level itself almost instantly when you release the downward pressure. If the car bounces several times, the shock absorber is worn out and should be replaced.

Removal and Installation

1971–72 OPEL AND 1971–73 GT

1. Remove the air cleaner assembly.
2. There is a plastic cover over the upper shock absorber mounting which must be removed.
3. Raise the car and support it on jackstands.
4. Remove the upper attaching nuts.
5. Remove the lower attaching nut.
6. Compress the shock absorber and remove it from the car.

NOTE: *Always replace the upper and lower bushings when replacing the shock absorber.*

7. Install the lower mounting first and tighten the nut to 30 ft lbs.
8. Install the upper mounting nuts and tighten until the distance from the top of the nut to the top of the stud is about ½ in.

1971–74 1900 AND MANTA

1. Raise the car and support it on jackstands.
2. Remove the upper attaching nuts, the lower attaching nuts, and compress the shock absorber.

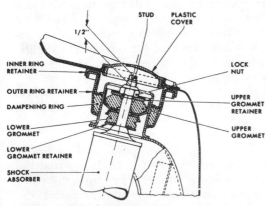

Shock absorber upper parts

3. Remove the shock absorber from the car.

4. When reinstalling, always replace the rubber grommets on the upper and lower mountings.

5. Install the lower attaching nut and tighten to 30 ft lbs.

6. Install the upper attaching nuts on the studs and tighten until the top of the nut is ½ in. from the top of the stud.

UPPER BALL JOINT

Removal and Installation

ALL MODELS

1. Raise the car under the spring or lower control arm.

Removing upper ball joint

NOTE: *Always support the vehicle safely before working under it.*

2. Remove the cotter pin and castle nut from the upper ball joint stud.

3. Using either a puller or a fork type separator, remove the ball joint stud from the steering knuckle.

4. Remove the two bolts which retain the ball joint to the upper control arm.

5. When installing the new ball joint, position the off-center holes in the flange toward the steering knuckle spindle.

6. Install the two upper control arm-to-ball joint nuts. Tighten to 29 ft lbs.

7. Install the upper ball joint stub in the steering knuckle and tighten the castle nut to 29 ft lbs on the 1971–72 Opel and 1971–

73 GT and tighten to 40 ft lbs on the 1971–74 1900 and Manta.

8. Install a new cotter pin.

NOTE: *After installing new ball joints, always have the front end alignment checked for proper caster and camber.*

LOWER BALL JOINT

Removal and Installation

Because this operation is critical to the front end geometry and cannot in our estimation be successfully undertaken without a variety of special tools and equipment, it has been eliminated from this guide. If the lower ball joints are judged defective, the vehicle should be taken to a qualified repair shop.

FRONT END ALIGNMENT

Opel suspensions include two control arms (an upper and a lower) which are attached to the chassis by hinges. The hinges permit the outer ends of the control arms to move up and down in relation to the chassis as the vehicle travels over bumps in the road surface, while keeping the outer ends from moving forward or backward.

The outer ends of the control arms are kept an equal distance apart by steering knuckles. The steering knuckles are held in place at top and bottom by ball joints. The wheel spindles extend outward from about the middle of the steering knuckles. The ball joints permit the upward and downward motion of the steering knuckles and the turning motion required for cornering, while keeping them vertical. Tie rods link them to the steering gear.

The upper and lower ends of the steering knuckles are not the same distance from the chassis; the upper end is closer. Therefore, the wheel spindles tend to angle downward and lift the vehicle slightly whenever the wheels are not pointed straight ahead.

A list of various terms used in wheel alignment, with their definitions, follows.

Camber

The wheel is not positioned vertically on most vehicles, but is angled so that the upper edge is further away from the chassis than is the lower edge. Angling the

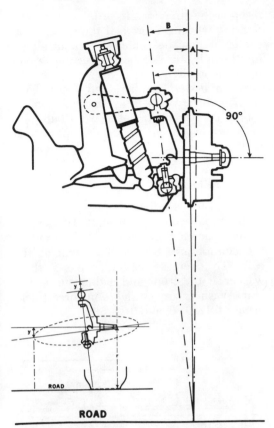

Camber (A), Steering Knuckle Inclination (B), and Included Angle (C); To turn wheel (r), the steering knuckle and chassis must move upward (y)

wheel in this manner makes better use of the tire tread during cornering.

Caster

The vehicle has caster if the upper end of the steering knuckle is positioned slightly behind the lower end. Caster helps the vehicle's steering return to the straight-ahead position, and improves directional stability.

Steering Axis Inclination

Steering axis inclination results from the fact that the upper end of the steering knuckle is closer to the chassis than the lower end. This angular mounting is what causes the vehicle to lift slightly during cornering. The car's weight thus tends to help the steering return to the center and to aid directional stability.

Included Angle

The included angle is the sum of the steering axis inclination and the caster angles. It is the angle between a line drawn between the two mounting points of the steering knuckle and a line drawn vertically through the center of the wheel.

In each of the above definitions, an imaginary angle between the vertical and the centerline of the wheel or the steering knuckle is described. On an alignment chart, these angles are referred to in degrees of positive caster, camber, etc. If the angle is listed as zero, the unit in question is to be perfectly vertical. If a figure of less than zero is listed, the unit should be angled in the opposite direction. For example, negative casters refers to an adjustment which positions the upper end of the steering knuckle ahead of the lower end, rather than behind.

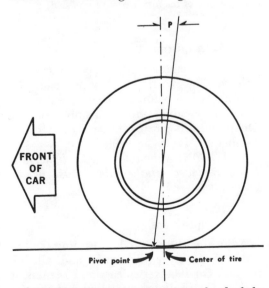

Positive Caster (P); the pivot point ahead of the center line of the tire holds the wheel stable

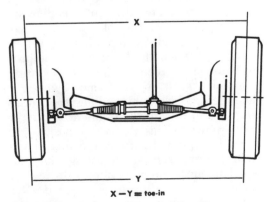

Toe-in is shown looking down at the front suspension from above; the front of the car is at the bottom of the drawing

Toe-In

When the front wheels are stationary, they are closer together at the front than at the rear. Aligning the wheels in this manner compensates for various frictional forces that alter the angles between the wheels when the vehicle is moving. Thus, the wheels are brought into a parallel position, relative to each other, as the vehicle gains speed. Toe-in is measured in inches; the difference between the distance separating the front and rear centerlines of the wheels.

Tracking

During straight-line operation, the vehicle's rear wheels must duplicate, or run parallel to, the paths of the front wheels. To measure the accuracy of a vehicle's tracking, measure the distance from the right-side lower ball joint to a point on the left side of the rear axle, and repeat the measurement for the left-side lower ball joint and a similar point on the right side of the rear axle. You may wish to drop a plumb line from each of these four points to the ground and mark the spots in order to avoid interference from various parts of the vehicle's undercarriage. The two diagonal lines should be equal in length to within 1/4 in. Otherwise, the frame of the vehicle is bent or the rear axle is off center.

The rear wheels may also be checked for toe-in or toe-out by measuring between the inner surfaces of the tires at front and rear. Toe-in or toe-out in excess of manufacturer's specifications indicates a bent rear axle.

There is a special machine designed to check the alignment of the front wheels. Caster is first adjusted to specifications by moving the upper control arm. This may be accomplished by repositioning shims, changing the length of a strut with adjusting nuts, or by repositioning the mounting point of a strut on the frame. Camber is then accomplished by pulling the entire control arm toward the frame or forcing it further away. This involves repositioning shims equally at the front and rear of the control arm, turning adjusting nuts an equal amount, or repositioning a strut.

On all vehicles, toe-in is adjusted after caster and camber are correct by turning the adjusting sleeves on the tie rods. These sleeves should be turned in equal amounts

in opposite directions in order to keep the steering wheel centered. If the wheel is off center, it may be centered without affecting toe-in by turning both adjusting sleeves in the same direction.

When caster, camber, and toe-in have been adjusted, steering axis inclination should be correct. If not, a worn ball joint or bent suspension or steering part is at fault.

Caster Adjustment

The caster is adjusted by placing shims on the upper control arm shaft. To increase caster, place a thin washer at the front of the control arm and a thick one at the rear. To decrease caster, place a thick washer at the front and a thin one at the rear. Washers are available in three thicknesses: 0.12, 0.36, and 0.24.

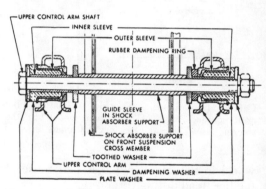

Cross-section of the upper control arm shaft

Camber Adjustment

The only camber adjustment possible is achieved by rotating the upper ball joint flange 108°. Factory settings are for the smallest possible positive camber on the Opels and GT and for the smallest negative camber on Mantas and 1900's.

CAUTION: *When the upper ball joints are replaced, the camber must be rechecked.*

Toe-in Adjustment

Adjustment is effected by turning the tie-rod sleeves on early Opels and all GT models. On 1900 series cars and Mantas, it is done by turning the axial joint of the tie-rod.

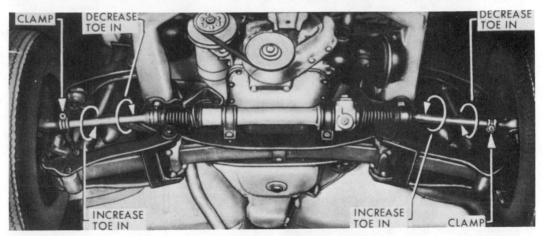

Toe-in adjustment on the tie-rods

Alignment Troubleshooting Chart

Front Wheel Shimmy

1. Tire inflation uneven or low.
2. Tires improperly mounted or wheels improperly balanced.
3. Incorrect caster.
4. Incorrect toe-in.
5. Uneven tire wear.
6. Excessively worn wheel bearings.
7. Worn ball joints.
8. Bent steering knuckle(s).
9. Inoperative shock absorbers.

Excessive Tire Wear

1. Both edges wear: insufficient pressure.
2. Center wears: excessive pressure.
3. One edge wears evenly: incorrect camber or toe-in, or damaged suspension parts.
4. One edge wears unevenly: incorrect camber or toe-in, insufficient pressure, improper wheel balance, or loose steering linkage.
5. Unequal wear between tires: unequal pressures or tire size, incorrect camber or toe-in, loose or bent steering linkage.

Vehicle Wanders

1. Tire pressures incorrect or unequal.
2. Incorrect caster, camber, or toe-in.
3. Loose or worn bushings anywhere in front suspension.
4. Rear axle position improper or frame bent.
5. Badly worn shock absorbers.

Car Pulls to One Side

1. Uneven tire pressures.
2. Incorrect caster, camber, or toe-in.
3. Brakes improperly adjusted.
4. Wheel bearings improperly adjusted.
5. Bent steering knuckle or other suspension component.
6. Improper tracking.

Wheel Alignment

Year	Model	CASTER①		CAMBER		Toe-in (in.)	WHEEL PIVOT RATIO (deg)	
		Range (deg)	Pref Setting (deg)	Range (deg)	Pref Setting (deg)		Inner Wheel	Outer Wheel
1971–	Opel	1–3	2	½–1½	1	⅟₃₂–⅛	20	18½
1975	GT	2–4	3	½–1½	1	⅟₃₂–⅛	20	18½
	1900	3½–6½	5	1½N–½N	1N	⅛–³⁄₁₆	20	19¼

① Permissible deviation from left to right wheel is 1 degree maximum
Note: All figures are positive unless specified negative (N).

Hard Steering

1. Low tire pressures.
2. Inadequate front-end lubrication.
3. Incorrect caster.
4. Improper steering gear adjustment.
5. Sagging front spring.

Steering

Opels use a rack and pinion steering gear to provide optimum handling and ease of maintenance. The steering gear pinion shaft is connected to the lower end of the steering column and it moves the rack gear to the left and right transmitting the turning motion of the steering wheel to the tie-rods and steering arms.

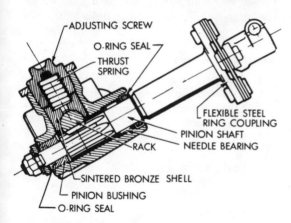

Cross-section of the steering gear

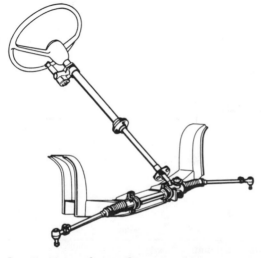

Steering gear with tie-rods

The steering gear housing is held to the crossmember by rubber bushings and clamps. The bushings prevent the transferral of noise and vibration to the body of the car.

The rack and pinion are held in mesh by a thrust spring and shell which are adjustable. The pressure of the thrust spring is varied by using an adjusting screw; this thrust spring forces a bronze shell against the rack which in turn is held against the pinion. This system effectively reduces backlash in the steering and avoids road shock.

STEERING WHEEL, TURN SIGNAL SWITCH, AND IGNITION SWITCH

These units are mounted in the steering column. Since they are not serviceable without lowering the steering column, service should be reserved for qualified personnel.

The steering column is collapsible and, in order to work on these components, it must be disassembled from the dash mountings and lowered into the passenger compartment. Any shock delivered to the system will collapse the column and render it useless. The column is held in place with shear bolts which must be removed by drilling and the use of reverse thread devices. This type of service is not in the realm of home repair.

STEERING GEAR ADJUSTMENTS

1. Set the steering gear to the high point by turning the front wheels straight ahead with the steering wheel centered.
2. Thread the adjusting screw into the steering gear housing until a resistance is felt. By threading the adjusting screw into the housing when the gear is on the high point, the bronze shell on the end of the thrust assembly is forced against the rack so that it is blocked.
3. Back off the adjusting screw ⅛ to ¼ of a turn.
4. Tighten the locknut to 43 ft lbs of torque.
5. Fill the area under the pinion shaft rubber boot with steering gear lubricant (SAE 90) and slide the boot into position.

STEERING LINKAGE

Removal and Installation

ALL OPEL AND GT
(EXCEPT 1900 AND MANTA)

1. Loosen the clamp which secures the flexible coupling to the steering shaft.

2. Remove the stop bolt from the underside of the steering column and pull the steering wheel straight back about 3 in.

Mast guide stop bolt

NOTE: *The stop bolt referred to secures the steering shaft bushing to the mast jacket.*

3. Remove the cotter pin located on the left and right tie-rod ends and unscrew the nuts.

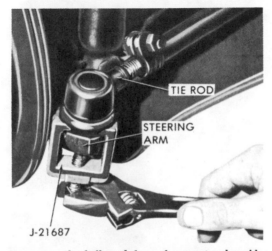

J-21687

Removing the ball stud from the steering knuckle

4. Remove the ball studs of the tie-rod ends from the steering arms. This can be done with a puller or by shocking the stud with one hammer positioned behind and one in front.

5. Remove the four attaching bolts which hold the steering gear to the front crossmember and lift off the steering gear assembly and tie-rods.

6. To install, position the steering gear and tie-rods on the front suspension crossmember and tighten the attaching bolts to 18 ft lbs.

7. Place the tie-rod ball studs in the steering arms and install the nuts. Tighten the nuts to 29 ft lbs and lock them in position with new cotter pins.

8. Turn the steering wheel so that the flat or cutout surface on the lower portion of the steering shaft is parallel to the flexible coupling bolt hole.

9. Install the lower end of the steering shaft to the flexible coupling and adjust the dimension between the steering wheel hub and the directional signal switch housing cover to $\frac{1}{8}$–$\frac{3}{32}$ of an inch. Tighten the flexible coupling bolt and nut to 15 ft lbs.

10. Install the stop bolt in the steering column.

11. Turn the steering wheel from lock-to-lock (full right to full left) to be sure it is operating smoothly. If it does not, go back and recheck all assembly procedures.

OPEL 1900 AND MANTA

1. Remove the splash shield from lower deflector panel and both side members.

CLAMP BOLT

2. Remove the clamp bolt which secures the flexible coupling to the steering shaft.

3. Remove the cotter pins and nuts from the tie-rod ends.

4. Separate the tie-rod from the steering arm.

5. Disconnect the steering gear housing from the suspension crossmember.

6. Remove the steering gear with the tie-rods.

7. To install: position the steering at the high point. This is done by pointing the front wheels straight ahead with the steering wheel spokes pointed downward at an oblique angle. The elongated cutout of the lower steering mast must coincide with the clamp bolt hole of the pinion flange.

8. Place the steering gear on the front suspension crossmember and tighten the attaching bolts to 29 ft lbs.

9. Position the tie-rod studs onto the steering arms and install the nuts. Tighten them to 29 ft lbs. Lock the nuts in position with new cotter pins.

10. Install the lower end of the steering shaft into the flexible coupling and tighten the clamp bolt to 22 ft lbs.

11. Attach the guard plate and deflector.

12. Operate the steering from lock-to-lock (full left to full right) and watch for smooth operation.

Chapter Nine

Brakes

Opels equipped with the 1.1 engine have four wheel drum brakes. All other models utilize front disc brakes and larger rear drum brakes. The disc brakes use two-piston fixed calipers and solid discs. The drum brakes are not self-adjusting and must be manually adjusted.

Hydraulic System

MASTER CYLINDER

Removal and Installation

1. Disconnect and plug the brake lines where they enter the master brake cylinder.
2. Remove the two bolts that secure the master cylinder to the cowl wall.
3. Depress the brake pedal slightly and remove the master cylinder from the support bracket and brake booster.
4. Inside the car, remove the trim pad above the pedal assembly. Then remove the actuating pushrod nut from the brake pedal and slide the assembly out.
5. Pour out the brake fluid and lift it out of position.
6. Installation is the reverse of removal.

Overhaul

1. Screw the static pressure valve out of the housing.

2. Push the piston into the cylinder to a point where a rod $\frac{1}{10}$ in. thick will slip into the feed port to hold the piston in this position.
3. Remove the stop screw at the bottom and the circlip at the booster end of the housing and take out both pistons together with the springs.
4. Unscrew the stop screw from the rear-brake-circuit piston. Remove the remaining parts.
5. Clean the master cylinder parts with brake fluid and dry with compressed air. Clean the compensating and feed ports.
6. Polish the cylinder bore and pistons.
Maximum piston diameter: 0.82 in.
Minimum piston diameter: 0.81 in.
7. Replace the rubber seals and static pressure valve.
8. Coat all parts with brake fluid for reassembly.
9. Assemble the intermediate piston and insert it into the cylinder bore with thrust spring and spring seat. The smaller diameter of the tapered thrust spring must face the piston.
10. With a drift, push the piston into the housing and insert a rod into the feed port.
11. Install the stop screw with a new seal ring.
12. Insert the preassembled piston for the rear brake circuit into the cylinder bore and install the circlip into the groove in the housing.

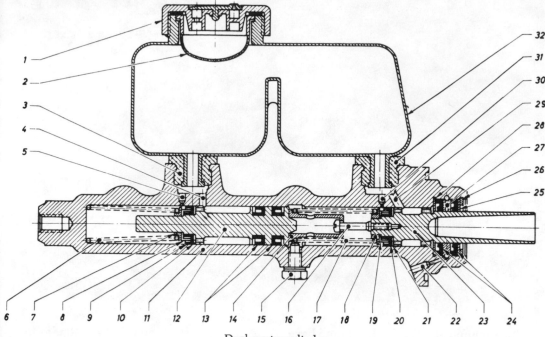

Dual master cylinder

1. Cover with seal ring
2. Screen
3. Sealing plug
4. Feed port
5. Compensating port
6. Piston spring
7. Piston spring collar
8. Support ring
9. Primary seal
10. Plate
11. Dual brake master cylinder housing
12. Intermediate piston (for front brake circuit)
13. Secondary seal
14. Stop sleeve
15. Stop screw with seal ring
16. Stop screw
17. Piston spring
18. Piston spring collar
19. Support ring
20. Primary seal
21. Plate
22. Drain port
23. Piston (rear brake circuit)
24. Secondary seals
25. Stop plate
26. Circlip
27. Intermediate ring
28. Stop plate
29. Feed port
30. Compensating port
31. Sealing plug
32. Twin brake fluid container

13. Check the piston for free movement. NOTE: *If required, place washers under the head of the stop screw.*

14. Push the piston partly into the housing and remove the rod from the feed port.

15. Screw in the new static pressure valves.

16. Coat the new sealing plugs thinly with brake fluid and insert them into the housing.

17. Push the twin brake fluid container into the sealing plugs.

BRAKE BOOSTER

The brake booster reduces required foot pressure for braking by approximately 25%. The booster is mechanically controlled by the foot pedal and conveys this pressure, along with an engine vacuum assistance, to the dual master cylinder. A vac-

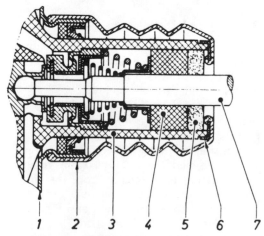

Cross-section of the brake booster

1. Brake booster housing
2. Protective cap
3. Control housing
4. Filter
5. Sound deadener
6. Retainer
7. Thrust rod

uum control valve prevents air from flowing back into the booster when the engine is not running. The valve must be replaced when defective.

Checking Brake Booster Operation

The operation of the brake booster can be checked easily.

1. With the engine off, use up all vacuum by depressing the brake pedal several times.

2. Hold the pedal down and start the engine. As vacuum builds, the pedal will move farther (held under the same foot pressure) as power is developed by the booster.

Removal and Installation

1. Disconnect the brake lines from the master cylinder.

2. Disconnect the vacuum line from the brake booster.

3. Remove the four attaching nuts and washers from the support.

4. On the GT, remove the master cylinder support-to-fender skirt bolts.

5. Again only on the GT, loosen the thrust rod lock nut and unscrew the piston push-rod while holding the master cylinder and brake booster.

6. On the 1900 and Manta, remove the clevis attaching nut and bolt at the pedal.

7. Remove the master cylinder and booster as a unit.

8. Detach the master cylinder from the booster.

9. Install the assembly in the reverse order of removal.

BLEEDING

Bleed the brake system to remove air from the brake cylinders. Air, being compressible, cushions fluid movement from the brake pedal to the wheel cylinders. Braking effectiveness is reduced accompanied by pedal sponginess. Bleed the disc brakes first. Bleed the rear wheels before the front ones when all brakes are drum type. After filling the reservoir to MAX level, clean dirt from the bleeder valve, remove the cap, and fit the valve with a hose to drain the fluid into a jar. The hose prevents fluid from seeping to the lining.

Open the valve ½ turn, depress the brake pedal, and allow it to return slowly. Continue bleeding until the fluid is free of air

bubbles. Keep the pedal depressed until the bleeder valve is closed.

NOTE: *Keep the fluid level high in the reservoir to prevent air from entering the line at the master cylinder. Discard the fluid discharged during the bleeding operation.*

Complete flushing of the brake system is recommended whenever new parts are installed. Fluid with any trace of mineral oil should not be used to flush the system.

Front Disc Brakes

DISC BRAKE PADS

Inspection and Replacement

1. Disc brake friction pads can be checked for wear without disassembling the caliper if a gauge is available that measures the distance from the inside of one friction pad backing plate to the other when the brake is engaged.

NOTE: *Both brake friction pads must be replaced if either pad is worn down to a thickness of 0.08 in. or less.*

2. If no gauge is available, tap the dowel pins from the brake caliper toward the center of the car after the pin retainer has been removed.

GAUGE   CALIPER ASSEMBLY

Measuring friction pad thickness

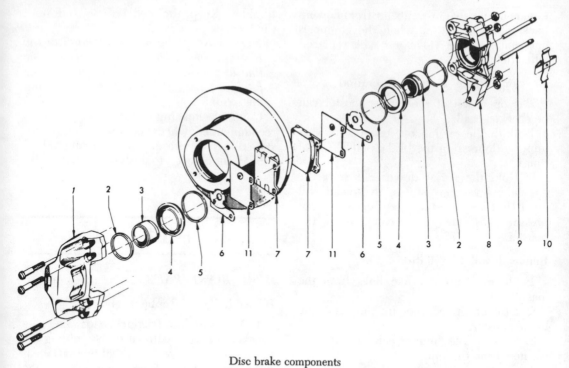

Disc brake components

1. Caliper rim half	5. Clamp rings	9. Dowel pins for friction pads
2. Rubber fluid seals	6. Retainer plates	10. Cross-shaped retaining spring
3. Hollow pistons	7. Friction pads	11. Pad backing plate
4. Rubber seals	8. Caliper mounting half	

3. Mark the friction pads for later reassembly and pull the pads from the caliper. NOTE: *Oily, cracked, or defaced pads need replacement.*

4. Pads themselves must measure at all times greater than 0.08 in. thick.

5. Remove high spots on the friction pads with a cut stone file before reinstalling.

6. If installing new friction pads, force both caliper pistons into their caliper bores completely with a clamp. NOTE: *Open the bleeder valve on the caliper to prevent brake reservoir overflow.*

7. Replace the friction pad retaining spring.

8. Press the brake pedal several times to seat the pads. Bleed and add brake fluid.

9. Avoid forceful braking for 125 miles to break in the pads.

DISC BRAKE CALIPERS

Removal and Installation

1. Remove the caliper from the wheel backing plate.

2. Loosen the brake line at the union, unfasten the caliper and brake hose bracket, and remove the brake pipe (plugging the hose at the union on their collars) and make sure that the clamp rings are correctly positioned on the seals.

3. Push the retainer plates into the pistons with the handle of a screwdriver.

Overhaul

NOTE: *Caliper halves are not disassembled for repair work.*

1. From the opening for friction pads, lift the retainer plates from each piston.

2. Next, pry the clamp rings from the rubber seals and remove the seals. Keep the twin parts from the two halves separated.

3. Check the caliper piston seals and clamp rings for deterioration or damage. Clean ring recesses with *denatured* alcohol.

NOTE: *A special clamp (J-22429) is recommended for forcing the pistons from the caliper halves.*

4. New rubber seals are recommended for reinstallation with cleaned clamp rings.

5. Make sure that the seals are securely seated.

6. Attach the brake pipe and caliper to the front end, making sure that the mating surfaces of the caliper and steering knuckle are clean and smooth.

7. Tighten the caliper attaching bolts to 50 ft lbs.

BRAKE DISC (ROTOR)

Removal and Installation

1. Unbolt the caliper and suspend it on a piece of heavy wire.

NOTE: *Do not stress the brake hose.*

2. Remove the wheel hub.

3. Support the wheel backing plate in a vise and unbolt the disc hat from the hub using a star wrench.

4. The disc may now be pulled from the hub.

CAUTION: *Do not drive the hub out of the disc.*

5. The disc is installed in the reverse order of removal.

6. When installing the disc on the hub, ensure that the mating surfaces are free of dirt, and torque the star bolts to 36 ft lbs.

7. Before installing the disc on the car, repack the wheel bearings.

Disc Inspection

The discs should be inspected visually for scratches, nicks, or scoring. The discs may be checked for lateral runout using a dial indicator mounted perpendicular to the disc, $\frac{1}{2}$ in. from its circumference. Disc parallelism is checked with a micrometer.

Minimum thickness of brake disc: 0.390 in.

Maximum unevenness: 0.002 in.

Maximum lateral runout: 0.001 in.

If runout or parallelism exceed the above specifications, the disc should be machined or replaced.

NOTE: *In no case should the disc be machined beyond the minimum thickness. If it is impossible to true the disc without exceeding this figure, the disc should be replaced.*

WHEEL BEARINGS

Removal and Installation

1. Remove the front wheels.

2. Remove the front wheel bearing hub cap and spindle nut.

3. Pull the rotor hub assembly off of the spindle. Be careful not to drop the outer bearing.

NOTE: *On cars equipped with disc brakes, it will be necessary to remove the caliper assembly before removing the rotor and hub assembly.*

4. Thoroughly clean the bearings of old lubricant and press fresh grease into the bearing.

NOTE: *Both inner and outer front bearings should be repacked with grease. For best results, both sides of the car should be repacked at the same time.*

5. Place the hub assembly on the spindle and install the spindle nut in the reverse order of removal.

Adjustments

When reinstalling the hub assembly onto the spindle, it is important to set the free-play in the bearing to prevent damage.

1. Install the hub assembly onto the spindle.

2. Place the outer bearing into position and install the spindle nut.

3. Tighten the spindle nut until all free-play is removed from the wheel bearing.

NOTE: *Do not overtighten the nut. This will cause binding of the bearing on its race and will cause excessive wear.*

4. Reinstall the bearing hub cap and re-check free-play.

Drum Brakes

Adjustment

FRONT OR REAR

Each shoe has an individual adjustment eccentric located on the backing plate. An arrow indicates the correct direction to turn for adjustment.

1. Jack up the car and support it on stands.

2. Rotate the wheels to make sure that the brake drums are turning freely.

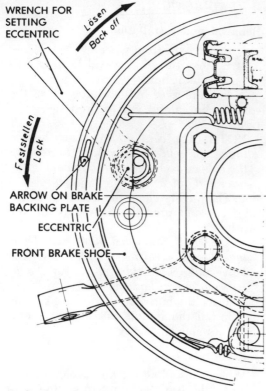

WRENCH FOR
SETTING
ECCENTRIC

Lösen
Back off

Feststellen
Lock

ARROW ON BRAKE
BACKING PLATE

ECCENTRIC

FRONT BRAKE SHOE

Brake shoe adjustment

3. Turn the drum toward the front while adjusting the forward eccentric (in the direction of the arrow). Stop when the shoe begins to drag on the drum and then back off on the eccentric until the drum is just free to turn.

4. Repeat the above step for the rear shoe, but turn the drum in the opposite direction.

5. Lower the car and check brake operation.

BRAKE DRUMS

Removal and Installation

FRONT

1. Remove the wheels, bearing hub cap, and spindle nut.

2. Pull the drum and hub assembly from the spindle being careful not to drop the outer bearing.

3. Installation is the reverse of removal.

REAR

1. Support the rear of the car and remove the rear wheels.

2. Remove the rear drums by pulling them off of the hub.

3. Install in the reverse order of removal.

Inspection

1. The drums should be checked for cracks, scoring, and concentricity.

2. Slight scores may be polished out using emery cloth. Eccentricity or serious scores should be removed by turning the drum providing the maximum diameter is not exceeded.

Maximum eccentricity of drum: 0.004 in.

NOTE: *Eccentricity is measured by comparing the diameter of the inner and outer edge of the machined surface in two places, 90° apart.*

Drums may be turned a maximum of 0.030 in.

3. To regain center contact with the brake shoes, grind the linings to 0.02 in. under drum diameter.

4. Before reinstalling the brake drum, inspect all brake pipe and hose connections for fluid leakage. Tighten these connections and apply heavy pressure to the brake pedal to recheck the seal.

5. Inspect the rear wheel backing plate for leaks from the wheel bearing oil seals. Replace the seals if needed.

6. Check all backing plate bolts for tightness.

7. Clean all dirt away from assemblies and repack the wheel bearings.

8. If a rear wheel backing plate was removed, use new gaskets lightly coated with grease. Torque the plate to 21 ft lbs.

9. Seal the outside of the backing plate near the brake shoe hold-down springs with body sealing compounds.

BRAKE SHOES

Removal and Installation

FRONT OR REAR

1. Raise the front of the car and support it safely.

2. Remove the front wheels and drum assemblies.

3. Remove the upper and lower brake shoe return springs.

4. Remove the brake shoe hold-down springs and retainers.

5. Remove the shoes from the backing plate.

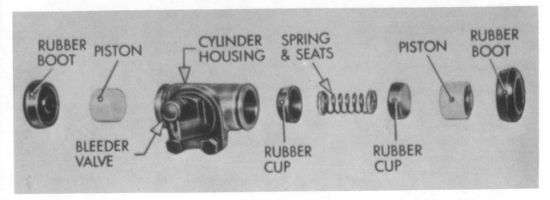

Drum brake wheel cylinder

6. Clean all dirt from the drum and backing plate and inspect all fittings and parts.

7. Installation is the reverse of removal.

WHEEL CYLINDERS

Removal and Installation

1. Remove the front wheels, drums, and brake shoes from the backing plates.

2. Disconnect the brake lines from the back of the wheel cylinder.

3. Unbolt the wheel cylinder and remove it from the backing plate.

4. Installation is the reverse of removal. NOTE: *After installation be sure to bleed the system of all air.*

Overhaul

1. Carefully pull the lower edges of the wheel cylinder boots away from the cylinders and note if the interior is wet—an indication of brake fluid seepage past the piston cup. If so, cylinder overhaul is required.

2. Clean dirt from all surrounding surfaces and then disconnect and seal off the brake line (tape is often satisfactory for sealing).

3. Remove the cylinder from the backing plate.

4. Dismantle the boots, pistons, cups and spring from the cylinder.

5. Remove the bleeder valve.

6. Discard the boots and cups; clean all other parts with fresh brake fluid. NOTE: *Use no fluid containing even a trace of mineral oil.*

7. Light scratches and corrosion can be polished from the pistons and bore with fine emery cloth or steel wool.

8. Dip all parts in brake fluid and reassemble.

9. After installation, adjust the brakes and road test for performance.

WHEEL BEARINGS

Removal and Installation

1. Remove the front wheels and bearing hub cap. Unscrew the spindle nut.

2. Pull the drum and hub assembly from the spindle. Be careful not to drop the outer bearing.

3. Thoroughly clean the bearing of old lubricant and press fresh grease into the bearing. NOTE: *Both inner and outer front bearings should be repacked with grease. For best results, both sides should be repacked at the same time.*

4. Place the drum and hub assembly onto the spindle and install the spindle nut.

5. Tighten until free-play is removed and reinstall the wheel onto the car.

Adjustments

1. Install the hub assembly onto the spindle.

2. Place the outer bearing onto the spindle and install the spindle nut.

3. Tighten the spindle nut until all free-play is removed from the wheel bearing. NOTE: *Do not tighten the nut. It will cause binding of the bearing on its race and therefore, excessive wear.*

4. Reinstall the bearing hub cap and recheck free-play.

Parking Brake

CABLE

Removal and Installation

1. Raise the car and support it securely.
2. Release the parking brake and disconnect the return spring.
3. Remove the adjusting nut from the parking brake equalizer.
4. Disconnect the parking brake cable at the rear connections.
5. Remove the cable from the car.
6. Install in the reverse order of removal.

Adjustment

1. Lift the rear of the vehicle and support it with jackstands.
2. Release the parking brake lever and loosen the nut in front of the equalizer.
3. Pull the brake lever up three notches (clicks), and tighten the nut behind the equalizer until the rear brakes begin to bind.
4. Tighten the nut in front of the equalizer.
5. Lubricate the cable in the area of the equalizer to ensure proper operation.

Brake Specifications

All measurements are given in in.

Year	Model Displacement (liters)	Master Cylinder Bore	WHEEL CYLINDER OR CALIPER PISTON BORE				BRAKE DISC OR DRUM DIAMETER				New Pad or Lining Thickness
			Front		Rear		Front		Rear		
			Disc	Drum	Disc	Drum	Disc	Drum	Disc	Drum	
1971	1.1	$\frac{3}{4}$	N.A.	$\frac{15}{16}$	——	$\frac{5}{8}$	N.A.	7.88	——	7.88	0.197
1971	1.9	$\frac{13}{16}$	1.89 (GT) 1.77	——	——	$\frac{5}{8}$	9.37	——	——	9.060	0.550
1973–75	1.9	$\frac{13}{16}$	1.89	——	——	$\frac{5}{8}$	9.37①	——	——	9.060	0.550

① 1975—9.68 in.

Doors

Removal and Installation

1970 OPEL, 1971–75 1900 AND MANTA

NOTE: *Prior to driving out the upper and lower hinge pins, remove the plastic plugs which are positioned in the hinge sleeve.*

Grind or file off the underside of the door check link rivet and drive out the rivet. Using Opel tool #J-21688 or another appropriate tool, drive out the door hinge pins and lift off the door.

Removing the hinge pin

GT

The door hinge is bolted to the body and to the door assembly. Simply remove the bolts from the hinge and remove the door.

DOOR PANELS

In order to remove the door panels you must have the tools to remove the window regulator handle and the inside door handle escutcheon.

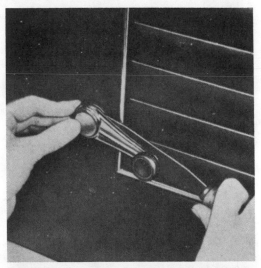

Using the tool to remove the window regulator handle

Positioning the tool on slide lock spring

1. Remove the front window regulator handle by inserting a tool similar to the one shown between the handle and the nylon disc behind it. Slide the lock spring outward and remove the handle.

2. Remove the door inside handle escutcheon.

3. Remove the door lock knob.

4. Remove the arm rest.

5. Remove the door panel.

6. Prior to installing the door panel be certain that the water deflector foil is inserted in the lower door slot. Then reassemble the door panel and related parts.

Locks

Removal and Installation

DOOR

1. Remove the door panel.

2. Remove the door lock knob.

3. Remove the inside door handle.

4. On the lock side scribe the position of the guide rail bolt and unscrew the bolt; push the guide rail downward and remove it through the access hole.

5. Reinstall in the reverse order of removal.

NOTE: *On Manta Rallye and Luxus models do not remove the guide rail.*

TRUNK

The trunk lid lock is removed from inside the luggage compartment by removing the two attaching screws.

The lock cylinder is held in place by a $1\frac{3}{16}$ in. nut and can be removed with a deep well socket when the trunk lid is almost horizontal.

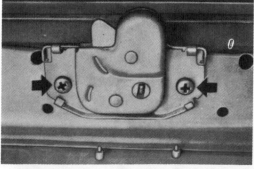

Trunk lid lock attaching screws

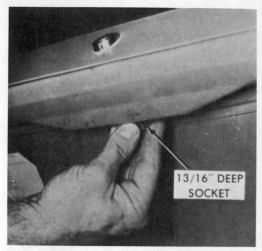

Removing the trunk lid lock cylinder

Hood and Trunk Lid

Both of these body components are bolted to their respective hinges. If they are removed, they can be realigned properly by scribing hinge marks on the underside.

Sunroof Adjustments

1. Adjust the front sunroof height by closing the sunroof and loosening the screws which secure the front guides. Rotate the height adjustment ring until the desired height is obtained.

2. Readjust the guides outward so that the guides just touch the sides of the rails

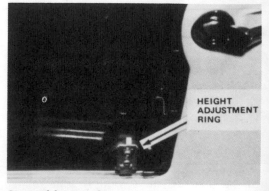

Sun roof front guide

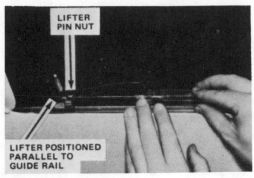

Lifter pin adjusting screw

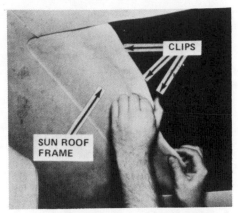

Separating the sun roof frame from the panel

and are not wedged against the rail sides. Tighten the screws.

NOTE: *The guides should lightly contact the guide rail and have about 0.02 in. of clearance.*

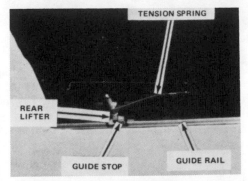

Rear sun roof lifter positioned 90° to the guide rail

are in a horizontal position. Loosen the lifter pin nut and turn the lifter pin to raise or lower the level of the sunroof.

NOTE: *The above procedures should be performed with the sunroof frame separated from the panel.*

Fuel Tank

Removal and Installation

1971 OPEL

1. Disconnect the battery to avoid an electrical spark while the air around the car is full of gasoline vapors.

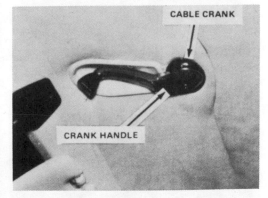

Sun roof cranking handle and cable crank

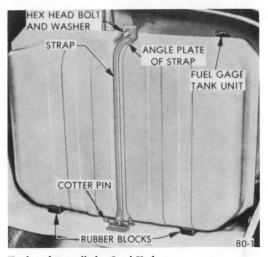

Fuel tank installed—Opel Kadett

3. Adjust the rear height by making sure that the rear sunroof guides are at a 90° angle to the guide rail. If they are not, remove the crank handle and cable crank and position the guides properly. Reinstall the handle and crank.

4. Open the sunroof until the rear lifters

2. Disconnect the wire from the fuel gauge tank unit.

3. Disconnect the vent hose from the tank.

4. Remove the tank filler cap.

5. Disconnect the rubber hose from the short metal fuel line and drain the fuel tank.

6. Slide the rubber grommet down and disconnect the fuel line from the tank.

7. Remove the fuel tank retaining strap bolt and retaining straps from inside the luggage compartment.

8. Lift the fuel tank off of the rubber spacers and pull the tank toward the center of the luggage compartment.

CAUTION: *Do not damage the filler neck seal.*

9. Remove the fuel screen from the tank by removing the threaded fuel line fitting.

10. When reinstalling the unit be careful to not damage the filler neck seal when you are fitting the filler neck to the fender. Place the tank on the insulating blocks and install the retaining strap and bolts. Connect the fuel lines and wire to the gauge. Connect the battery and fill the tank. Check all lines and connections for leaks as well as making sure that the tank is firmly held in place with the retaining straps and bolts.

1971–75 OPEL 1900 AND MANTA

1. Using a pinch clamp, close the connecting hose between the tank and the fuel line that goes to the fuel pump.

2. Loosen the hose clamp and pull off the fuel line.

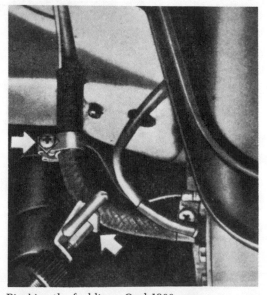

Pinching the fuel line—Opel 1900

3. Remove the filler cap and unscrew the four screws which hold the filler neck to the side panel.

4. Pull off the fuel tank hose and plug the connecting tubes on the tank.

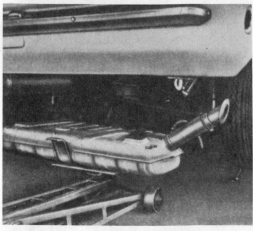

Removing the fuel tank—Opel 1900

5. Using a jack topped with a wooden board about 12 in. square, support the fuel tank and unscrew the strap. Lower the fuel tank from the car.

6. The installation procedure is the reverse of removal.

GT

1. Disconnect the battery.

2. Remove the rubber cap and unscrew the fuel line from the tank in order to drain the unit.

Fuel line attachment—Opel GT

Spare tire hold-down and brackets—Opel GT

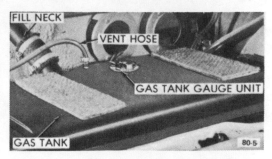

Top view of fuel tank—Opel GT

3. Remove the spare tire and the jack.
4. Remove the spare tire hold-down and brackets.
5. Remove the spare tire support panel.
6. Remove the spare tire support attaching brackets; they are attached to the rear wheel housing panel and are covered with sound deadening material.
7. Remove the fuel tank vent hose and filler hose.
8. Remove the fuel tank gauge wire and the tank attaching bolts.
9. Remove the tank from the car.

10. Install in the reverse order of removal.

FUEL LINES (ALL MODELS)

NOTE: *All fuel lines used on Opels are plastic and have an outside diameter of 0.240 in. Plastic lines are not flared. If replacement is necessary, see an Opel parts department. The line must be made flexible by placing it in hot water. Mold it to the shape of the old line and install in the same position. Be sure to replace all the insulating grommets to prevent chafing.*

Appendix

General Conversion Table

Multiply by	To convert	To	
2.54	Inches	Centimeters	.3937
30.48	Feet	Centimeters	.0328
.914	Yards	Meters	1.094
1.609	Miles	Kilometers	.621
.645	Square inches	Square cm.	.155
.836	Square yards	Square meters	1.196
16.39	Cubic inches	Cubic cm.	.061
28.3	Cubic feet	Liters	.0353
.4536	Pounds	Kilograms	2.2045
4.226	Gallons	Liters	.264
.068	Lbs./sq. in. (psi)	Atmospheres	14.7
.138	Foot pounds	Kg. m.	7.23
1.014	H.P. (DIN)	H.P. (SAE)	.9861
——	To obtain	From	Multiply by

Note: 1 cm. equals 10 mm.; 1 mm. equals .0394″.

Conversion—Common Fractions to Decimals and Millimeters

INCHES			INCHES			INCHES		
Common Fractions	Decimal Fractions	Millimeters (approx.)	Common Fractions	Decimal Fractions	Millimeters (approx.)	Common Fractions	Decimal Fractions	Millimeters (approx.)
1/128	.008	0.20	11/32	.344	8.73	43/64	.672	17.07
1/64	.016	0.40	23/64	.359	9.13	11/16	.688	17.46
1/32	.031	0.79	3/8	.375	9.53	45/64	.703	17.86
3/64	.047	1.19	25/64	.391	9.92	23/32	.719	18.26
1/16	.063	1.59	13/32	.406	10.32	47/64	.734	18.65
5/64	.078	1.98	27/64	.422	10.72	3/4	.750	19.05
3/32	.094	2.38	7/16	.438	11.11	49/64	.766	19.45
7/64	.109	2.78	29/64	.453	11.51	25/32	.781	19.84
1/8	.125	3.18	15/32	.469	11.91	51/64	.797	20.24
9/64	.141	3.57	31/64	.484	12.30	13/16	.813	20.64
5/32	.156	3.97	1/2	.500	12.70	53/64	.828	21.03
11/64	.172	4.37	33/64	.516	13.10	27/32	.844	21.43
3/16	.188	4.76	17/32	.531	13.49	55/64	.859	21.83
13/64	.203	5.16	35/64	.547	13.89	7/8	.875	22.23
7/32	.219	5.56	9/16	.563	14.29	57/64	.891	22.62
15/64	.234	5.95	37/64	.578	14.68	29/32	.906	23.02
1/4	.250	6.35	19/32	.594	15.08	59/64	.922	23.42
17/64	.266	6.75	39/64	.609	15.48	15/16	.938	23.81
9/32	.281	7.14	5/8	.625	15.88	61/64	.953	24.21
19/64	.297	7.54	41/64	.641	16.27	31/32	.969	24.61
5/16	.313	7.94	21/32	.656	16.67	63/64	.984	25.00
21/64	.328	8.33						

Conversion—Millimeters to Decimal Inches

mm	inches	mm	inches	mm	inches	mm	inches	mm	inches
1	.039 370	31	1.220 470	61	2.401 570	91	3.582 670	210	8.267 700
2	.078 740	32	1.259 840	62	2.440 940	92	3.622 040	220	8.661 400
3	.118 110	33	1.299 210	63	2.480 310	93	3.661 410	230	9.055 100
4	.157 480	34	1.338 580	64	2.519 680	94	3.700 780	240	9.448 800
5	.196 850	35	1.377 949	65	2.559 050	95	3.740 150	250	9.842 500
6	.236 220	36	1.417 319	66	2.598 420	96	3.779 520	260	10.236 200
7	.275 590	37	1.456 689	67	2.637 790	97	3.818 890	270	10.629 900
8	.314 960	38	1.496 050	68	2.677 160	98	3.858 260	280	11.032 600
9	.354 330	39	1.535 430	69	2.716 530	99	3.897 630	290	11.417 300
10	.393 700	40	1.574 800	70	2.755 900	100	3.937 000	300	11.811 000
11	.433 070	41	1.614 170	71	2.795 270	105	4.133 848	310	12.204 700
12	.472 440	42	1.653 540	72	2.834 640	110	4.330 700	320	12.598 400
13	.511 810	43	1.692 910	73	2.874 010	115	4.527 550	330	12.992 100
14	.551 180	44	1.732 280	74	2.913 380	120	4.724 400	340	13.385 800
15	.590 550	45	1.771 650	75	2.952 750	125	4.921 250	350	13.779 500
16	.629 920	46	1.811 020	76	2.992 120	130	5.118 100	360	14.173 200
17	.669 290	47	1.850 390	77	3.031 490	135	5.314 950	370	14.566 900
18	.708 660	48	1.889 760	78	3.070 860	140	5.511 800	380	14.960 600
19	.748 030	49	1.929 130	79	3.110 230	145	5.708 650	390	15.354 300
20	.787 400	50	1.968 500	80	3.149 600	150	5.905 500	400	15.748 000
21	.826 770	51	2.007 870	81	3.188 970	155	6.102 350	500	19.685 000
22	.866 140	52	2.047 240	82	3.228 340	160	6.299 200	600	23.622 000
23	.905 510	53	2.086 610	83	3.267 710	165	6.496 050	700	27.559 000
24	.944 880	54	2.125 980	84	3.307 080	170	6.692 900	800	31.496 000
25	.984 250	55	2.165 350	85	3.346 450	175	6.889 750	900	35.433 000
26	1.023 620	56	2.204 720	86	3.385 820	180	7.086 600	1000	39.370 000
27	1.062 990	57	2.244 090	87	3.425 190	185	7.283 450	2000	78.740 000
28	1.102 360	58	2.283 460	88	3.464 560	190	7.480 300	3000	118.110 000
29	1.141 730	59	2.322 830	89	3.503 903	195	7.677 150	4000	157.480 000
30	1.181 100	60	2.362 200	90	3.543 300	200	7.874 000	5000	196.850 000

To change decimal millimeters to decimal inches, position the decimal point where desired on either side of the millimeter measurement shown and reset the inches decimal by the same number of digits in the same direction. For example, to convert .001 mm into decimal inches, reset the decimal behind the 1 mm (shown on the chart) to .001; change the decimal inch equivalent (.039″ shown) to .00039″).

Tap Drill Sizes

National Fine or S.A.E.		
Screw & Tap Size	Threads Per Inch	Use Drill Number
No. 5	44	37
No. 6	40	33
No. 8	36	29
No. 10	32	21
No. 12	28	15
1/4	28	3
5/16	24	1
3/8	24	Q
7/16	20	W
1/2	20	29/64
9/16	18	33/64
5/8	18	37/64
3/4	16	11/16
7/8	14	13/16
1 1/8	12	1 3/64
1 1/4	12	1 11/64
1 1/2	12	1 27/64

National Coarse or U.S.S.		
Screw & Tap Size	Threads Per Inch	Use Drill Number
No. 5	40	39
No. 6	32	36
No. 8	32	29
No. 10	24	25
No. 12	24	17
1/4	20	8
5/16	18	F
3/8	16	5/16
7/16	14	U
1/2	13	27/64
9/16	12	31/64
5/8	11	17/32
3/4	10	21/32
7/8	9	49/64
1	8	7/8
1 1/8	7	63/64
1 1/4	7	1 7/64
1 1/2	6	1 11/32

Decimal Equivalent Size of the Number Drills

Drill No.	Decimal Equivalent	Drill No.	Decimal Equivalent	Drill No.	Decimal Equivalent
80	.0135	53	.0595	26	.1470
79	.0145	52	.0635	25	.1495
78	.0160	51	.0670	24	.1520
77	.0180	50	.0700	23	.1540
76	.0200	49	.0730	22	.1570
75	.0210	48	.0760	21	.1590
74	.0225	47	.0785	20	.1610
73	.0240	46	.0810	19	.1660
72	.0250	45	.0820	18	.1695
71	.0260	44	.0860	17	.1730
70	.0280	43	.0890	16	.1770
69	.0292	42	.0935	15	.1800
68	.0310	41	.0960	14	.1820
67	.0320	40	.0980	13	.1850
66	.0330	39	.0995	12	.1890
65	.0350	38	.1015	11	.1910
64	.0360	37	.1040	10	.1935
63	.0370	36	.1065	9	.1960
62	.0380	35	.1100	8	.1990
61	.0390	34	.1110	7	.2010
60	.0400	33	.1130	6	.2040
59	.0410	32	.1160	5	.2055
58	.0420	31	.1200	4	.2090
57	.0430	30	.1285	3	.2130
56	.0465	29	.1360	2	.2210
55	.0520	28	.1405	1	.2280
54	.0550	27	.1440		

Decimal Equivalent Size of the Letter Drills

Letter Drill	Decimal Equivalent	Letter Drill	Decimal Equivalent	Letter Drill	Decimal Equivalent
A	.234	J	.277	S	.348
B	.238	K	.281	T	.358
C	.242	L	.290	U	.368
D	.246	M	.295	V	.377
E	.250	N	.302	W	.386
F	.257	O	.316	X	.397
G	.261	P	.323	Y	.404
H	.266	Q	.332	Z	.413
I	.272	R	.339		

ANTI-FREEZE INFORMATION

Freezing and Boiling Points of Solutions
According to Percentage of Alcohol or Ethylene Glycol

Freezing Point of Solution	Alcohol Volume %	Alcohol Solution Boils at	Ethylene Glycol Volume %	Ethylene Glycol Solution Boils at
20°F.	12	196°F.	16	216°F.
10°F.	20	189°F.	25	218°F.
0°F.	27	184°F.	33	220°F.
−10°F.	32	181°F.	39	222°F.
−20°F.	38	178°F.	44	224°F.
−30°F.	42	176°F.	48	225°F.

Note: above boiling points are at sea level. For every 1,000 feet of altitude, boiling points are approximately 2°F. lower than those shown. For every pound of pressure exerted by the pressure cap, the boiling points are approximately 3°F. higher than those shown.

ANTI-FREEZE CHART

Temperatures Shown in Degrees Fahrenheit
+32 is Freezing

Quarts of **ETHYLENE GLYCOL** Needed for Protection to Temperatures Shown Below

Cooling System Capacity Quarts	1	2	3	4	5	6	7	8	9	10	11	12	13	14
10	+24°	+16°	+4°	−12°	−34°	−62°								
11	+25	+18	+8	−6	−23	−47								
12	+26	+19	+10	0	−15	−34	−57°							
13	+27	+21	+13	+3	−9	−25	−45							
14			+15	+6	−5	−18	−34							
15			+16	+8	0	−12	−26							
16		+17	+10	+2	−8	−19	−34	−52°						
17		+18	+12	+5	−4	−14	−27	−42						
18		+19	+14	+7	0	−10	−21	−34	−50°					
19		+20	+15	+9	+2	−7	−16	−28	−42					
20			+16	+10	+4	−3	−12	−22	−34	−48°				
21			+17	+12	+6	0	−9	−17	−28	−41				
22			+18	+13	+8	+2	−6	−14	−23	−34	−47°			
23			+19	+14	+9	+4	−3	−10	−19	−29	−40			
24			+19	+15	+10	+5	0	−8	−15	−23	−34	−46°		
25			+20	+16	+12	+7	+1	−5	−12	−20	−29	−40	−50°	
26				+17	+13	+8	+3	−3	−9	−16	−25	−34	−44	
27				+18	+14	+9	+5	−1	−7	−13	−21	−29	−39	
28				+18	+15	+10	+6	+1	−5	−11	−18	−25	−34	
29				+19	+16	+12	+7	+2	−3	−8	−15	−22	−29	
30				+20	+17	+13	+8	+4	−1	−6	−12	−18	−25	

For capacities over 30 quarts divide true capacity by 3. Find quarts Anti-Freeze for the ⅓ and multiply by 3 for quarts to add.

For capacities under 10 quarts multiply true capacity by 3. Find quarts Anti-Freeze for the tripled volume and divide by 3 for quarts to add.

To Increase the Freezing Protection of Anti-Freeze Solutions Already Installed

Cooling System Capacity Quarts	Number of Quarts of **ETHYLENE GLYCOL** Anti-Freeze Required to Increase Protection													
	From +20°F. to					From +10°F. to					From 0°F. to			
	0°	−10°	−20°	−30°	−40°	0°	−10°	−20°	−30°	−40°	−10°	−20°	−30°	−40°
10	1¾	2¼	3	3½	3¾	¾	1½	2¼	2¾	3¼	¾	1½	2	2½
12	2	2¾	3½	4	4½	1	1¾	2½	3¼	3¾	1	1¾	2½	3¼
14	2¼	3¼	4	4¾	5½	1¼	2	3	3¾	4½	1	2	3	3½
16	2½	3½	4½	5¼	6	1¼	2½	3½	4¼	5¼	1¼	2¼	3¼	4
18	3	4	5	6	7	1½	2¾	4	5	5¾	1½	2½	3¾	4¾
20	3¼	4½	5¾	6¾	7½	1¾	3	4¼	5½	6½	1½	2¾	4¼	5¼
22	3½	5	6¼	7¼	8¼	1¾	3¼	4¾	6	7¼	1¾	3¼	4½	5½
24	4	5½	7	8	9	2	3½	5	6½	7½	1¾	3½	5	6
26	4¼	6	7½	8¾	10	2	4	5½	7	8¼	2	3¾	5½	6¾
28	4½	6¼	8	9½	10½	2¼	4¼	6	7½	9	2	4	5¾	7¼
30	5	6¾	8½	10	11½	2½	4½	6½	8	9½	2¼	4¼	6¼	7¾

Test radiator solution with proper hydrometer. Determine from the table the number of quarts of solution to be drawn off from a full cooling system and replace with undiluted anti-freeze, to give the desired increased protection. For example, to increase protection of a 22-quart cooling system containing Ethylene Glycol (permanent type) anti-freeze, from +20°F. to −20°F. will require the replacement of 6¼ quarts of solution with undiluted anti-freeze.